Sons of the Revolution

The Constitution of the Society of the Sons of the Revolution

and by-laws and register of the New York Society

Sons of the Revolution

The Constitution of the Society of the Sons of the Revolution
and by-laws and register of the New York Society

ISBN/EAN: 9783337238223

Printed in Europe, USA, Canada, Australia, Japan

Cover: Foto ©Andreas Hilbeck / pixelio.de

More available books at **www.hansebooks.com**

EXEGI MONUMENTUM ÆRE PERENNIUS.

The Constitution

OF THE

Society of Sons of the Revolution

AND

By-Laws and Register

OF THE

New York Society.

NEW YORK :
EXCHANGE PRINTING COMPANY.
1892.

OFFICERS

OF THE

GENERAL SOCIETY.

General President,
HON. JOHN LEE CARROLL,
Of the District of Columbia Society.

General Vice-President,
HON. WILLIAM WAYNE.
Of the Pennsylvania Society.

General Secretary,
JAMES MORTIMER MONTGOMERY,
Of the New York Society.

General Assistant Secretary,
TIMOTHY MATLACK CHEESMAN, M. D.,
Of the New York Society.

General Treasurer,
RICHARD McCALL CADWALADER,
Of the Pennsylvania Society.

General Assistant Treasurer,
ARTHUR HENRY DUTTON,
Of the District of Columbia Society.

General Chaplain,
REV. DANIEL CONY WESTON, D. D.,
Of the New York Society.

(3)

NEW YORK SOCIETY

INSTITUTED	FEBRUARY 22, 1876.
REORGANIZED - - -	DECEMBER 4, 1883.
INCORPORATED UNDER THE LAWS OF THE STATE OF NEW YORK,	MAY 3, 1884.

INCORPORATORS.

JOHN AUSTIN STEVENS,

JOHN COCHRANE,

AUSTIN HUNTINGTON,

*GEORGE H. POTTS,

FREDERICK SAMUEL TALLMADGE,

~GEORGE WASHINGTON WRIGHT HOUGHTON,

ASA BIRD GARDINER,

THOMAS HENRY EDSALL,

*JOSEPH W. DREXEL,

JAMES MORTIMER MONTGOMERY,

JAMES DUANE LIVINGSTON,

J. BLEECKER MILLER,

ALEXANDER R. THOMPSON, JR.

OFFICERS OF THE NEW YORK SOCIETY FROM ITS REORGANIZATION, DECEMBER 4, 1883.

☆

Elected	PRESIDENTS.	Retired
1883	John Austin Stevens,	1884
1884	Frederick Samuel Tallmadge,	——

VICE-PRESIDENTS.

1883	John Cochrane,	1884
1884	Thomas Henry Edsall,	1886
1886	Elbridge T. Gerry,	1888
1888	Floyd Clarkson,	——

SECRETARIES.

1883	Austin Huntington,	1884
1884	*George Washington Wright Houghton,	1886
1886	James Mortimer Montgomery,	——

ASSISTANT SECRETARY.

1891	Edward Trenchard,	——

TREASURERS.

1883	*George H. Potts,	1885
1885	F. J. Huntington,	1885
1885	Austin Huntington,	1886
1886	Asa Coolidge Warren,	1887
1887	Arthur Melvin Hatch,	——

REGISTRARS.

1887	Asa Coolidge Warren,	1889
1889	Henry Thayer Drowne,	1891
1891	Charles Isham,	——

HISTORIANS.

1888	Austin Huntington,	1889
1889	John Canfield Tomlinson,	1891
1891	Henry Wyckoff Le Roy,	——

CHAPLAINS.

1889	Rev. Daniel Cony Weston, D. D.,	1889
1889	Rev. Brockholst Morgan,	——

SONS OF THE REVOLUTION

IN THE

STATE OF NEW YORK.

INSTITUTED • • • • • • • • • • • FEBRUARY 22, 1876.
REORGANIZED • • • • • • • • • • • • DECEMBER 4, 1883.
INCORPORATED UNDER THE LAWS OF THE STATE OF NEW YORK • MAY 3, 1884.

OFFICERS.

President.

FREDERICK SAMUEL TALLMADGE, - 145 Broadway, New York.

Vice-President.

BVT. LT.-COL. FLOYD CLARKSON, - - 39 Broadway, New York.

Secretary.

JAMES MORTIMER MONTGOMERY, - 56 Wall Street, New York.

Assistant Secretary.

EDWARD TRENCHARD, - - - - - - 56 Wall Street, New York.

Treasurer.

ARTHUR MELVIN HATCH, - - - - 14 Nassau Street, New York.

BOARD OF MANAGERS.

ASA BIRD GARDINER, LL. D.,
BRADISH JOHNSON, JR.,
CHARLES HORNBLOWER WOODRUFF,
WILLIAM CARPENDER,
ROBERT LENOX BELKNAP,
ROBERT OLYPHANT,
JOHN CANFIELD TOMLINSON,
GOUVERNEUR M. SMITH, M. D.,
WILLIAM GASTON HAMILTON.

Registrar.   *Historian.*

CHARLES ISHAM.   HENRY WYCKOFF LE ROY

Chaplain.

REV. BROCKHOLST MORGAN.

OFFICE OF THE SOCIETY, 56 WALL STREET.

(7)

SONS OF THE REVOLUTION
IN THE
STATE OF PENNSYLVANIA.

INSTITUTED APRIL 3, 1888.

INCORPORATED UNDER THE LAWS OF THE STATE OF PENNSYLVANIA SEPTEMBER 29. 1890.

OFFICERS.

President.
Hon. WILLIAM WAYNE, - - - Paoli, Pa.

Vice-President.
RICHARD McCALL CADWALADER, 710 Walnut[Street. Philadelphia, Pa.

Secretary.
GEORGE HORACE BURGIN, M. D., Chilton Avenue, Germantown, Pa.

Treasurer.
ROBERT PORTER DECHERT. - - 406 S. Broad Street, Philadelphia, Pa.

Registrar.
JOHN WOOLF JORDAN, - - - 1300 Locust Street, Philadelphia, Pa.

Historian.
JOSIAH GRANVILLE LEACH, - - 733 Walnut Street, Philadelphia, Pa.

Chaplain.
Rev. GEORGE WOOLSEY HODGE, - 334 S. 13th Street, Philadelphia, Pa.

BOARD OF MANAGERS.

BVT.-MAJOR JAMES EDWARD CARPENTER.
ISAAC CRAIG,
WILLIAM HENRY EGLE, M. D..
REV. HORACE EDWARD HAYDEN,
WILLIAM MACPHERSON HORNOR.
CHARLES HENRY JONES,
ELON DUNBAR LOCKWOOD,
THOMAS McKEAN,
Hon. SAMUEL WHITAKER PENNYPACKER. LL. D.

DELEGATES TO THE GENERAL SOCIETY.

HERMAN BURGIN, M. D.,   BVT.-MAJ. JAMES EDWARD CARPENTER,
JOSIAH GRANVILLE LEACH,   Hon. CLIFFORD STANLEY SIMS.
Hon. SAMUEL WHITAKER PENNYPACKER. LL. D.

ALTERNATES.

THOMAS HEWSON BRADFORD, M. D..
ARTHUR VINCENT MEIGS, M. D.,
JOHN CADWALADER,
Hon. JAMES TYNDALE MITCHELL, LL. D..
GEORGE RANDOLPH SNOWDEN.

(8)

SONS OF THE REVOLUTION

IN THE

DISTRICT OF COLUMBIA.

INSTITUTED MARCH 11, 1889.
INCORPORATED UNDER THE LAWS OF THE UNITED STATES DECEMBER, 1889.

OFFICERS.

President.
Hon. JOHN LEE CARROLL, Washington, D. C.

Vice-President.
REAR ADMIRAL FRANCIS ASBURY ROE, U. S. Navy.

Secretary.
PICKERING DODGE, 1827 Jefferson Avenue, Washington, D. C.

Treasurer.
ALEXANDER BROWN LEGARÉ, 1728 I Street, Washington, D. C.

Registrar and Historian.
GAILLARD HUNT, 1466 Rhode Island Avenue.

Chaplain.
REV. GEORGE WILLIAM DOUGLAS, D. D.

BOARD OF MANAGERS.

LEWIS JOHNSON DAVIS,
REAR ADMIRAL SAMUEL RHOADES FRANKLIN, U. S. Navy.
COMMODORE JAMES AUSTIN GREER, U. S. Navy.
ARCHIBALD HOPKINS.
ALBION K. PARRIS,
CHARLES WORTHINGTON.
B. LEWIS BLACKFORD,
H. B. CILLEY.

DELEGATES TO THE GENERAL SOCIETY.

Hon. JOHN LEE CARROLL,
REAR ADMIRAL SAMUEL RHOADES FRANKLIN, U. S. Navy,
CAPTAIN DANIEL MORGAN TAYLOR, U. S. Army,
CHARLES WORTHINGTON,
BVT. MAJOR-GENERAL NICHOLAS LONGWORTH ANDERSON.

SONS OF THE REVOLUTION

IN THE

STATE OF IOWA.

INSTITUTED APRIL. 19, 1890.

OFFICERS.

President.

RIGHT REV. WILLIAM STEVENS PERRY, D. D. (*Oxon.*), LL. D., D. C. L., BISHOP OF IOWA.

Vice-President.

SAMUEL FRANCIS SMITH, Davenport, Iowa.

Secretary.

EDWARD SEYMOUR HAMMATT, Davenport, Iowa.

Treasurer.

ESEK STEERE BALLORD, Davenport, Iowa.

Chaplain.

VERY REV. CHARLES REUBEN HALE, D. D., LL. D., Davenport, Iowa.

Registrar and Historian.

JOHN HUBBARD STURGIS, Burlington, Iowa.

BOARD OF MANAGERS.

RT. REV. WILLIAM STEVENS PERRY,
SAMUEL FRANCIS SMITH,
EDWARD SEYMOUR HAMMATT.
ESEK STEERE BALLORD,
VERY REV. CHARLES REUBEN HALE,
JOHN HUBBARD STURGIS,
REV. WILLIAM SALTER,

CHARLES WHITAKER,
HUITT ROSS,
EDWARD HAMLIN HAZEN,
WILLIAM PERRY BRADY,
REV. PETER CLARK WOLCOTT,
JOHN ELY BREADY,
ENOCH MEAD.

DELEGATES TO THE GENERAL SOCIETY.

RT. REV. WILLIAM STEVENS PERRY, WILLIAM PERRY BRADY, EDWARD SEYMOUR HAMMATT.

ALTERNATES.

SAMUEL FRANCIS SMITH.   ESEK STEERE BALLORD, ENOCH MEAD.

(10)

SONS OF THE REVOLUTION

IN THE

STATE OF NEW JERSEY.

Instituted January 6, 1891.

OFFICERS.

President.
Hon. S. MEREDITH DICKINSON, Trenton, N. J.

Vice-President.
CLEMENT H. SINNICKSON, Salem, N. J.

Secretary.
JOHN ALEXANDER CAMPBELL, Trenton, N. J.

Treasurer.
HUGH HENDERSON HAMILL, Trenton, N. J.

Registrar.
FOSTER CONARROE GRIFFITH, Trenton, N. J.

Historian.
MORRIS HANCOCK STRATTON, Salem, N. J.

Board of Managers.

Hon. GEORGE MAXWELL ROBESON,
GARRETT DORSET WALL VROOM,
BAYARD STOCKTON,
CHRISTOPHER H. BERGEN,
PETER L. VOORHEES,
Bvt. Brig.-Gen. S. DUNCAN OLIPHANT,
HUGH HENDERSON HAMILL,
WILLIAM JOHN POTTS,
WILLIAM ELMER, M. D.

Delegates to the General Society.

Hon. GEORGE MAXWELL ROBESON,
WILLIAM JOHN POTTS,
Bvt. Brig.-Gen. S. DUNCAN OLIPHANT,
MALCOLM MacDONALD,
PETER L. VOORHEES.

11

SONS OF THE REVOLUTION

IN THE

STATE OF GEORGIA.

Instituted May 22, 1891.

OFFICERS.

President.
Colonel JOHN SCREVEN.

Vice-President.
JOSEPH GASTON BULLOCH, M. D.

Secretary.
WILLIAM HARDEN, 59 Gordon Street, Savannah. Ga.

Assistant Secretary.
GEORGE M. GADSDEN.

Treasurer.
WARING RUSSELL.

Registrar.
JOHN SULLIVAN SCHLEY.

Chaplain.
Rev. LACHLAN C. VASS, D. D.

BOARD OF MANAGERS.

Hon. WILLIAM DEARING HARDEN,   THOMAS F. SCREVEN.
PHILIP M. RUSSELL,   GRANTHAM I. TAGGART,
JOHN S. SHIVERS,   FRANCIS S. LATHROP.
WILLIAM DANIEL GRANT (Atlanta),   BEIRNE GORDON.
AUGUSTUS OEMLER.

DELEGATES TO THE GENERAL SOCIETY.

Hon. WILLIAM DEARING HARDEN,   WILLIAM HARDEN.
WILLIAM DANIEL GRANT (Atlanta),   Rev. LACHLAN C. VASS, D. D.,
Col. JOHN SCREVEN.

ALTERNATES.

THOMAS PINCKNEY HUGER,   GEORGE M. GADSDEN,
HARVEY JOHNSON (Atlanta),   HUGH V. WASHINGTON (Macon),
JOSEPH G. BULLOCH, M. D.

(12)

SONS OF THE REVOLUTION

IN THE

COMMONWEALTH OF MASSACHUSETTS.

ORGANIZED IN FANEUIL HALL OCTOBER 1, 1891.
INCORPORATED UNDER THE LAWS OF THE COMMONWEALTH OF MASSACHUSETTS OCTOBER 1, 1892.

OFFICERS.

President.
WILLIAM LEVERETT CHASE.

Vice-President.
HAZARD STEVENS.

Treasurer.
FRANK HARRISON BRIGGS, 45 High Street, Boston.

Secretary.
HENRY DEXTER WARREN, Hotel Berkeley, Boston.

Registrar.
WALTER KENDALL WATKINS.

Historian.
FRANCIS ELLINGWOOD ABBOTT, LL. D.

BOARD OF MANAGERS.

PROFESSOR EBEN NORTON HORSFORD,   WALTER GILMAN PAGE.
ANDREW ROBESON,   WINTHROP WETHERBEE.
WILLIAM CURTIS CAPELLE,   GILBERT HODGES.
ARTHUR HENRY DUTTON.   THEODORE HAROLD CLAPP.
        CHARLES HOWARD BAILEY, JR.

DELEGATES TO THE GENERAL SOCIETY.

WILLIAM LEVERETT CHASE,
FRANCIS ELLINGWOOD ABBOTT, LL. D.,
ANDREW ROBESON,
ALFRED BROOKS FRY.

ALTERNATES.

RIGHT REVEREND PHILLIPS BROOKS, BISHOP OF DIOCESE OF MASSACHUSETTS,
REVEREND EDWARD EVERETT HALE, D. D., LL. D.,
PROFESSOR EBEN NORTON HORSFORD,
HOWARD EATON HAYDEN.

(13)

THE NAME OF WASHINGTON.

Sons of the youth and the truth of the nation,—
  Ye that are met to remember the man
Whose valor gave birth to a people's salvation,—
  Honor him now ; set his name in the van.
    A nobleness to try for,
    A name to live and die for—
      The name of Washington !

Calmly his face shall look down through the ages—
  Sweet yet severe with a spirit of warning ;
Charged with the wisdom of saints and of sages :
  Quick with the light of a life-giving morning.
    A majesty to try for,
    A name to live and die for—
      The name of Washington !

Though faction may rack us, or party divide us,
  And bitterness break the gold links of our story.
Our father and leader is ever beside us.
    Live and forgive ! But forget not the glory
    Of him whose height we try for;
    A name to live and die for—
      The name of Washington !

Still in his eyes shall be mirrored our fleeting
  Days, with the image of days long ended :
Still shall those eyes give, immortally, greeting
  Unto the souls from his spirit descended.
    His grandeur we will try for ;
    His name we'll live and die for—
      The name of Washington !

Geo. Parsons Lathrop.

(11)

Certificate of Incorporation.

WE, John Austin Stevens, John Cochrane, Austin Huntington, George H. Potts, Frederick S. Tallmadge, Joseph H. Drexel, George W. W. Houghton, Asa Bird Gardiner, Thomas H. Edsall, James M. Montgomery, James Duane Livingston, John Bleecker Miller, and Alexander R. Thompson, Jr., all being residents of the State of New York, do hereby certify that we desire to form a Society, pursuant to the provisions of an Act entitled "An Act for the incorporation of Societies or Clubs for certain lawful purposes," passed by the Legislature of the State of New York, May 12th, 1875, and of the several Acts extending and amending said Act.

That the corporate name of the said Society is to be "SONS OF THE REVOLUTION."

That the objects of said Society are social and patriotic, and that said Society is to be formed for the purpose of perpetuating among their descendants the memory of the brave men who periled their lives and interests in the war of the Revolution to wrest the American Colonies from British dominion.

That the number of the managers who shall direct the concerns of said Society shall be thirteen.

That the names of such managers for the first year are John Austin Stevens, John Cochrane, Austin Huntington, George H. Potts, Frederick S. Tallmadge, Joseph W. Drexel, George W. W. Houghton, Asa Bird Gardiner, Thomas H. Edsall, James M. Montgomery, James Duane Livingston, John Bleecker Miller, and Alexander R. Thompson, Jr.

That the principal office of said Society is to be in the city of New York.

In witness whereof, we have hereunto, and to the duplicate hereof, set our hands and affixed our seals this twenty-ninth day of April, 1884.

In presence of as to all but		
John Bleecker Miller,	JOHN AUSTIN STEVENS,	[L. S.]
	JOHN COCHRANE,	[L. S.]
EDWARD H. STROBEL.	AUSTIN HUNTINGTON,	[L. S.]
	GEORGE H. POTTS,	[L. S.]
As to John Bleecker Miller,	FREDERICK S. TALLMADGE,	[L. S.]
	GEORGE W. W. HOUGHTON,	[L. S.]
FREDK. E. FISHEL.	ASA BIRD GARDINER,	[L. S.]
	THOMAS H. EDSALL,	[L. S.]
	JOSEPH W. DREXEL,	[L. S.]
	JAMES MORTIMER MONTGOMERY,	[L. S.]
	JAMES DUANE LIVINGSTON,	[L. S.]
	ALEXANDER R. THOMPSON, JR.,	[L. S.]
	JOHN BLEECKER MILLER.	[L. S.]

STATE OF NEW YORK,
CITY AND COUNTY OF NEW YORK, } *ss.:*

On this 29th day of April, 1884, before me personally appeared John
Austin Stevens, John Cochrane, Austin Huntington, George H. Potts,
Frederick S. Tallmadge, George W. W. Houghton, Joseph W. Drexel,
Asa Bird Gardiner, Thomas H. Edsall, James Mortimer Montgomery, James
Duane Livingston, and Alexander R. Thompson, Jr., to me known to be
twelve of the individuals described in and who executed the foregoing
certificate, and they severally before me signed the said certificate, and
acknowledged that they executed the same for the purposes therein mentioned.

EDWARD H. STROBEL,
Notary Public,
New York County.

STATE OF NEW YORK,
CITY AND COUNTY OF NEW YORK, } *ss.:*

On this 1st day of May, 1884, before me personally appeared John
Bleecker Miller, to me known to be one of the individuals described in and
who executed the foregoing certificate, and he, before me, signed the said
certificate, and acknowledged that he executed the same for the purposes
therein mentioned.

FREDK. E. FISHEL,
Notary Public,
Suffolk County.

Certificate filed in New York County.

[ENDORSED.]

CERTIFICATE OF INCORPORATION.

I hereby approve of the incorporation of the Society of the "Sons of the
Revolution," and consent that the within Certificate of Incorporation be
filed.

GEORGE C. BARRETT, J.

New York City, May 2, 1884.

(16)

Constitution of the General Society.

It being evident, from a steady decline of a proper celebration of the National holidays of the United States of America, that popular concern in the events and men of the war of the Revolution is gradually declining, and that such lack of interest is attributable, not so much to the lapse of time and the rapidly increasing flood of immigration from foreign countries, as to the neglect on the part of descendants of Revolutionary heroes to perform their duty in keeping before the public mind the memory of the services of their ancestors and of the times in which they lived; therefore, the Society of the Sons of the Revolution has been instituted to perpetuate the memory of the men, who, in the military, naval and civil service of the Colonies and of the Continental Congress, by their acts or counsel, achieved the Independence of the country, and to further the proper celebration of the anniversaries of the birthday of Washington, and of prominent events connected with the war of the Revolution; to collect and secure for preservation the rolls, records and other documents relating to that period : to inspire the members of the Society with the patriotic spirit of their forefathers ; and to promote the feeling of friendship among them.

The General Society shall be divided into State Societies, which shall meet annually on the day appointed therefor in their respective by-laws, and oftener if found expedient : and at such annual meeting the reasons for the institution of the Society shall be considered, and the best measures for carrying them into effect adopted.

The State Societies at every annual meeting shall choose a president, a vice-president, a secretary, a registrar, a treasurer, a chaplain, and such other officers as may by them respectively be deemed necessary, and a board of managers, all of whom shall retain their respective positions until their successors are duly chosen.

Each State Society shall cause to be transmitted annually or oftener to the other State Societies, a circular letter calling attention to whatever may be thought worthy of observation respecting the welfare of the Society or of the general union of the States, and giving information of the officers chosen for the year ; and copies of these letters shall also be transmitted to the General Secretary to be preserved among the records of the General Society.

The State Societies shall regulate all matters respecting their own affairs, consistent with the general good of the Society ; judge of the qualification of their members or of those proposed for membership, subject, however, to the provisions of this Constitution ; and expel any member, who, by conduct unbecoming a gentleman or a man of honor, or by an opposition to the interests of the community in general or of the Society in particular, may render himself unworthy to continue in membership.

In order to form funds that may be respectable, each member shall contribute upon his admission to the Society and annually thereafter, such sums as the by-laws of the respective State Societies may require ; but any of such State Societies may provide for the endowment of memberships by the payment of proper sums in capitalization, which sums shall be properly invested as a permanent fund, the income only of which shall be expended.

The regular meeting of the General Society shall be held every three years, and special meetings may be held upon the order of the General President or upon the request of two of the State Societies, and such meetings shall consist of the General Officers and a representation not exceeding five deputies from each State Society, and the necessary expenses of such meeting shall be borne by the State Societies.

At the regular meeting, a General President, Vice-President, Secretary, Assistant Secretary, Treasurer, Assistant Treasurer, and Chaplain shall be chosen by a majority of the votes present, to serve until the next regular general meeting, or until their successors are duly chosen.

At each general meeting the circular letters which have been transmitted by the several State Societies shall be considered, and all measures taken which shall conduce to the general welfare of the Society.

The General Society shall have power at any meeting to admit State Societies thereto, and to entertain and determine all questions affecting the qualifications for membership in or the welfare of any State Society as may by proper memorial be presented by such State Society for consideration.

Any male person above the age of twenty-one years, of good character, and a descendant of one who, as a military, naval or marine officer, soldier, sailor or marine, in actual service, under the authority of any of the thirteen Colonies or States or of the Continental Congress, and remaining always loyal to such authority, or a descendant of one who signed the Declaration of Independence, or of one who, as a member of the Continental Congress or of the Congress of any of the Colonies or States, or as an official appointed by or under the authority of any such legislative bodies, actually assisted in the establishment of American Independence by services rendered during the war of the Revolution, becoming thereby liable to conviction of treason against the government of Great Britain, but remaining always loyal to the authority of the Colonies or States, shall be eligible to membership in the Society.

The Secretary of each State Society shall transmit to the General Secretary a list of the members thereof, together with the names and official designations of those from whom such members derive claim to membership, and thereafter upon the admission of members in each State Society, the Secretary thereof shall transmit to the General Secretary information respecting such members similar to that herein required.

The Society shall have an insignia, which shall be a badge suspended from a ribbon by a ring of gold ; the badge to be elliptical in form, with escaloped edges, one and one-quarter inches in length, and one and one-eighth inches in width ; the whole surmounted by a gold eagle, with wings displayed, inverted : on the obverse side a medallion of gold in the centre, elliptical in form, bearing on its face the figure of a soldier in Continental uniform, with musket slung ; beneath, the figures 1775 : the medallion surrounded by thirteen raised gold stars of five points each upon a border of dark blue enamel. On the reverse side in the centre a

medallion corresponding in form to that on the obverse, and
also in gold, bearing on its face the Houdon portrait of
Washington in bas-relief, encircled by the legend, "Sons
of the Revolution ;" beneath, the figures 1883 ; and upon the
reverse of the eagle the number of the badge to be engraved ; the medallion to be surrounded by a plain gold
border, conforming in dimensions to the obverse ; the ribbon
shall be dark blue, ribbed and watered, edged with buff, one
and one-half inches wide, and one and one-half inches in
displayed length.

The insignia of the Society shall be worn by the members
on all occasions when they assemble as such for any stated
purpose or celebration, and may be worn on any occasion of
ceremony ; it shall be carried conspicuously on the left
breast, but members who are or have been officers of the
Society may wear the insignia suspended from the ribbon
around the neck.

The custodian of the insignia shall be the General Secretary, who shall issue them to members of the Society under
such proper rules as may be formulated by the General
Society, and he shall keep a register of such issues wherein
each insignia issued may be identified by the number
thereof.

The seal of the Society shall be one and seven-eighths
inches in diameter, and shall consist of the figure of a Minute-man in Continental uniform, standing on a ladder leading to a belfry ; in his left hand he holds a musket and an
olive branch, whilst his right grasps a bell-rope : above, the
cracked Liberty Bell : issuing therefrom a ribbon bearing
the motto of the Society, *Exegi monumentum aere perennius* ;
across the top of the ladder on a ribbon, the figures 1776 ;
and on the left of the Minute-man, and also on a ribbon, the
figures 1883, the year of the formation of the Society ; the

whole encircled by a band three-eighths of one inch wide; thereon at the top thirteen stars of five points each; at the bottom the name of the General Society, or of the State Society to which the seal belongs.

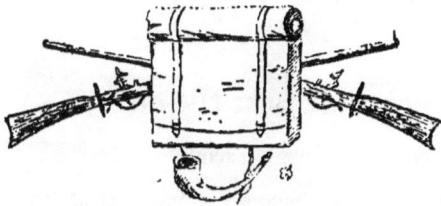

Society

Sons of the Revolution

In the State of New York.

INSTITUTED	-	-	-	FEBRUARY 22, 1876.
REORGANIZED	-	-	-	DECEMBER 3, 1883.
INCORPORATED	-	-	MAY 3, 1884.

Constitution.

Preamble.

WHEREAS, it has become evident from the decline of proper celebration of such National holidays as the Fourth of July, Washington's Birthday, and the like, that popular interest in the events and men of the War of the Revolution is less than in the earlier days of the Republic :

AND WHEREAS, this lack of interest is to be attributed not so much to lapse of time as to the neglect on the part of descendants of Revolutionary heroes to perform their duty of keeping before the public mind the memory of the services of their ancestors, and of the times in which they lived, and of the principles for which they contended ;

THEREFORE, the Society of the "SONS OF THE REVOLUTION" has been instituted, to perpetuate the memory

of the men who, in military, naval or civil service, by their
acts or counsel, achieved American Independence ; to promote and assist in the proper celebration of the anniversaries of Washington's Birthday, the Battles of Lexington
and Bunker Hill, the Fourth of July, the Capitulations of
Saratoga and Yorktown, the *formal* Evacuation of New
York by the British Army, on the 3d of December, 1783,
as a relinquishment of territorial sovereignty, and other
prominent events relating to or connected with the War
of the Revolution ; to collect and secure for preservation
the manuscript rolls, records and other documents and
memorials relating to that War ; to inspire among the
members and their descendants the patriotic spirit of their
forefathers ; to inculcate in the community in general sen-
timents of Nationality and respect for the principles for
which the patriots of the Revolution contended ; to assist
in the commemorative celebration of other great historical
events of National importance, and to promote social inter-
course and the feeling of fellowship among its members.

ARTICLE I.

Name of Society.

The Society shall be known by the name, style and title
of " SONS OF THE REVOLUTION."

ARTICLE II.

Membership.

Any male person, above the age of twenty-one years,
shall be eligible to membership in the "SONS OF THE REVO-
LUTION" who is descended from an ancestor, as the propositus, who, either as a military, naval or marine officer,
soldier, sailor, or marine, or official in the service of any

one of the thirteen original Colonies or States, or of the National Government representing or composed of those Colonies or States, assisted in establishing American Independence during the War of the Revolution, between the 19th day of April, 1775, when hostilities commenced, and the 19th day of April, 1783, when they were ordered to cease.

Provided: That when the claim of eligibility is based on the service of an ancestor in the "minute men" or "militia," it must be satisfactorily shown that such ancestor was actually called into the service of the State or United States, and performed garrison or field duty ; and

Provided further: That when the claim of eligibility is based on the service of an ancestor as a "sailor" or "marine," it must in like manner be shown that such service was other than shore duty and regularly performed in the Continental Navy, or the Navy of one of the original thirteen States, or on an armed vessel, other than a merchant ship, which sailed under letters of marque and reprisal, and that such ancestor of the applicant was duly enrolled in the ship's company, either as an officer, seaman, or otherwise than as a passenger ; and

Provided further: That when the claim of eligibility is based on the service of an ancestor as an "official," such service must have been performed in the civil service of the United States, or of one of the thirteen original States, and must have been sufficiently important in character to have rendered the official specially liable to arrest and imprisonment, the same as a combatant, if captured by the enemy, as well as liable to conviction of treason against the Government of Great Britain.

Service in the ordinary duties of a civil office, the performance of which did not *particularly* and *effectively* aid the American Cause shall not constitute eligibility.

Provided further: That when there shall be no surviving issue in direct lineal succession from an officer, soldier, sailor or marine who died or was killed while in actual service as aforesaid, or from an officer who received, by formal resolve, the approbation of the Continental Congress for revolutionary services, or from a Signer of the Declaration of Independence, the claim of eligibility shall descend and be limited to one representative at a time in the nearest collateral line of descent from such propositus, who may be otherwise qualified as herein required, and to be designated by the Society; and no other descendants in collateral lines shall be admitted in right of any services whatever.

In the construction of this article, the Volunteer Aides de Camp of General Officers in Continental Service, who were duly announced as such and who actually served in the field during a campaign, shall be comprehended as having performed qualifying service.

The civil officials and military forces of the State of Vermont, during the War of the Revolution, shall also be comprehended in the same manner as if they had belonged to one of the thirteen original States.

No service of an ancestor shall be deemed as qualifying service for membership in the "SONS OF THE REVOLUTION" where such ancestor, after assisting in the cause of American Independence, shall have subsequently either adhered to the enemy, or failed to maintain an honorable record throughout the War of the Revolution.

No person shall be admitted unless he be eligible under one of the provisions of this Article nor unless he be of good moral character and be judged worthy of becoming a member.

ARTICLE III.

Officers.

The officers of the Society of the "SONS OF THE REVO-LUTION" shall be a President, a Vice-President, a Secretary, a Treasurer, a Registrar, and a Chaplain, who shall be chosen by ballot at every annual meeting from among the members thereof.

ARTICLE IV.

Board of Managers.

The Board of Managers of the Society shall be fifteen, namely : the President, the Vice-President, the Secretary, the Treasurer, the Registrar, and the Chaplain, *ex-officio*, and nine others who shall be chosen by ballot at every annual meeting from among the members of the Society.

ARTICLE V.

Admission of Members.

Every application for membership shall be made in writing, subscribed by the applicant, and approved by two members over their signatures. Applications shall contain, or be accompanied by, proof of eligibility, and such applications and proofs shall be submitted to the Board of Managers, who shall have full power to determine the qualifications of the applicant.

Payment of the initiation fee and subscription to the declaration required by the Constitution of this Society shall be a pre-requisite of membership.

ARTICLE VI.

Declaration.

Every member shall declare upon honor that he will endeavor to promote the purposes of this Institution and

observe the "Constitution" and "By-Laws" of this Society,
and, if he be a citizen of the United States, shall declare that
he will support the Constitution of the United States. Such
declaration shall be in writing, and subscribed by the member making it.

ARTICLE VII.

Institution Considered.

At every meeting the purposes of the Institution will
be fully considered and the best measures to promote them
adopted. No question, however, involving the party politics
of the Day within the United States shall ever be discussed
or considered in any meeting of the "SONS OF THE REVO-
LUTION."

ARTICLE VIII.

Commemorations.

It shall be a standing Regulation that the members shall,
when practicable, hold a commemorative celebration and
dine together at least once every year.

ARTICLE IX.

Seal.

The seal of the Society of the "SONS OF THE REVOLU-
TION" shall be one and seven-eighths of an inch in diameter,
and shall consist of the figure of a "Minute-man" in Continental uniform. standing on a ladder leading to a belfry,
and holding in his left hand a musket and an olive branch,
and grasping in his right hand a bell-rope. Above. the
cracked "Liberty bell"; issuing therefrom a ribbon. bearing the motto of the "SONS OF THE REVOLUTION" : "Exegi
Monumentum Ære Perennius." Across the top of the
ladder, on a ribbon, the figures "1776," and at the left of

the Minute-man, and also on a ribbon, the figures "1883," the year of the Centennial commemoration of the permanent evacuation by the British army of American territory; the whole encircled by a band three-eighths of an inch wide; thereon at the top thirteen stars of five points each, and at the bottom the legend, "SONS OF THE REVOLUTION;" the following being a fac-simile thereof:

The Secretary shall be the custodian of the seal, which shall be identical in every particular with this description.

ARTICLE X.

Insignia.

The insignia of the "SONS OF THE REVOLUTION" shall consist of a badge pendant from the ribbon by a ring of gold.

The badge shall be elliptical in form, with escaloped edges, one and one-quarter inches in length, and one and one-eighth inches in width; the whole surmounted by a gold eagle, with wings displayed, inverted. On the obverse side a medallion of gold in the centre, elliptical in form, bearing on its face the figure of a soldier in Continental uniform, with musket slung. Beneath, the figures "1775;" the medallion surrounded by thirteen raised gold stars of five points each upon a border of dark blue enamel.

On the reverse side, in the centre, a medallion, corresponding in form to that on the obverse, and also in gold, bearing on its face Houdon's portrait of Washington in bas-relief, encircled by the legend, "SONS OF THE REVOLUTION." Beneath the figures "1883," and upon the reverse of the eagle, the number of the particular badge engraved; the medallion surrounded by a plain gold border conforming in dimensions to the obverse, upon which members may have their names engraved in script.

The ribbon shall be dark blue, ribbed and watered, edged with buff, one and one-half inches wide and one and one-half inches in displayed length

The insignia shall be worn by the members conspicuously and only on the left breast on all occasions when they shall assemble as such for any stated purpose or celebration. The badge shall never be worn as an article of jewelry.

The Treasurer of the Society shall procure and issue the insignia to the members and shall keep a record of all issued by him.

Such insignia shall be returned to the Treasurer of the Society by any member who may formally withdraw or resign or be expelled, but otherwise it shall be deemed an heirloom.

No member shall receive more than one badge, unless to replace one, the loss or destruction of which shall first be satisfactorily established.

The following being a fac-simile of such insignia :

"OBVERSE."   " REVERSE."

On occasions other than the meetings for any stated purpose or celebration, members may wear a rosette of the prescribed ribbon and pattern in the upper button-hole of the left lapel of the coat.

The Treasurer shall procure and issue the rosettes to members.

The following being a fac-simile of the same, which shall not exceed fifteen millimetres in diameter :

ARTICLE XI.

Alterations and Amendments.

No alteration nor amendment of the Constitution of this Society shall be made unless notice thereof shall be duly given in writing, signed by the member proposing the same, at a meeting of the Society, nor unless the same shall be adopted at a subsequent meeting, held at least thirty days after such notice, by a vote of three-fourths of the members present.

By-Laws.

--- -- --

SECTION I.

Initiation Fee, Dues and Contributions.

The initiation fee shall be ten dollars ; the annual dues, five dollars, which shall be payable on or before the first day of January in every year. The payment at one time of seventy-five dollars shall thenceforth exempt the member so paying from the payment of annual dues.

Any member who may contribute two hundred and fifty dollars to the " Permanent Fund " of the Society shall be exempt from the payment of annual dues, and this exemption shall extend in perpetuity to his lineal successors in membership from the same propositus, one at a time, who may be selected for such exemption by the Society.

SECTION II.

Permanent Fund.

There shall be a " Permanent Fund," to be derived from contributions, and to remain forever to the use of the Society, the income only of which shall be expended.

SECTION III.

President.

The President, or in his absence the Vice-President, or in his absence a chairman *pro tempore*, shall preside at all meetings of the Society and of the Board of Managers, and shall exercise the usual functions of a presiding officer, under general parliamentary rules, subject to an appeal to the Society, in proper cases under those rules. The President shall be, *ex officio*, a member of all committees other than the Committee on Nominations. He shall have power to convene the Board of Managers and appoint the place of such meeting when called by him.

He shall also perform such other representative duties on behalf of the Society, either personally or by correspondence, as it or the Board of Managers may find desirable or necessary, or as customarily appertain to his office, and he shall enforce a strict observance of the Constitution and By-Laws of the Society.

In case of his decease, resignation, neglect to serve, or inability from any cause to act as President, the duties of the office shall devolve on the Vice-President, until the vacancy caused by such decease, resignation, or neglect to serve, shall be filled, or until the inability shall cease.

SECTION IV.

Secretary.

The Secretary shall conduct the *general* correspondence of the Society and keep a record thereof. He shall notify all qualified and accepted candidates of their admission, and perform such other duties as the Society, or Board of Managers, or his office, may require of him. He shall have charge of the seal, certificates of incorporation, by-laws, historical and other documents and records of the Society other than those required to be deposited with the Registrar, and shall affix the seal to all properly authenticated certificates of membership, and transmit the same without delay to the member for whom it shall be issued or to his proper representative. He shall also notify the Registrar of all admissions to membership, and transmit to him the applications and proofs of eligibility of all persons so admitted. He, together with the presiding officer, shall, when necessary, certify all acts of the Society, and, in proper cases, authenticate them under seal. He shall have charge of all printing and publications directed by the Society or by the Board of Managers. He shall give due notice of the time and place of all meetings of the Society, and of the Board of Managers, and shall attend the same. He shall keep fair and accurate records of all the proceedings and orders of the Society, and of the Board of Managers, and shall give notice to the several officers of all votes, orders, resolves, and proceedings of the Society or of the Board of Managers, affecting them or appertaining to their respective duties; and, at the annual meeting, and oftener, if required, shall report to the Society the names of those candidates who have been admitted to membership, and also the names of those members whose resignations or voluntary withdrawals have been consented to and accepted, and also the names of those members who have been expelled, or dropped for non-payment of dues, or for failure to substantiate claim of descent. In his absence from any meeting, a Secretary *pro tempore* may be designated therefor, unless the Assistant Secretary shall be present to act in such capacity.

SECTION V.

Treasurer.

The Treasurer shall collect and keep the funds and securities of the Society; and as often as those funds shall amount to one hundred dollars they shall be deposited in

some bank in the City of New York, which shall be designated by the Board of Managers, to the credit of the
Society of the "SONS OF THE REVOLUTION," and such funds
shall be drawn thence on the check of the Treasurer for the
purposes of the Society only. Out of these funds he shall pay
such sums only as may be ordered by the Society, or by the
Board of Managers, and shall perform such other duties as
the Society, or Board of Managers, or his office, may require
of him. He shall keep a true account of his receipts and
payments, and, at each annual meeting, render the same to
the Society, with a full statement of the financial condition
of the Society, when a committee shall be appointed to
audit his accounts.

For the faithful performance of his duty, he shall give
such security as the Society, or Board of Managers in lieu
of its action thereon, may from time to time require.

SECTION VI.

Registrar.

The Registrar shall receive from the Secretary, file and
keep of record all the proofs upon which memberships have
been granted, declarations of members on admission of
adherence to the Constitution and By-Laws of the Society,
together with a list of all diplomas countersigned by him,
and all documents, rolls, or other evidences of service in
the War of the Revolution of which the Society may
become possessed ; and he, under the direction of the Board
of Managers, shall make or cause to be made for file in his
office, copies of such original or certified documents as the
owners thereof may not be willing to leave permanently in
the keeping of the Society.

SECTION VII.

Chaplain.

The Chaplain shall be a regularly ordained minister of a Christian denomination, and it shall be his duty to open and close all meetings with customary chaplaincy services, and perform such other duties as ordinarily appertain to such office.

SECTION VIII.

Historian.

The Board of Managers shall have power to appoint an Historian, who shall keep a detailed record, to be deposited with the Secretary, of all the historical and commemorative celebrations of the Society; and he shall edit and prepare for publication such historical addresses, essays, papers and other documents of an historical character, other than a Register of Members, as the Secretary may be required to publish; and at every annual meeting, if there shall be a necrological list for the year then closing, he shall submit the same, with carefully prepared biographies of the deceased members.

SECTION IX.

Assistant Secretary.

The Board of Managers shall have power to appoint an Assistant Secretary, who shall assist the Secretary in the performance of such duties of that office as the latter may, from time to time, devolve upon him, and may, in such cases, give required notices, and certify, and authenticate, when necessary, any acts, documents or records of the Society.

In case of the absence of the Secretary from any meeting of the Society or of the Board of Managers, or of his decease, resignation, neglect to serve, or inability from any cause to act in that capacity, the duties of the office shall devolve on the Assistant Secretary until the Secretary shall return, or until the vacancy caused by such decease, resignation, or neglect to serve, shall be filled, or until the inability shall cease.

SECTION X.

Board of Managers.

The Board of Managers shall judge of the qualifications of every candidate who shall make proper application for admission to the Society, and shall have power to admit him to membership therein, if found eligible under the Constitution of this Society. Three negative votes shall be a rejection of the applicant.

They may, through the Secretary, call special meetings of the Society at such times as they may see fit; and they may arrange for commemorative celebrations by the Society.

They shall recommend plans to the Society for promoting its purposes, and, when practicable, may digest and prepare business for its meetings, and shall supervise all publications issued in its name, and decide whether copies of records or other documents or papers may be furnished on request of any party, in cases not pertaining directly to the business of the Society, and the proper conduct of its affairs.

They shall generally superintend the interests, and shall have the control and management of the affairs and funds of the Society. They shall also perform such duties as may be prescribed by the Constitution and By-Laws, or required by any Standing Rule or Resolve of the Society; provided, *however*, that they shall at no time be required to take any action nor contract any debt for which they shall be jointly or severally liable. They shall be competent to consent to and to accept the resignation or voluntary withdrawal from membership of any enrolled member of the Society.

They may require the attendance of any member of the Society, or any official or Committee thereof. at any meeting. for consultation and advice.

The Board of Managers shall meet as often as they may desire, or at the call of the President. or upon the written request of any three members of the same, addressed to the Secretary.

A majority of the Board of Managers shall be a quorum for the transaction of business.

At every annual meeting they shall submit to the Society a general report of their proceedings during the year then closing, and at such other time as may be required by the Society.

SECTION XI.

Expulsion and Suspension.

The Board of Managers shall have power to expel any enrolled member of this Society who, by a conduct inconsistent with a gentleman and a man of honor, or by an opposition to the interests of the Community in general or of this Society in particular, may render himself unworthy to continue a member, or who shall persistently transgress, or, without good excuse, willfully neglect or fail in the performance of any obligation enjoined by the Constitution or By-Laws or any standing Rule of this Society. *Provided,* that such member shall have received at least ten days' notice of the complaint preferred against him, and of the time and place for hearing the same, and have been thereby afforded an opportunity to be heard in person.

Whenever the cause of expulsion shall not have involved turpitude nor moral unworthiness, any member thus expelled may. upon the unanimous recommendation of the Board of Managers. but not otherwise. be restored to membership by the Society at any meeting.

The Board of Managers shall also have power to drop from the Roll the name of any enrolled member of the Society who shall be at least two years in arrears in the payment of dues, and who, on notice to pay the same. shall fail and neglect to do so within ten days thereafter. and upon being thus dropped, his membership shall cease and determine ; but he may be restored to membership at any time by the Board of Managers, on his application therefor. and upon his payment of all such arrears and of the annual dues from the date when he was dropped to the date of his restoration. The Board of Managers may also suspend any officer from the performance of his duties, for cause ; which proceeding must be reported to the Society and acted upon by it within thirty days, either by rescision of the suspension or removal of the suspended officer from office. or otherwise the suspension shall cease.

SECTION XII.

Vacancies and Terms of Office.

Whenever an officer of this Society shall die, resign, or neglect to serve. or be suspended, or be unable to properly perform the duties of his office, by reason of absence, sickness or other cause. and whenever an office shall be vacant. which the Society shall not have filled by an election, the Board of Managers shall have power to appoint a member to such office *pro tempore*, who shall act in such capacity until the Society shall elect a member to the vacant office, or until the inability due to " suspension. absence. sickness or other cause" shall cease. *Provided*, however, that the office of President or Secretary shall not thus be filled by the Board of Managers, when there shall be a Vice-President or Assistant Secretary to enter upon the duties of those offices respectively.

In like manner, the Board of Managers may supply vacancies among its members, under the same conditions and limitations ; and in case any member thereof, other than an officer, shall be absent from three consecutive meetings of the same, his place therein may be declared vacant by the Board of Managers and filled by an appointment which shall continue in full effect until the Society shall elect a successor.

Subject to these provisions, all officers of the Society, and the members of the Board of Managers, shall, from the time of their election or appointment, continue in their respective offices until the next annual meeting, and until their respective successors shall be duly chosen.

SECTION XIII.

Resignation.

No resignation or voluntary withdrawal from membership of any member enrolled in this Society shall become effective as a release from the obligations thereof, unless consented to and accepted by the Board of Managers.

SECTION XIV.

Disqualification.

No person who may be enrolled as a member in this Society shall be permitted to continue in membership where the proofs of claim of qualification by descent shall be found to be defective and insufficient to substantiate such claim,

or not properly authenticated. The Society, or the Board of
Managers, may, at any time after thirty days' notice to such
person to properly substantiate or authenticate his claim,
require the Secretary to erase his name from the list of
members, and such person shall thereupon cease to be a
member : *Provided*, he shall have failed or neglected to
comply satisfactorily with such notice.

Where the Board of Managers shall direct the erasure of
a person's name for a cause comprehended under this section, such person shall have a right of appeal to the next
annual meeting of the Society ; but he shall not be restored
to membership unless by a vote of three-fourths of the
members present on that occasion, or at a subsequent meeting to which the consideration of the appeal may have
been specifically postponed.

SECTION XV.

Annual and Special Meetings.

The Society shall hold an annual meeting in the city of
New York on the third day of December in every year, at
which a general election of officers and managers, by ballot,
shall take place, except when such date shall fall on Sunday,
in which case the meeting shall be held on the following day.

In such election the polls shall be open one and one-half
hours, and a majority of the ballots given for any office or
for a manager shall constitute a choice therefor ; but, if on
the first ballot no member shall receive such a majority,
then a further balloting, in such case, shall forthwith take
place, in which a plurality of votes given shall determine
the choice therefor. During any election the regular Order
of Business may be proceeded with.

Special meetings shall be held by direction of the Board
of Managers, or upon the written request of thirty members

of the Society, at such time and place as said Board may
direct. At such special meeting no business shall be trans-
acted except such as shall be specified in the notice therefor.

One week's notice of time and place of annual or special
meetings shall be given by publication in two daily news-
papers in the city of New York, and by mailing through the
post-office in said city a written or printed notice to every
member of the Society.

At all meetings of the Society thirty members shall constitute a quorum for the transaction of business.

The meetings of the Society for business shall be generally conducted according to Parliamentary Law, and the
following Order of Business shall, as far as the same may
be applicable, be followed :

Order of Business :

1. Meeting called to order by Presiding Officer.
2. Prayer by the Chaplain.
3. Reading of minutes of prior meetings not previously
acted upon.
4. Election of officers and managers, when necessary.
5. Communications from or Report of Board of Managers.
6. Reports of Officers.
7. Reports of Special Committees.
8. Unfinished business.
9. Written communications requiring action of the
Society.
10. Specially noticed business.
11. Notices of motion for subsequent meeting.
12. Miscellaneous business.
13. Reading of the Preamble to this Constitution.
14. Closing Prayer by the Chaplain.

SECTION XVI.

Service of Notices.

It shall be the duty of every member to inform the Secretary, by written communication, of his place of residence and of any change thereof, and of his post-office address.

Service of any notice under this Constitution or By-Laws upon any member of the Society, addressed to him at his last recorded place of residence or post-office address, and forwarded by mail, shall be deemed sufficient service of such notice.

SECTION XVII.

Recommendation of Candidates.

No member shall approve an application for membership in this Society unless he shall *know* the candidate to be worthy, and shall have satisfied himself by due examination of proofs that such candidate is eligible, and will, if admitted, be a desirable member.

SECTION XVIII.

Nominating Committee.

The Society may, at the annual meeting, choose a Nominating Committee, of nine members, to nominate officers and members of the Board of Managers, for election at the succeeding annual meeting.

In case the Society shall not choose such a Committee, the President shall, prior to every annual meeting, appoint such a Nominating Committee of nine members from among the members longest enrolled as such, who may consent to serve on such Committee, exclusive of officers or members of the Board of Managers.

The Nominating Committee shall select and nominate a ticket of the names proposed to fill the respective offices, to be elected by ballot, which ticket shall be printed and distributed as the " Regular Ticket " at the ensuing annual election.

In order to secure as far as may be in the Board of Managers stability in procedure and familiarity with precedents in the business affairs of the Society, every Nominating Committee shall, in making nominations for the suffrages of the Society of members of said Board other than those who are *ex-officio* members, so arrange their recommendations as to provide for the retirement annually of not less than three nor more than four of those who shall have served longest continuously on said Board, and for the continuance of a proportionate number.

SECTION XIX.

Decease of Members.

Upon the decease of *any* member residing within the State of New York, notice thereof, and of the time and place of the funeral, shall be given by the Secretary by publication, and it shall thereupon become the duty of the members, when practicable, to attend the obsequies.

Any member, upon being informed of the decease of a member, shall make it his business to see that the Secretary is promptly notified of the fact, which fact shall also, in due time, be communicated to the Society.

SECTION XX.

Certificate of Membership.

Every member shall be entitled to receive a certificate of membership, which shall be authenticated by the President and Secretary, and countersigned by the Registrar of the

46

Society, and to which the seal of the "SONS OF THE REVO-
LUTION" shall be affixed. The certificate shall be in form
following :

"SONS OF THE REVOLUTION."

Be it known that.........................has been duly
admitted a member of this Institution in right of the services
of.............................in the cause of American
Independence during the War of the Revolution.

Dated at the City of New York this....day of..........,
in the year of our Lord........thousand........hundred and
........., and of the Independence of the United States of
America the.........

....
President of the Society.

| I. S. |

....
Secretary of the Society.

....
Registrar.

SECTION XXI.

Marshal.

The President of the Society may, from time to time, in
his discretion, designate a member to act, under his direction, as Marshal for the Society in its commemorative celebrations, parades and other meetings, and to perform such
duties as usually appertain to such a position.

SECTION XXII.

Alterations or Amendments.

No alteration nor amendment of the By-Laws of this
Society shall be made unless notice thereof shall be duly
given in writing, signed by the member proposing the same,
at a meeting of the Society, nor unless the same shall be
adopted at a subsequent meeting, held at least thirty days
after such notice, by a vote of two-thirds of the members
present.

"IN THE NAME OF THE GREAT JEHOVAH AND THE CONTINENTAL CONGRESS!..."

An Address

ON

"Ticonderoga: or the Defeat of the Old World in the New,"

DELIVERED AT THE BERKELEY LYCEUM, MONDAY, MAY 11, 1891,
BEFORE THE SOCIETY,

By Professor Henry P. Johnston.

MR. PRESIDENT AND MEMBERS OF THE
"SOCIETY OF THE SONS OF THE REVOLUTION."

Ladies and Gentlemen:

In his noble address at the dedication of Bunker Hill monument nearly seventy years since, Daniel Webster, rising into national fame, eulogized the American Revolution as the grandest achievement of modern times—the saving event of the age, shining in relief as a wonder to the nations and a blessing to mankind.

Fulsome praise this, we would say, to bestow upon a movement whose effects had yet to mature, and whose resulting political system was hardly accepted as existing beyond its experimental stage. But Webster's estimate, based upon fact and faith and consciousness of American destiny, has been more than confirmed.

A wonder and a blessing! Indulging for a moment in the conceit this occasion may justify—where in all history have we had the spectacle of a provincial community bravely breaking its connection with a powerful government and venerated associations, and that, too, upon a nice issue of constitutional principle and cabinet policy ; then bounding forward on a great career, vigorous, confident, resourceful, developing by normal processes, expanding rapidly and prodigiously, avoiding disruption by a mighty struggle, and taking its place within the rounded century as one of the leading nations of the globe ? And where so much of opportunity for all men; where such freedom of person and opinion; where so little felt the finger of authority, and where such regard for authority; where so much self-respect in every social grade, rooted in the sense of common equality in citizenship; where more confidence in the sufficiency of governmental forms; where any greater disposition shown to expose dangers that may threaten them, and where, in general, any healthier state of society ? For in such things we must speak by comparison. A blessing, also, in the broader sense that we have inspired something like a world-faith in self-government. Not to speak of the acknowledged influence our example has had upon Continental Europe, the branch of the race to which we belong—what we call the Anglo-Saxon—has everywhere felt the leaven and is engaged in working out a common problem. In line with our own land to-day stands our Mother Country, England, a monarchy in form, in reality a free representative government. In line stands her great colony, Canada, a confederation of practically self-governing States; and in line stands that more distant but growing group, which is now moving to present itself to the world as the new Commonwealth of Australia. This galaxy of communities, claiming a place in the fore-front of civilization, and representing a population of one hundred and twenty millions, stands avowedly on the platform of principles of which the American Revolution and the American Constitution are the most prominent exponents. The Anglo-Saxon race, the world over, is to-day in its popular trend and sympathies democratic—in its political forms and relations, republican.

To appreciate the full significence of this Revolution we must associate together a series of distinct struggles—we must combine a series of distinct results; and appropriately so on the present anniversary, for of all the spots endeared to us by the valor and sacrifices of the men of " Seventy-six." Ticonderoga alone stands forth as the witness and symbol of the conflicts which proved decisive.

We remember the Revolution as having assured to us independence and a larger measure of self-government. This was the immediate outcome of that struggle, which in turn was a historical development of the English Revolution of 1688, and earlier efforts on the part of Englishmen to limit the prerogative of the Crown. All the way through our ancestral life we meet with the demand for rights and privileges. The American movement stands as the latest step forward in the same line, with the boon of independence super-added—a boon secured through the necessities of the situation. But the Revolution did more than close the traditional dispute with royalty at home. As being fought out on distant soil it had other relations. It closed and fittingly crowned a succession of struggles waged both in Europe and America affecting the future of the New World. It closed the struggle for possession in America a matter of the greatest moment to this nation; for we are apt to forget that our influence and proud position in the eye of the world is due not to our independence and our republican system alone. Our National grandeur lies in our expanse. Not the republic of the United States, but the dominant, the all but illimitable republic is the attraction we present; and this, it will be recalled, has come about not simply through our contest with England in the last century.

Turn back to the earlier situation. It is a striking fact in the history of this Continent—bordering, indeed, upon the romantic—that after its discovery and settlement by four leading powers of Europe—Spain, France, Holland and England—and after successive struggles on their part for supremacy here, it has passed out of the control of all of them. Not since the old Roman world succumbed to the Teutonic invader has there been anything more impressive in the course of events than this release of America from the grasp of Europe.

It had been the dream of the Spaniard that the regions brought to light through the faith of Columbus, and explored with so much zeal and hazard by his successors, would expand his dominions into an empire unmatched in wealth and grandeur, and whose power would overawe every rival. The ground of his hope seemed as good as his title to the soil. His sailors had, in fact, traced out a new world. They first skirted the coasts of South America, mapping it in its present shape as a distinct continent, hitherto unknown. They first crept along the line of the Isthmus and the deep indenture of the Gulf of Mexico, dropping into and giving names to the rivers and bays, and they first settled on our eastern and western coasts. The Spaniard planted himself in the West Indies, in South America, in Mexico, in California, and in Florida, asserted his exclusive sovereignty over these new regions and gloried in his expansion. But his dreams have been disturbed. Fate has handled him without gloves. To-day he owns, save some islands, not a foot of soil in the vast America he discovered! The Frenchman, also, came this way. Under the buoyant Cartier he pushed northward, looking for a turn in the endless coast, and thus discovered the St. Lawrence. Under Champlain and the Jesuit Fathers he penetrated to the Lakes trading with the natives, groping and wandering as he traded, until he reached the Mississippi. With a keen relish for exploration he descended the river, paddled up its tributaries, and, for the first time, laid out its course, and opened up that imperial domain we call our interior—the valley of the Mississippi. It once belonged to the Frenchman, and for its retention he struggled desperately. But he lost all. To-day he owns no more here than the Spaniard! The Dutch had their turn. They came to buy and trade. Claiming un-occupied territory, they settled down in this vicinity in the most natural and comfortable way, laid the foundations of the metropolis of the New World, and in their trade and industries forecast the possibilities of our Empire State. But one day in the midst of their growing prosperity the worst of all the Stuarts turned them out without notice, and, perhaps, without good warrant. The Holland which first cleared this region for us, the Holland which was our first and constant friend in the Revolution, does not now even own an island here! And last, came the Englishman. He did more than all others, for he brought with him a population, settling continuously along our coast for seven hundred miles. He planted villages and towns, organized society, established civil government ; in fact, created a new member for his empire—the American colonies. He crowded or pushed all rivals out. The Spaniard was kept down at the Gulf, the Frenchman yielded to his superior might, the Dutch were made of no account. All went. Destiny, as it was read in the last century, waved the English flag over this continent. But to-day another waves here. All that the Englishman retains on this side is Canada, and he holds that as a sort of confession that he could keep no more!

Here is a succession of events from which a nation-drama, as it were, might be composed, with no lack of material in the way of shifting scene and effective climax; and we can give it a sounding title—the " Humiliation of Europe in America."

If Europe is not here to-day, Europe alone is responsible. Her powers attempted to monopolize Nature's gift of a continent to the world, as they had so often wrested and monopolized territory at home. They overreached themselves, and lost. Europe is not here because of the soulless, iron mould in which her course has been forced to run for centuries. Rivalries, jealousies, state-craft, ambition, grasping policies, have been more often than not the springs of the "international incident" there, with retribution following. Proud Spain, for example, with the wealth of the New World in her lap, assumed to dictate, coerce and crush, until her enemies and her rivals, singly and in combination, succeeded in the course of two centuries to trim her plumage and relegate her to the position of a fourth-rate power. Her humiliation came, in part, in the shape of a weakened hold on America by the time of our Revolution, due to her enforced weakness at home. France and England succeeded to her supremacy. Then, between these two, came the giant conflicts of the last century, resulting in the expulsion of the French from America. England thus was left supreme. At the close of the Seven Years' War, or our French and Indian war in 1763, the British Empire stood at the height of its power. Influential in Continental diplomacy, mistress of the seas, the foundations of her Indian dominion laid, her American colonies undisturbed by the presence of either France or Holland, and Spain not to be feared, Britain ruled as never before.

And what now remained to humble *her?* What could exclude *her* from America? It is the same story. Her own Europeanism— traditional Europeanism, as she had imbibed it—explains all. Those Colonies! To her superficial eye they were but part of herself— three million British subjects inconveniently separated from her by an ocean, nothing more. In her pride and blind egotism, England, and we mean here official England, failed to observe that one hundred and fifty years of colonial life had eradicated the Old World impress among those people; that they had cut loose from the past; that the influence of isolation, throwing them upon their own resources, had developed a strong, self-reliant race; that--derived mainly, it is true, from the root and loins of old England the new soil, the new clime, the new surroundings, the new self-culture, the new political education, had bred in them something like a variation of the stock. England had failed to observe that in 1775 her colon-

ists had grown into a fifth element here, practically native to
America and unknown to Europe; and when she came to deal with
it, contrast and collision were inevitable. England's exclusive com-
mercial policy—not unlike what Spain's had been—her narrow sense
of political justice, her ultra views of authority, her Old World self-
assertion, brought about the rupture, and we have the American
Revolution with its result. The old England, the European England,
was finally excluded herself from these shores. The succession of
struggles for possession here was closed, leaving the new American
dominant with a noble stretch of territory, from the Lakes to Florida,
from the Atlantic to the Mississippi. The certainty of our future expansion was then and there fixed. Spain still lay west and south of
us, but Spain was needy and elfete, and time would add to our pos-
sessions all that we might seek.

The Revolution thus brought us into an inheritance of magnifi-
cent domain, as well as into the full inheritance of rights, privileges
and autonomy. The former has been necessary to impress ourselves
and the world with the blessings of the latter. A contracted republic,
confined to a strip upon this coast, such as we might have been, had
European contests resulted differently, would doubtless be respected,
but it could not develop, nor command, nor inspire. Let us rejoice
that we have here no "pent-up Utica;" no Switzerland—happy republic, shining in the heart of Europe, but cooped up in mountain
cantons, with her neutrality guaranteed by monarchies; no Holland
of old, with glorious history, in the enjoyment of whose fruits we
share, but outstripped and overawed by armed powers on every side;
no isolated city democracies, the pride of antiquity, but doomed to
absorption and extinction. No! we, ourselves, and the sympathetic
world glory in seeing here not a republic in pigmy form, but an out-
stretched colossus, the "wonder" of Webster's anticipation—not a
beacon light, but a new and radiant sun, whose blaze and warmth
and glowing splendor penetrate to every corner and compel the attention and reflection of mankind.

Ticonderoga! This society, in whose organization we have a most
happy conception realized, fittingly recalls such memories of the
Revolution. The great "dead past" of a nation is not dead. As
well tell us that the roots of the giant oak are dead, because they are

buried under the surface. That never can be dead which alone will account for what Carlyle so beautifully describes as "the leafy, blossoming present." Ticonderoga and all the other fields of that conflict remind us of things done, the atmosphere of whose influence is a living breath to-day. To us assembled this evening Ticonderoga presents itself in all its historical significance as associated with events and results that have made possible our enormous territorial growth. It plays a striking part in the humiliation of Europe. It recalls the two greatest of the struggles for possession here. It is the silent witness of the defeat of both France and England in America.

The old fortress, now ruined and crumbling, at the southern end of Lake Champlain, has stood there, once rebuilt, for one hundred and thirty-six years. In 1755 the French established themselves at that point, and put up what Parkman calls "their redoubtable stronghold" with which they expected to command, with other points, the entire lake region, and connect with points to the South and West that would secure the Ohio and Mississippi Valleys. For four years the contest was carried on for the control of the fortress, in which figured prominently such leaders as Montcalm and Dieskau, Amherst, Abercromby, Sir William Johnson, Howe, Williams and Lyman. In the summer of 1759 success fell to Amherst, and the French lost Ticonderoga and their positions to the northward. This important blow, with Wolfe's signal victory at Quebec in the same year, put the finish to French dominion in America. Our most dangerous contestant for the territory here was expelled, to be followed twenty years later by England herself.

What we especially celebrate on this occasion is the second capture of Ticonderoga—its loss to Britain at the outbreak of the Revolution, May 10, 1775. While not a leading event as a military achievement, we cannot fail to recall that there have been single incidents in history, not fully appreciated at the time, which magnify as they recede and their meaning becomes better understood. Have we not here an illustration? Certain points then suggest themselves: What place and prominence shall we give the capture of the fortress in the valuation of Revolutionary events? To whom belongs the credit of conceiving or planning it? What men won the laurels of the exploit?

The position of Ticonderoga, in relative importance, was not unlike that of ancient Thermopylæ. Both of them were gateways—gateways between northern and southern lands and dominion. Each controlled a situation, and was alike a menace and a defence. Down through memorable and tragic Thermopylæ have poured successively Persian, Macedonian, Roman, Gaul and Turk, to devastate Grecian fields and wipe out Grecian freedom. Around Ticonderoga in actions much less striking in history, true, but scarcely less significant in results, Frenchman, Englishman and American have played their part. The strategic value of that post, as demonstrated in the French and Indian War, had been enhanced by the time of the Revolution. Powerfully reinforced, and under vigorous military administration, Ticonderoga was capable of becoming a standing source of danger to New York and New England. The same reasons that impelled so many men from those sections of the country to march against it in 1758 and '59 would impel still more to march in 1775 and '76. Recalling the topography of that region, it will be observed that, in British hands, Ticonderoga would have been made the capital point in a chain of posts and fortifications, stretching from the St. Lawrence to the southern end of Lake George, and possibly carried to the Hudson only fifty miles above Albany. With St. John securing the Sorel River to the northward, with a fleet of bateaux and gunboats controlling Lake Champlain; with the strong works at Crown Point restored; with Ticonderoga and Mount Independence rendered unassailable; with Lake George free and protected by Fort William Henry; with Canada as a base of supplies, and with the savage as an ally, the position of the enemy would have seriously embarrassed American plans and movements in the northern field. Operating from such a line and front, it would have been possible for the British to undertake or threaten, in each year of the war, what Burgoyne attempted in 1777. They could have moved directly upon Albany, or frequently repeated expeditions like those to Bennington and Oriskany, keeping the settlements in Northern New York, in Vermont, New Hampshire, Western Massachusetts and Connecticut in a chronic state of alarm. As a consequence, those States would have been compelled to provide for a general defence in that quarter, and so far have been weakened in ability to contribute men and supplies for the wider Continental demand. This complication could not but have affected unfavorably every campaign of the Revolution.

Fortunately, however, the early capture of Ticonderoga forestalled these unwelcome probabilities, and immediately turned the advantage to the American arm of the balance. Upon the seizure of the fort the colonists moved northward, took possession themselves of Crown Point, sailed the length of Lake Champlain, and by the autumn found Montreal in their hands. Instead of suffering themselves to be crowded back upon their own settlements, they carried the war into the enemy's country. Their strategy was of the highest order, for it pushed the field of immediate operations two hundred miles away from their neighborhood up to the line of the St. Lawrence, and in addition put the enemy on the defensive. Was it not precisely this that Demosthenes urged the Athenians to do when the wily Philip of Macedon threatened descent upon Greece? " Strengthen our northern colonies," said the great, earnest orator; "fight Philip where he is, at home!" But lethargy following a long period of supremacy and fading public spirit had beset Athens, and her citizens could not be roused. Those fertile, robust colonists of '75, however, who had never read a Phillipic nor ever heard of Macedon, became for the moment generals under the impulse of their new and absorbing cause. That early surprise of Ticonderoga proved far more than an incident. It was military forecast. It gave us territory; it gave us time; it gave us confidence; it saved us our settlements; it gave us many cannon then much needed; and it signally facilitated military operations elsewhere in the field. We must credit it with most valuable advantages secured and proportionate dangers avoided.

And what was the exploit? An old story often told, but still bright as the firesides around which that story was told again and again in that day among our northern hills and valleys. It was an exploit at which our hardy ancestors were adepts—a bit of skillful by-play, a well-laid surprise, the leap of a panther out of the woods, the swoop of an eagle upon its prey!

In the month of April, 1775, when the war opened, you would have found Captain Delaplace's Company of the Twenty-Sixth Regiment of British regulars doing so-called garrison duty at the old fort. It numbered less than fifty men. What they were there for was, perhaps, to them a puzzle, and no doubt a sleepy, idle life they had of it. Had they sniffed the danger in the air there would have been work enough on hand, repairing walls and watching the roads. But turn in another direction. In that same month of April, the moment the Lexington Alarm was sounded and war was accepted as inevitable, you would have found many men all over New England and New York looking instinctively toward Ticonderoga. Can there be any doubt of this? There were some thousand old soldiers of the previous war still living in those colonies whose thoughts would immediately revert to that strategic point. It was the one point to which they were marched in the old campaigns. If it was important then it was still more important now, and the necessity of securing it for the colonies at once presented itself. John Brown of Pittsfield advised the Massachusetts Provincial Congress to seize it "as soon as possible." Benedict Arnold talked of it on his march from New Haven to Lexington. Parsons, Wyllys, Mott and others of Connecticut, Ethan Allen and his Green Mountain Boys, Adams and Hancock of Boston—and how many more?—all had the matter in mind and at heart. But the men among the multitude whom we have to do with are the men who acted. It is the men who took time by the forelock and the fort by surprise that interest us on an occasion like this.

Two expeditions against the fortress were set on foot simultaneously in two different quarters. The one best planned and first "mobilized" succeeded. Should we be surprised to learn that its starting point was Hartford, Connecticut? Not, when we recall that colony's exertions to do her part with her neighboring colonies to keep Ticonderoga in English hands in the French and Indian War. Her anxiety for its possession was none the less active in the present crisis, and she was ready for the enterprise. The last days of the April session of the Assembly at Hartford had been devoted to the serious and exciting business of war preparation. Profoundly moved by the Lexington Alarm, popular sentiment in favor of resistance had acquired overwhelming force. Young men were arming, old men advising. As everywhere else, energetic leaders and newly appointed officers discussed measures, plans, prospects. They canvassed the field in public and private, in knots and groups, on the corner and at the hearthstones; and the uppermost question with them all was—"Lexington means war—the next move what?" It was a question that could have found more than one answer, but one of those groups answered it in its own way and thereby became famous. It was answered in a very resolute, practical and telling fashion. Those men offset the Lexington raid by promptly seizing Ticonderoga—and in the step we have a touch of righteous retaliation as well as good strategy.

The Hartford enterprise initiated secretly, and was at once private and semi-official. Who first urged the project, who was the moving spirit in the company, we cannot venture to say with certainty. One of their number, Colonel Samuel H. Parsons, of New London, leaves us this brief record in the case : "On my way to Hartford," he writes to Joseph Trumbull, "I fell in with Captain Arnold, who gave me an account of the state of Ticonderoga, and that a great number of brass cannon were there. On my arrival at Hartford, Col. Sam. Wyllys, Mr. Deane and myself first undertook and projected taking that fort; and with the assistance of three other persons procured money, men, etc., and sent out on this expedition without any consultation with Assembly or others." "This I mention," adds Parsons, "only for this reason, that 'tis matter of diversion to me to see the various competitors for the honor of concerting and carrying this matter into execution contending so strenuously about a matter, in the execution of which all concerned justly deserve applause." With other records in corroboration we are thus in possession of the names of at least three of the originators of and prime movers in the Connecticut scheme—Parsons, Wyllys, Deane. It is equally clear that the name of Benedict Arnold should be associated with these three as an originator, but his efforts, it will appear, were identified with another undertaking.

The sinews of the expedition, money and men, were provided forthwith. Borrowing upon their own notes three hundred and eighty pounds from the State Treasury, Parsons and his associates, increased to eleven, placed the funds in the hands of three trusted individuals—Phelps, Mott and Romans—with directions to proceed to Western Massachusetts and the Green Mountain settlements, and there organize a force to capture the fort. They were to act according to their best judgment. From Hartford to Ticonderoga is a distance, as the road goes, of two hundred miles. At Salisbury, Conn., on the route, the three men in question were joined by thirteen others, selected for their known integrity, loyalty and enthusiasm. Among them were Bigelow, Bull, Blagden, Babcock, Halsey, Nichols and others, subsequently meritorious officers in the Continental army. These sixteen men were the nucleus of the expedition in the field.

At Salisbury they agreed to make their way on horseback, unarmed, like casual travellers or traders, to the town of Sheffield, Massachusetts, where they proceeded to plan and execute. Two of their number were sent West to Albany to buy provisions and put them on the road to Ticonderoga. The rest pushing on to Pittsfield the next day found there some willing spirits who joined heart and soul in the enterprise; among them John Brown and Colonel Easton. These two advised the Connecticut party to enlist men from that vicinity, and accordingly Mott and Easton struck out to Williamstown and Jericho and quickly picked up forty resolute volunteers. Sixty men now in the party, and all headed by different roads for Bennington in the Grants. There more men were sent off with Connecticut money to buy provisions, and two others, Phelps and Hiccock, were entrusted with the secret mission of proceeding in advance to spy out the fortress, Joshua-like, and report its condition. Phelps shrewdly played the lumbering countryman passing that way, and dropped in to be shaved by the garrison barber. He found matters as he hoped to find them, and returned to report that the redcoats were still listless and unsuspicious.

At Bennington also we meet with one of the striking figures of the exploit—Ethan Allen ! The pride of the Green Mountain Boys, eccentric and fearless, with one hundred and fifty comrades of his own stamp, he added momentum to the force and picturesqueness to the character of the expedition. Bennington is sixty miles from Ticonderoga. As the object of the enterprise could no longer be concealed, small parties of men were sent out on all the roads leading to the fortress, with orders to delay every person they met. But even with this precaution it is remarkable that no lurking tory or treacherous volunteer, with an eye to the reward for information he might expect from the British, found his way to the fort in the five days that intervened before the surprise. On Sunday night, May 7, all were at Castleton, twenty miles southwest of the coveted stronghold. Here final organization was effected. A sort of military Executive Committee was formed, with Mott at the head, while Allen was placed in command of the force, now over two hundred strong, with Easton as second and Seth Warner as third.

And here at Castleton suddenly appeared another figure no less striking than Allen's—Benedict Arnold ! As yet unknown he boldly presented himself in camp, with the startling demand upon the Com-

mittee to surrender the command of the expedition to himself. Who
was he, they asked, and why such assumption of authority ?

With Arnold is associated the second enterprise for the capture of
Ticonderoga referred to. After his conversation in the matter with
Colonel Parsons at Hartford, he marched on with his company to
Boston to find that its services were not in immediate demand. The
Ticonderoga suggestion absorbed his mind. Whether he had first
proposed the surprise to Parsons or whether Parsons conceived of it
after the conversation may never be known, but that both men immediately acted upon the hint, and independently of each other, is a
matter of history. How Parsons' activity culminated we have seen.
Arnold was equally prompt and energetic, and is deserving of about
the same meed of praise for his personal efforts that one would
award to any individual of the expedition in hand. Instead of re-
turning to Hartford to associate himself with Parsons and the others—
and here, no doubt, we see the assertion of his high-born spirit and
ambition to command—he turned immediately to the Massachusetts
authorities and urged them to undertake the surprise on their own
account. Succeeding in his application, he received a commission as
a Massachusetts Colonel, and was given due authority to raise a regiment in the western part of the colony and seize Ticonderoga.
Without delay he set out on his secret errand, and arrived at Castleton only to find, as we have seen, that the Connecticut party had
forestalled him. Not to be baffled, however, he made the claim that
the chief command belonged to him as holding the highest commission and from the highest authority. But the expedition was
fully organized, and had accepted the authority of the Connecticut
party, which, though private and self-constituted, was known to be
representative and semi-official as supported by a loan from the public
Treasury. Arnold's demand, accordingly, was scouted and resisted.
Much parley and angry talk ensued, with the result that the new-
comer was compelled to yield his point and accept an honorary but
honorable place at the head of the force as a *quasi* leader side by
side with Ethan Allen.

On the heels of the Arnold episode came the report into camp that
the Ticonderoga garrison had at last got wind of the Yankee enterprise and were prepared to receive it. But nothing would daunt
those determined souls. Half were frontiersmen—all that we are
accustomed to imagine as embodied in the make-up of the Green

Mountain Boy. They were not to be frightened. Mott declared he would not return to Hartford until he had at least marched around the fortress if he could not get in. All showed the spirit of the old Spartan, when told that in a coming action with the Persians he would find their arrows pouring in so thickly as to hide the sun. " Well," was his confident reply, " so much the better! we shall then have the advantage of fighting in the shade!"

Finally, on the night of May 9, the determined band reaches Shoreham, on the eastern side of Lake Champlain, and prepares to cross to Ticonderoga opposite, a distance of two miles. Ferriage is slow from lack of boats, and at 4 o'clock on the next morning, in spite of Allen's and Arnold's best exertions, not more than eighty-five men are over. As daylight will discover the movement to the enemy, the attack must be made at once, and fully alive to this the leaders waste no time. Allen stops a moment to harangue the company, closing with some such words as these :—" Friends and fellow soldiers : I now propose to advance before you, and in person conduct you through the gate; for we must this morning either quit our pretensions to valor or possess ourselves of this fortress in a few minutes; and inasmuch as it is a desperate attempt (which none but the bravest men dare undertake), I do not urge it on any contrary to his will. You that will undertake it, voluntarily, poise your firelocks!" Every musket comes to the front, and all push forward with Allen and Arnold conspicuous at their head. As they near the sally-port of the frowning work, a sentinel snaps his musket and quickly retreats. The main gate is found closed, but the narrow wicket is open, and through it the party dashes impetuously one by one, and immediately re-forms in the centre of the parade. The garrison is asleep! Ticonderoga is taken!

As the awakened regulars came tumbling out of their quarters they were instantly made prisoners. And as for Ethan Allen, can the pen do him more graphic honor than he receives from the artist's pencil in the illustration on the programme of the evening ? Roused from his dreams of security by some rude thumping on his door, the Commander of the post made his appearance in the uniform of the hour, and with a flickering light beheld the stalwart, threatening form of the Green Mountain Alexander. A pointed conversation thereupon took place, and one form of it is as good as another. The form we like the best—that which can never be erased from our

63

school books or our histories—is the best authenticated.* "By what authority do you demand the surrender of this fort?" exclaimed the British hero in white. The intensity of the confusion that must have overcome him in Allen's answer can only be imagined! "*In the name of the Great Jehovah and the Continental Congress!*" replied his captor, and the beginning of the end of England's domination in America was sealed!

Ticonderoga with Thermopylæ to-day are things of the past. Hardly can they appear in a famous rôle again. Modern engines of war and modern military methods have disarmed them of their importance. And yet they remain representative names. Thermopylæ may no longer have its terrors, but along the Rhine and the Danube what? Mighty contests of the recent past and contests yet to come. Ancient Europe in one respect finds its counterpart—a more brilliant counterpart—in modern Europe. War there still remains an imminent and a blighting possibility. With us Ticonderoga has no counterpart. No fortresses loom up like shadows within our borders; no standing armies wither the hand of industry. We rejoice that this is so to-day at least, and may it ever be! And for this situation, the greatest of blessings, let us profoundly acknowledge our indebtedness to the American Revolution. It was that Revolution that sounded here the death-knell of the old world system of rival *separate* States, divided from each other by walls and battlements and glittering arms, and dedicated this Continent to the system of *United* States, locked in a common national brotherhood under the sheltering panoply of peace.

---

* Allen's reply appears first in Goodwin's "American Revolution," under date of August, 1775. It is also given by Allen in his autobiography or narrative. The exclamation has been treated with some humor and sarcasm, as being highly bombastic and without point. The Continental Congress, it is claimed, had not yet, by a few hours, convened at Philadelphia, and its authority was a mere shadow. It will be recalled, however, that the First Congress, which had adjourned only a few months before, formed the American "Association," to whose authority the Whig element subscribed, and then provided for its own successor. Delegates to the latter, or Second Congress, were then (May, 1775) assembling at Philadelphia to proceed with the deliberations, and advise as the situation might demand. The two Congresses were looked upon as essentially a continuous body, representing a new governing force in the Colonies which the emergency had created. It was the talk of the day; its advice respected; its recommendations carried out. To Allen and his men it was anything but a shadow, and in demanding the fortress, the authority of Congress, whether given or not, was the one authority to evoke. The reply came naturally.

MEMBERSHIP ROLL.

1891. ABBOT. EVERETT VERGNIES,   712

> Great-great-grandson of Major Abiel Abbot (1741–1809),
> Muster-Master and Paymaster, with rank of Cap-
> tain, in Colonel Nahum Baldwin's Regiment New
> Hampshire Militia, raised to reinforce the Continental
> Army at New York, September 16, 1776; 2d Major
> 5th Regiment New Hampshire Militia, December 11,
> 1776; Major in Colonel Moses Nichol's Regiment
> New Hampshire Militia, raised to reinforce the Conti-
> nental Army at Ticonderoga, June 29, 1777; 1st Ma-
> jor 5th Regiment New Hampshire Militia. March 30,
> 1781; Member of New Hampshire Provincial Con-
> gress. 1777, 1779 and 1780.

1885. ABNEY, JOHN RUTLEDGE.

> Great-great-grandson of Lieutenant William Abney, of
> Major Andrew Williamson's Battalion South Carolina
> Militia.

1887. ABORN, ROBERT W.,   11

> Grandson of Privateersman Daniel Aborn, Commander
> of the Privateer Sloop-of-War "Chance" of Rhode
> Island.

1886. ADAMS, CHARLES H.,   91

> Grandson of Ensign Anthony Egbertse (1753–1833), 1st
> Regiment Albany County Militia, Colonel Jacob
> Lansing, Jr., New York.

Elected.

No. of
Insignia.

1891. ADDOMS. SAMUEL KISSAM,   57

Grandson of Lieutenant Jonas Addoms, of New York
(1753-1837), 2d Regiment Continental Corps of Artillery, Colonel John Lamb.

1891. ALDEN. CHARLES HENRY, Lieutenant-Colonel and Surgeon, U. S. A.,   678

Grandson of Private Henry White (1752-1837), Private
in Captain Sabin Mann's Company, Colonel Hardee's
Regiment Massachusetts Militia, April, 1775.
Also, Grandson of Private Eliab Alden (1762-1841),
Private in Captain Joshua White's Company, Colo-
nel Eben Sprout's Regiment Massachusetts Militia,
"Dartmouth Alarm," May, 1778, and in Expedition
to Rhode Island, 1779.

1891. ALEXANDER, HENRY EUGENE,

Great-grandson of Surgeon Thomas Noble Stockett
(1717-1802), 1st Lieutenant in Captain Thomas Wat-
kin's Company, South River Battalion, Anne Arun-
del County (Maryland) Militia, February 13, 1776; 2d
Surgeon's Assistant to Colonel William Richardson's
Battalion, Maryland Flying Camp Militia, September
26, 1776; later Surgeon Maryland Line; then transferred to Recruiting Department, and served to close
of war.

1891. ALLEN. JOHN PLATT,   649

Great-great-grandson of Captain Daniel Platt (1738-
1826), Ensign in Captain John Ely's Company 6th
Regiment Connecticut Line, Colonel S. H. Parsons,
May 1, 1775; 1st Lieutenant in 4th Battalion Connecticut Militia, November 6, 1777; Captain in Colonel Worthington's Regiment Connecticut Militia,
July, 1779; Lieutenant in Captain Wright's Company of Militia, "New Haven Alarm," 1779.

Also, Great-grandson of Private Aaron Hall (1760–
1839), Captain Stephen Hall's Company 7th Regiment
Connecticut Line, Colonel Heman Swift, May 24,
1777.

Also, Great-grandson of Private Archelaus Allyn (1749–
1828), Private in Captain Isaac Cook's Company
Wallingford (Connecticut) Militia, "Lexington
Alarm," April 19, 1775; Private in 2d Company, Cap-
tain Street Hall, 7th Regiment Connecticut Line,
Colonel Charles Webb, July 8, 1775.

1890. ALLEN, THEODORE LATHROP,   437

Great-grandson of Lieutenant Solomon Allen (1751–
1821), 2d Regiment Continental Light Dragoons,
Lieutenant-Colonel Jameson, Conn.

1891. ANDERSON, JOHN SCHUYLER,   579.

Great-great-grandson of Josiah Hornblower, Speaker of
Lower House (Assembly) Provincial Congress, New
Jersey, 1780; Member of Upper House (Council),
1781–4.

1890. ANDERSON, JOSEPH LONGWORTH, *M. D.*,   458

Grandson of Lieutenant-Colonel Richard Clough Anderson (1750–1826), Captain 5th Regiment Virginia
Continental Infantry, January 26, 1776; Major 1st
Regiment Virginia Continental Infantry, February
10, 1778; later, Lieutenant-Colonel 6th Regiment Virginia Continental Infantry.

1890. ANDERSON, LARZ, 2d,

Great-grandson of Lieutenant-Colonel Richard Clough
Anderson (1750–1826), Captain 5th Regiment Virginia
Continental Infantry, January 26, 1776; Major 1st
Regiment Virginia Continental Infantry, February
10, 1778; later, Lieutenant-Colonel 6th Regiment Vir-
ginia Continental Infantry.

68

Elected.		No. of Insignia.

1891. ANDREWS, JAMES M.,   505

Great-grandson of Corporal Miles Andras (1735 ——),
Captain Hezekiah Willes' Company, Colonel Wol-
cott's Regiment Connecticut Militia, December, 1775.
Also, Great-grandson of Private Abel Whitlock, Pri-
vate in Captain Samuel Comstock's Company, 9th
Regiment Connecticut Militia, Lieutenant-Colonel
John Mead, August, 1776; Private in Captain Lock-
wood's Company, Connecticut Coast Guards, 1780.

1888. ANGELL, MALCOM HENRY,   214

Great-grandson of Colonel Israel Angell, Major Rhode
Island Militia, 1775; Major 11th Regiment Continental Infantry, Colonel Hitchcock, 1776; Lieutenant-Colonel 2d Battalion Rhode Island Continental
Infantry, Colonel Hitchcock, 1776.

1888. ANTHONY, RICHARD AMERMAN,   159

Great-grandson of Captain Nicholas N. Anthony, 3d
Regiment New York County Militia, Colonel
Abraham P. Lott.

1890. ARMS, FRANK THORNTON,

Great-great-grandson of Sergeant Henry Mason (1759–
1836), Sergeant in Captain Latham's Company of
Connecticut Artillery, stationed at Groton March 6,
1781, wounded at Groton Heights, September 6, 1781.
Also, Great-great-grandson of Ensign Daniel Billings
(1750–1801), Sergeant in 3d Company, Captain Samuel Prentice, 6th Regiment Connecticut Militia, Colonel S. H. Parsons, 1775; Ensign 10th Regiment
Connecticut Line, Colonel S. H. Parsons, 1775.

Also, Great-great-great-grandson of Captain John Williams (1739–1781), Private in Captain McClelland's Company Woodstock (Connecticut) Militia, Lexington Alarm, April, 1775; Private in Captain John Chapman's Company 6th Regiment Connecticut Militia, Colonel S. H. Parsons, May 6, 1775; Ensign in 4th Company, Captain Wheeler, 4th Battalion, Colonel Samuel Selden, Connecticut Militia; Lieutenant in Captain William Stanton's Company, 8th Regiment Connecticut Militia, Lieutenant-Colonel Oliver Smith, September 8, 1776; Captain in Colonel Obadiah Johnson's Regiment Connecticut Militia, January 1, 1778, served in Rhode Island; Captain in Connecticut Militia, New Haven Alarm, July, 1779; Captain in 8th Regiment Connecticut Militia, 1780; killed in action at Groton Heights, September 6, 1781.

Also, Great-great-great-great-grandson of Private Elnathan Perkins (1717–1781), Connecticut Militia, killed in action at Groton Heights, September 6, 1781.

Also, Great-great-grandson of Captain Peter Comstock (1732–1802), 3d Regiment Connecticut Militia, Colonel Jonathan Latimer, 1781.

1890. ARMSTRONG, PHILANDER B.,   432

Great-grandson of Private Henry Eads (1755–1841), Captain Thomas Morseland's Company, Colonel Brown's Regiment Maryland Militia, 1776 to 1782.

1891. ARNOLD, FRANK,   573

Great-grandson of Surgeon Philip Padelford (1753–1815), Surgeon's Mate, Colonel Thomas Carpenter's Regiment Rhode Island Militia, 1778, and served on ship-of-war "General Mifflin," 1780.

Also, Great-great-grandson of Captain-Lieutenant James Arnold (1723-1793), 3d Lieutenant 1st Company Warwick (Rhode Island) Militia, Captain Job Randall, 1776; Captain Lieutenant Kent County (Rhode Island) Militia, 1778; Signer of the Declaration of Independence of Rhode Island, 1776; Assistant to the Governor of Rhode Island, 1775, 1776, 1778, 1780; Member of Rhode Island Council of War, 1777; Member of Rhode Island Assembly, 1775. 1782; Justice of the Court of Common Pleas for Warwick, 1782-3.

1890. ARNOLD, JAMES OLIVER,

Great-great-grandson of Caleb Arnold (1725 1784), Member of Rhode Island Provincial Congress, 1773 to 1778, and Member Rhode Island War Committee. 1780.
Also, Great-grandson of Private William Arnold (1753-1806), Captain Stephen Kimball's Company, Rhode Island Militia, Colonel Daniel Hitchcock, 1775.

1890. AUSTIN, JOSEPH ELIOT,   420

Grandson of Fifer Appollus Austin (1760-1842), Captain Harmon's Company, 4th Regiment Connecticut Line, Colonel John Durkee, February 16, 1777.

1889. BABCOCK, HARRY SALTONSTALL,   103

Great-grandson of Colonel Harry Babcock (1736-1800), served as Volunteer at Boston, 1775; Colonel of 4th Regiment Rhode Island Continental Infantry, January, 1776; honorably discharged May, 1776, on account of illness.
Also, Great-great-grandson of Major-General Joshua Babcock (1707-1783), Major-General Rhode Island Colony Brigade, October, 1775; Chief Justice of Rhode Island, 1775; Member of State Council of War, 1775 to 1780; Member of Rhode Island Assembly, 1775, and Speaker of same. 1778.

1890. BABCOCK, HENRY DENISON, 411

Great-great-grandson of Colonel Harry Babcock (1736–
1800), served as Volunteer at Boston, 1775; Colonel
of 4th Regiment Rhode Island Continental Infantry,
January, 1776; honorably discharged May, 1776, on
account of illness.

Also, Great-great-great-grandson of Major-General
Joshua Babcock (1707–1783), Major-General Rhode
Island Colony Brigade, October, 1775; Chief Justice
of Rhode Island, 1775; Member of State Council of
War, 1775 to 1780; Member of Rhode Island Assem-
bly, 1775, and Speaker of same, 1778.

1892. BACON, WILLIAM POST HAWES,

Great-grandson of Private Richard Bacon (1757–1822),
Captain Hezekiah Welles' Company, Colonel Erastus
Wolcott's Regiment Connecticut State Troops, 1776,
at siege of Boston; Private in Captain J. P. Wylly's
Company, Colonel S. B. Webb's Regiment "Addi-
tional Continental," May 8, 1777; captured on Long
Island, December 10, 1777; Prisoner two years and
nine months; Private in Elisha Hopkins' Company
3d Regiment Connecticut Line, Colonel S. B. Webb,
January 1, 1781.

Also, Great-grandson of Elisha Skinner (1753–1823),
served in the Commissary's Department under Commissary-General Jeremiah Wadsworth of Connecticut.

Also, Great-great-grandson of Lieutenant Joseph Haws
(1727–1818), Captain Fairbanks' Company Massachusetts Militia, and representative to General Court,
1778–81.

1888. BADGER, WILLIAM WHITTLESLEY, 193

Great-grandson of Colonel Joseph Badger, 10th Regiment New Hampshire Militia, 1776.

72

1891. BAKER, GEORGE LIVINGSTON,

Great-grandson of Private Jesse Davidson (1758 ——),
Private in Captain James Gilmore's Company of
Windham (New Hampshire) Militia, July 8, 1775;
Private in Captain Jesse Wilson's Company, Colonel
Moses Nichol's Regiment New Hampshire Militia,
raised to reinforce the Northern Army, July 21, 1777.

1892. BAKER, REVEREND GEORGE STUART,   778

Great-grandson of Private Joseph Wheeler (1735-1793),
Private in Captain Samuel Stone's Company, Colonel
William Prescott's Regiment Massachusetts Militia,
"Lexington Alarm," April 19, 1775; Member of
Massachusetts Provincial Congress.

1889. *BAKER, PETER CARPENTER (died May 19, 1889),   537

Great-grandson of First Lieutenant Increase Carpenter,
Queens County Battalion Militia of New York.

1891. BALCH, COLLINS LAWTON,

Great-great-grandson of John Collins, of Rhode Isl-
and (1717-1795), Member Continental Congress, 1778-
80; Signer of the Rhode Island Declaration of Independence, March 4, 1776; Member of Rhode Island
Assembly, 1775-6.

1890. BALCH, LEWIS, M. D.,   457

Great-grandson of Colonel John Jay (1745-1829), Member of the Continental Congress; President of same
three years; prepared draft of Constitution of New
York, 1777, and appointed first Chief Justice under it;
Chairman of the New York Council of Safety; Member of the New York Provincial Congress; appointed
Colonel of 2d Regiment New York City Militia, October 27, 1775.

1890. BALDWIN, CHARLES MARVIN,

Great-great-grandson of Roger Sherman (1721-1793),
Member of Continental Congress from Connecticut,
1775 to 1789; Signer of the Declaration of Independence.

1890. BALDWIN, HENRY DE FOREST,

> Great-great-grandson of Roger Sherman (1721 1793),
> Member of Continental Congress from Connecticut,
> 1775 to 1789; Signer of the Declaration of Inde-
> pendence.

1891. BALDWIN, SIMEON,

> Great-grandson of Roger Sherman (1721 1793), Mem-
> ber of Continental Congress from Connecticut, 1775
> to 1789; Signer of the Declaration of Independence.

1889. BALDWIN, WALTER SHERMAN,   203

> Great-great-grandson of Private Benjamin Goldthwait,
> Captain David Parks' Company Massachusetts
> Militia, December 20, 1775.

1891. BANGS, ANSON CUYLER,   607

> Great-grandson of Captain John N. Bleecker (1739
> 1825), 6th Company Albany County Militia, Colonel
> Jacob Lansing, Jr., October 20, 1775; previously (Au-
> gust 3, 1775) Assistant Deputy Commissary-General
> Northern Department.

1891. BANKS, AUGUSTINE,

> Great-grandson of Private John Banks, Private in
> Captain Jonathan Dimon's Company, Connecticut
> Militia, Lexington Alarm, April 19, 1775; Private in
> Captain Ebenezer Hill's Company, Colonel Samuel
> Whiting's Regiment Connecticut Militia, October 5,
> 1777.
>
> *Also*, Great-grandson of Captain David Olmstead, Cor-
> poral 4th Company, Captain Joseph Hart, 7th Regi-
> ment Connecticut Militia, Colonel Charles Webb,
> August 7, 1775; Sergeant in Captain Benedict's Com-
> pany, Colonel Bradley's Battalion Connecticut Mili-
> tia, August 22, 1776; Captain in Colonel Roger Enos'
> Regiment Connecticut Militia, June 3, 1778 (on the
> Hudson); Captain in Connecticut "Provisional"
> Regiment, March, 1781.

74

Also, Great-grandson of Lieutentant John Foster (1742–1788), Captain Anther Smith's Company, Ulster County Militia, Colonel Jonathan Hasbrouck, October 11, 1775.

1891. BANKS, DAVID,   507

Grandson of Captain and Quartermaster David Banks (1743–1815), New Jersey Militia.

1892. BANISTER, REVEREND THOMAS LEWIS,

Great-grandson of Lieutenant-Colonel John Banister (1709–1790), Lawson's Brigade Virginia Line; Member of Virginia Convention, 1776–7; Member of Continental Congress, 1778–9; Signer of the Articles of Confederation, 1781.

1891. BARCLAY, JAMES SEARLE,   498

Great-grandson of Ensign John Barclay (1749–1816), Ensign Philadelphia Associators, 1776; Member of Philadelphia Light Horse, 1780.

1891. BARKER, FORDYCE DWIGHT,   33

Great-great-grandson of Major Abiel Abbot (1741–1809), Muster-Master and Paymaster, with rank of Captain, in Colonel Nahum Baldwin's Regiment New Hampshire Militia, raised to reinforce the Continental army at New York, Sept. 16, 1776; 2d Major 5th Regiment New Hampshire Militia, December 11, 1776; Major in Colonel Moses Nichols' Regiment New Hampshire Militia, raised to reinforce the Continental army at Ticonderoga, June 29, 1777; 1st Major 5th Regiment New Hampshire Militia, March 30, 1781; Member of New Hampshire Provincial Congress, 1777, 1779 and 1780.

1885. BARNARD. HORACE.

Great-grandson of Captain John Barnard (1722 ——),
Lieutenant 2d Company Colonel Erastus Wolcott's
Regiment Connecticut Militia, 1776; Lieutenant 1st
Company 6th Battalion Colonel John Chester Wads-
worth's Brigade Connecticut Militia, 1776; Captain
3d Regiment Connecticut Line, Colonel Samuel
Wyllys, 1777: retired by consolidation, January 1,
1781.

1890. BARNES, ALFRED CUTLER, 372

Great-grandson of Private Amos Morris (1726-1801),
Captain William Van Duersen's Company, Connecticut State Guards, stationed at New Haven
during the "Alarm," 1781.

1890. BARNES, HENRY BURR, 361

Great-grandson of Private Amos Morris (1726-1801).
Captain William Van Duersen's Company, Connecticut State Guards, stationed at New Haven
during the "Alarm," 1781.

1891. BARNES, WILLIAM D., 558

Great-grandson of Private Amos Morris (1726-1801).
Captain William Van Duersen's Company Connecticut State Guards, stationed at New Haven
during the "Alarm," 1781.

1891. BARROW, JAMES THOMAS, 514

Great-grandson of Lieutenant-Colonel John Brown
(1744-1780), served under Ethan Allen at Ticonderoga, 1775; in Arnold's Expedition to Canada and at
assault on Quebec, 1775-6; Lieutenant-Colonel Continental army, 1776; conducted the expedition against
Ticonderoga, 1777; killed in action in the Mohawk
Valley, 1780: Member of Massachusetts Committee
of Correspondence, 1774-5; Member of Massachusetts Provincial Congress, 1775.

1891. BARROWS, CHARLES CLIFFORD, *M. D.*,

> Great-grandson of Captain David Nye (1738-1816). Private in Captain Noah Fearing's Company Wareham (Massachusetts) Militia, "Lexington Alarm," April 19, 1775; Captain 14th Company 4th Regiment Plymouth County (Massachusetts) Militia, in Expedition to Rhode Island, December 10, 1776; Captain Wareham Company in Continental Service, January 13, 1778; Captain Wareham Militia, "Dartmouth Alarm," September 5, 1778; Captain of 2d Company Wareham Militia, "Falmouth Alarm," Colonel Sprout, September 1778; Captain 4th Regiment Plymouth County Militia, Lieutenant-Colonel White, in Expedition to Rhode Island, July 3, 1780; Member of Wareham Committee of Correspondence, March 27, 1780.

1891. BARROWS, ELLIOT THOMAS,

> Great-great-grandson of Lieutenant Nemiah Cobb (1752-1841), Private in Captain John Bridgham's Company, Colonel Cotton's Regiment Massachusetts Militia, October 7, 1775; Ensign in same, 1775; Private in Lieutenant Shurtleff's Company, Colonel Lathrop's Regiment Plymouth Militia, December 11, 1776, at Bristol, Rhode Island; Lieutenant in Captain Jesse Sturtevant's Company, Colonel John Jacob's Regiment, detached from the Militia to reinforce the Continental Army in Rhode Island, July 25, 1780; 1st Lieutenant 7th Company 1st Regiment Massachusetts Continental Infantry, July 1, 1781.

1891. BARROWS, IRA,

> Great-great-grandson of Lieutenant Aaron Barrows (1743-1801), Private in Captain Jabez Ellis' Company South Attleboro' (Massachusetts) Minute Men. "Lexington Alarm," April 19, 1775; Private same Company, Colonel Daggett's Regiment Massachusetts Militia, December, 1776; 2d Lieutenant in Captain Whitmarsh's Company, Colonel Thomas Carpenter's Regiment Massachusetts Militia, on Expedition to Rhode Island, 1778.

Elected.

No. of
Insignia.

1887. BARROWS, HENRY II.,

Great-grandson of Lieutenant Aaron Barrows (1743-1801), Private in Captain Jabez Ellis' Company South Attleboro' (Mass.) Minute Men, "Lexington Alarm," April 19, 1775; Private same company Colonel Daggett's Regiment Massachusetts Militia, December, 1776; 2d Lieutenant in Captain Whitmarsh's Company, Colonel Thomas Carpenter's Regiment Massachusetts Militia on Expedition to Rhode Island, 1778.

1891. BARTLETT, EZRA ALBERT, M. D.,

Great-grandson of Josiah Bartlett of New Hampshire (1728-1795), Signer of the Declaration of Independence; Member Continental Congress, 1775-8; Chief-Justice Court of Common Pleas, 1780; Justice Supreme Court, New Hampshire, 1782; Chief-Justice Supreme Court, New Hampshire, 1783.

1884. * BARTOW, MOREY HALE (died 1886),

Great-grandson of Captain Nathaniel Scribner, of Colonel Henry Luddington's Regiment New York Militia.

1889. BARTOW, SAMUEL BLACKWELL, JR.,

Great-great-grandson of Colonel Jacob Blackwell (1717 ——), Queens County Militia, and Member First New York Provincial Congress.

1889. BECKWITH, LEONARD FORBES,   102

Great-grandson of Colonel Jacob Blackwell (1717 ——), Queens County Militia, and Member First New York Provincial Congress.

1891. BEDELL, EDWIN,   508

Great-great-grandson of Private Reuben Collard, Sussex County Militia, New Jersey.
Also, Great-grandson of Private David Canfield, New Jersey Militia, died from wounds received in action at Springfield, New Jersey, December 16, 1776.

1889.   BEERS, LUCIUS H.,

Great-grandson of Private Robert Newell, Private 6th
Company, Captain Shipman, 7th Regiment Connect-
icut Militia in Continental Service, Colonel Charles
Webb, at Siege of Boston, 1775; Private in Captain
Kirtland's Company 6th Regiment Connecticut Line,
Colonel Return J. Meigs, April, 1777; Private Cap-
tain Baldwin's Company 7th Regiment Connecticut
Line, Colonel Heman Swift, June 28, 1780; Private
in Captain Selden's Company 4th Regiment Connect-
icut Line, Colonel Zebulon Butler, January 1, 1781.

1890.   BELDEN, CHARLES D.,   460

Great-great-grandson of 2d Lieutenant Jacob Van Tas-
sel, 2d Lieutenant in Colonel Joseph Drake's Regiment Westchester County Militia, March 17, 1777.

1886.   BELDEN, WILLIAM,

Grandson of Captain Ezekiel Porter Belden, Lieutenant Sheldon's Dragoons, Connecticut, 1776; Captain
same, 1777; resigned, 1780; previously 2d Lieutenant
in Colonel Bradley's Regiment Connecticut Militia,
1776.

1887.   BELKNAP, ROBERT LENOX (Life Member),   47

Great-grandson of Captain Samuel Belknap (1735-1821),
in command of Company of Militia which marched
from Woburn to Concord and Cambridge, April 19,
1775; Captain 1st Company 2d Regiment Middlesex
County Militia, May, 1776; Captain Colonel Brood's
Regiment Massachusetts Militia, October, 1775.
Also, Great-great-grandnephew and representative of
Major David Lenox (1753-1828), Captain 3d Pennsylvania Battalion, Colonel John Shee, 1776; captured
at Fort George, November 16, 1776, and a prisoner
eighteen months; exchanged, and appointed Aide-de-
Camp, with rank of Major, on staff of Major-General
Anthony Wayne, 1778.

1891. BELMONT, AUGUST. 503

Great-grandson of Christopher Raymond Perry (1761 1818), served on the "Mifflin." Commander Babcock; captured, confined in prison ship "Jersey;" escaped after three months' confinement; subsequently served as Midshipman on Continental frigate "Trumbull," Captain James Nicholson.

1890. BENET, LUDOVIC, 435

Great-grandson of Lieutenant-Colonel William Scudder, Sergeant in Captain McMire's Company, 1st Battalion 1st Establishment New Jersey Line, November 10, 1775; 1st Major 3d Regiment Middlesex County Militia, August 9, 1776; Lieutenant-Colonel same, September 6, 1777.

1886. BENJAMIN, ARTHUR BEDELL. 526

Grandson of Lieutenant Aaron Benjamin, Drummer 2d Company 5th Regiment Connecticut Militia, 1775; Ensign (1777), Lieutenant (1778), and Adjutant (1780), 8th Regiment Connecticut Line, Colonel John Chandler; detached as Adjutant, Meigs' Connecticut Light Regiment, and present at the storming of Stony Point, July 15, 1779; Adjutant 5th Regiment Connecticut Line, Lieutenant-Colonel Sherman, 1781; Lieutenant 3d Regiment Connecticut Line, Colonel S. B. Webb, 1783; Lieutenant in Colonel Heman Swift's "final formation," 1783.

1885. *BENJAMIN, FREDERICK A. (died October 3, 1891), 527

Son of Lieutenant Aaron Benjamin, Drummer 2d Company 5th Regiment Connecticut Militia, 1775; Ensign (1777), Lieutenant (1778), and Adjutant (1780), 8th Regiment Connecticut Line, Colonel John Chandler; detached as Adjutant, Meigs' Connecticut Light Regiment, and present at the storming of Stony Point, July 15, 1779; Adjutant 5th Regiment Connecticut Line, Lieutenant-Colonel Sherman, 1781; Lieutenant 3d Regiment Connecticut Line, Colonel S. B. Webb, 1783; Lieutenant in Colonel Heman Swift's "final formation," 1783.

Elected.   No. of
                                                                             Insignia.

1888. BENJAMIN, GEORGE POWELL,   264

Grandson of Private Nathan Benjamin, of Captain
John Minthorn's Company, Colonel John Hathorn's
Regiment, Orange County Militia, New York, Oc-
tober, 1779.

1888. BENJAMIN, JOHN,   536

Grandson of Lieutenant Aaron Benjamin, Drummer
2d Company 5th Regiment Connecticut Militia, 1775;
Ensign (1777), Lieutenant (1778), and Adjutant (1780),
8th Regiment Connecticut Line, Colonel John Chandler; detached as Adjutant, Meigs' Connecticut Light
Regiment, and present at the storming of Stony Point,
July 15, 1779; Adjutant 5th Regiment Connecticut
Line, Lieutenant-Colonel Sherman, 1781; Lieutenant
3d Regiment Connecticut Line, Colonel S. B. Webb,
1783; Lieutenant in Colonel Heman Swift's "final
formation," 1783.

1890. BENSEL, JOSEPH,

Great-grandson of Lieutenant William Tapp (1750–1796),
Ensign 5th Company 1st Regiment New York Line,
Colonel McDougal, 1775; 2d Lieutenant and Quartermaster same regiment, 1775; 2d Lieutenant in Colonel
Nicholson's Regiment, on service in Canada, 1776;
1st Lieutenant Captain Thomas De Witt's Company,
3d Battalion New York Line, Colonel Peter Gansevoort, 1776; resigned March 20, 1780.

1889. *BENSON, RICHARD HOFFMAN (died September 29, 1889),

Grandson of Lieutenant-Colonel Robert Benson, New
York Militia, Aide-de-Camp to Governor George
Clinton, Secretary New York Provincial Congress,
and Continental Commissary for Prisoners of War.

81

Elected.   No. of
                                                                Insignia
1889. BENTON, JOSIAH HENRY,   226

Great-grandson of Private Josiah Benton (1745-1826),
Private in Connecticut Militia from Tolland, "Lex-
ington Alarm," April 19, 1775; Private in 5th Com-
pany, Captain Willis, 2d Regiment Connecticut
Militia, Colonel Spencer, May 3, 1775; Private in
Captain Abram Tyler's Company, 17th Regiment
Connecticut Continental Infantry, Colonel Jedediah
Huntington, 1776; served in Battle of Long Island.

1890. BETTS, FREDERIC H.,   319

Grandson of Private Uriah Betts (1761-1841), Captain
Nathan Gilbert's Company, Colonel Samuel Whiting's Regiment Connecticut Militia, October 5, 1777;
served with Continental Army on the Hudson.

1891. BETTS, LOUIS FREDERICK HOLBROOK,

Great-grandson of Private Uriah Betts (1761-1841),
Captain Nathan Gilbert's Company, Colonel Samuel
Whiting's Regiment Connecticut Militia, October 5,
1777; served with Continental Army on the Hudson.

1889. BIBBY, ANDREW ALDRIDGE,

Great-grandson of Captain John Hughes, 1st Regiment
"Canadian" Continental Infantry, Colonel James
Livingston.

1890. BICKLEY, LAWRENCE WHARTON,   433

Great-great-grandson of Thomas Wharton, Jr. (1735-
1778), Member of Committee of Safety, President of
the Council of Safety, President of the Supreme
Executive Council of Pennsylvania, March 5, 1777;
died in office, May 22, 1778.

1889. BIGELOW, CLARENCE O.,

Great grandson of Adjutant Joel Bigelow, 1st Regiment
Cumberland County Militia, New York, July 24, 1782.

1890. BILLINGS, DAVID LANE, 419

Great-great-grandson of Private Samuel Billings (1718–
1781), Private in Captain Samuel Ransom's Company
of (Wyoming) Connecticut Militia, 1776: Private in
Captain Eldridge's Company, 1st Regiment Connecticut Line, Colonel Huntington, January 15, 1777;
Private in Groton Militia, killed in action at Groton
Heights, September 6, 1781.

Also, Great-grandson of Private John Billings, Private
in 5th Company, Captain James Chapman, 6th Regiment Connecticut Militia, Colonel S. H. Parsons,
May 5, 1775: Private in Preston Militia, served in
action at Groton Heights, September 6, 1781.

Also, Great-great-grandson of Captain Isaac Farwell
(1744-1791), 2d Lieutenant in Captain Amos Morrill's
Company, 1st Battalion New Hampshire Militia,
Colonel John Stark, April, 1775: 1st Lieutenant in
1st Company 3d Regiment New Hampshire Continental Infantry, Colonel Joseph Reed, 1775; Captain
1st Company 1st Regiment New Hampshire Continental Infantry, Colonel Cilley, November 7, 1776.

Also, Great-great-grandson of Captain Samuel Weth-
erbee (1745-1819), Private Massachusetts Militia,
January 25, 1776, served in Canada; Captain 5th
Company, Colonel Isaac Wyman's Regiment New
Hampshire Militia, June, 1776.

1890. BILLINGS, ELMER MANDEVILLE,

Grandson of Private Henry H. Mandeville (1760-1847),
Private New Jersey Militia under Captain Jonas
Ward, November, 1776; Private in Captain Ogden's
Company New Jersey Militia, January, 1777: Private
in Lieutenant Anthony Mandeville's Company Mil-
itia, December, 1778; Private in Captain Minard's
Company New Jersey Militia, 1779: also served in
New Jersey Militia, 1779-81.

83

Great-great-grandson of Private Samuel Billings (1718-
1781), Private in Captain Samuel Ransom's Company
of (Wyoming) Connecticut Militia, 1776; Private in
Captain Eldridge's Company 1st Regiment Connecticut Line, Colonel Huntington, January 15, 1777;
Private in Groton Militia, killed in action at Groton
Heights, September 6, 1781.

Also, Great-grandson of Private John Billings, Private
in 5th Company, Captain James Chapman, 6th Regiment Connecticut Militia, Colonel S. H. Parsons,
May 5, 1775; Private in Preston Militia, served in
action at Groton Heights, September 6, 1781.

Also, Great-great-grandson of Captain Isaac Farwell
(1744-1791), 2d Lieutenant in Captain Amos Morrill's
Company, 1st Battalion New Hampshire Militia,
Colonel John Stark, April, 1775; 1st Lieutenant in
1st Company 3d Regiment New Hampshire Continental Infantry, Colonel Joseph Reed, 1775; Captain
1st Company 1st Regiment New Hampshire Continental Infantry, Colonel Cilley, November 7, 1776.

Also, Great-great-grandson of Captain Samuel Weth-
erbee (1745-1819), Private Massachusetts Militia,
January 25, 1776, served in Canada; Captain 5th
Company, Colonel Isaac Wyman's Regiment New
Hampshire Militia, June, 1776.

1890. BILLINGS, OLIVER P. C.,   107

Great-grandson of Private Samuel Billings (1718-1781),
Private in Captain Samuel Ransom's Company of
(Wyoming) Connecticut Militia, 1776; Private in
Captain Eldridge's Company, 1st Regiment Connecti-
cut Line, Colonel Huntington, January 15, 1777;
Private in Groton Militia, killed in action at Groton
Heights, September 6, 1781.

Also, Grandson of Private John Billings, Private in
5th Company, Captain James Chapman, 6th Regiment Connecticut Militia, Colonel S. H. Parsons,
May 5, 1775; Private in Preston Militia, served in
action at Groton Heights, September 6, 1781.

Also, Great-grandson of Captain Isaac Farwell (1744-1791), 2d Lieutenant in Captain Amos Morrill's Company, 1st Battalion New Hampshire Militia, Colonel John Stark, April, 1775; 1st Lieutenant in 1st Company 3d Regiment New Hampshire Continental Infantry, Colonel Joseph Reed, 1775; Captain 1st Company 1st Regiment New Hampshire Continental Infantry, Colonel Cilley, November 7, 1776.

Also, Great-grandson of Captain Samuel Wetherbee (1745-1819), Private Massachusetts Militia, January 25, 1776, served in Canada; Captain 5th Company, Colonel Isaac Wyman's Regiment New Hampshire Militia, June, 1776.

1891. BINNEY, HAROLD,

Great-grandson of Private Josiah Talbot, Captain Samuel Fisher's Company, Colonel Titcomb's Regiment Massachusetts Militia.

1889. BISHOP, DAVID WOLFE, 162

Grandson of Captain David Wolfe, 2d Regiment New York State Militia Infantry (New York County) ; later, Assistant Quartermaster Continental Army.

1889. BISSELL, EUGENE, 748

Grandson of Ensign John Norton, Private in Connecticut Militia, "Lexington Alarm," April 19, 1775; Ensign in 18th Regiment Connecticut Militia, August 19, 1776.

Also, Grandson of Isaac Bissell, Private in Captain Elihu Kent's Company Suffield (Connecticut) Militia, "Lexington Alarm," April 19, 1775; Sergeant in Captain John Harmon's Company, Colonel Erastus Wolcott's Regiment Connecticut Militia, 1776; Private in Captain Simeon Sheldon's Company Connecticut Militia, "New Haven Alarm," July, 1779.

85

1889.   BISSELL, EUGENE, JR.,   **749**

Great-grandson of Ensign John Norton, Private in
Connecticut Militia, "Lexington Alarm," April 19,
1775; Ensign in 18th Regiment Connecticut Militia,
August 19, 1776.

Also, Great-grandson of Isaac Bissell, Private in Captain Elihu Kent's Company Suffield (Connecticut)
Militia, "Lexington Alarm," April 19, 1775; Sergeant in Captain John Harmon's Company, Colonel
Erastus Wolcott's Regiment Connecticut Militia,
1776; Private in Captain Simeon Sheldon's Company Connecticut Militia, "New Haven Alarm,"
July, 1779.

1887.   BISSELL, PELHAM ST. GEORGE,   **73**

Great-grandson of Isaac Bissell, Private in Captain
Elihu Kent's Company Suffield (Connecticut) Militia,
"Lexington Alarm," April 19, 1775; Sergeant in
Captain John Harmon's Company, Colonel Erastus
Wolcott's Regiment Connecticut Militia, 1776; Pri-
vate in Captain Simeon Sheldon's Company Con-
necticut Militia, "New Haven Alarm," July, 1779.

Also, Great-grandson of Captain John Wemple, 1st
Lieutenant 4th Company, 3d Battalion (Mohawk)
New York Militia, Colonel Frederick Fisher: Cap-
tain same Regiment, 1781.

1888.   BIXBY, ROBERT FORSYTH,

Great-great-grandson of Quartermaster David Poe,
Maryland Militia.

1890.   BLAKEMAN, CALDWELL ROBERTSON,   **456**

Great-grandson of Rev. James Caldwell (1734-1781),
Chaplain 3d Battalion, 1st Establishment New Jersey
Line, Deputy-Quartermaster and Assistant-Commis-
sary-General Continental Army ; murdered at Eliz-
abethport, November 24, 1781.

86

1890. BLAUVELT, ABRAM DEMAREST,

Great-grandson of Sergeant Joseph Blauvelt (1714–1789), of Captain John M. Hogencamp's Company, Colonel A. Hawkes Hay's Regiment Orange County Militia, New York.

Also, Great-great-grandson of Major Johannes James Blauvelt, Orange County Militia, New York, 1776.

1889. BLAUVELT, DAVID J.,

Grandson of Captain Thomas Blanch (1740–1823), of Colonel Asher Holmes' Regiment New Jersey State Volunteers in Continental Service.

1889. BLAUVELT, JOHN DE WITT,　　215

Great-grandson of Sergeant Joseph Blauvelt (1714–1789), of Captain John M. Hogencamp's Company, Colonel A. Hawkes Hay's Regiment Orange County Militia, New York.

Also, Great-great-grandson of Major Johannes James Blauvelt, Orange County Militia, New York, 1776.

1884. BLOODGOOD, ROBERT FANSHAWE,　　276

Great-grandson of Colonel and Brevet Brigadier-General Goose Van Schaick (1736–1789), Colonel 2d Regiment New York Militia, 1775; Colonel 5th Regiment New York Line, 1776; Colonel 1st Regiment New York Line, 1776; Brigadier-General by brevet at close of war.

1887. *BOLTON, JAMES CLINTON (died March 28, 1891),

Grandson of Brigadier and Brevet Major-General James Clinton (1736–1812), Colonel 3d Regiment New York Line, 1775; Brigadier-General Continental Army, 1776; Major-General Continental Army, by brevet, 1783.

1891. BOTT, JOSEPH WARNER,

Great-great-grandson of Lieutenant Joseph Little (——1791), Captain Ezekiel Giles' Company, from Plaistow, New Hampshire, September 28, 1777; joined the Northern Army at Saratoga, October, 1777.

87

1888. BOWEN, CLARENCE WINTHROP, 266

Great-great-grandson of Captain Mathew Bowen, Con-
necticut Militia.
Also, Great-great-grandson of Captain Isaac Gardner,
Massachusetts Militia.
Also, Great-grandson of Private Benjamin Tappan,
Massachusetts Militia.
Also, Great-grandson of Surgeon William Aspinwall,
Massachusetts Militia.

1884. BOWMAN, JOSEPH JOSLYN, 476.

Great-grandson of Major Joseph Bowman (1749 ——),
Ensign Captain Grainger's Company, Colonel Jonathan Ward's Regiment Massachusetts Militia, 1775;
2d Major 4th Regiment Worcester County Militia,
Colonel Jonathan Walker, 1776; Major in Colonel
Job Cushing's Regiment Massachusetts Bay Militia,
served in Northern Department, 1777.

1889. BRADISH, G. JOHNSTON, 377

Great-grandson of Captain John Williamson, 1st Regiment South Carolina Continental Infantry.

1890. BRADLEY, CYRUS SHERWOOD,

Great-grandson of Private Levi Bradley (1758–1829),
Fairfield Coast Guards, November 4, 1776; served in
the Danbury Raid, April, 1777.
Also, Great-great-grandson of Ensign Seth Bradley
(1735–1798), Ensign in Captain Eliphalet Thorp's
Company, 1st Battalion Connecticut State Troops,
Colonel Samuel Whiting, 1776.
Also, Great-great-grandson of Private Daniel Sher-
wood (1735–1819), in Captain Jonathan Dimon's Com-
pany Connecticut Militia, May, 1775; Private in
Fairfield Coast Guards, November 7, 1776; Clerk in
Captain George Burr's Company, Colonel Samuel
Whiting's Regiment Connecticut Militia, October,
1777.

Also. Great-great-grandson of Private John Dimon
(1730–1777), Connecticut Militia, taken prisoner in the
Danbury Raid, taken to New York, and died there
in the "Sugar House."

Also. Great-great-great-grandson of Simon Couch (1729–
1809), of Redding, Connecticut, authorized to raise
recruits for the Continental Army, 1781.

Also. Great-great-grandson of Private Gershom Bulkley. Captain Jonathan Dimon's Company, Connecticut Militia, 1775.

Also, Great-great-grandson of Private John Wakeman
(1731 ——), Private in Captain Jonathan Dimon's
Company Connecticut Militia, 1776; Private in Fairfield Coast Guards, October 28, 1776; Private in Captain George Burr's Company, Colonel Samuel Whiting's Regiment Connecticut Militia, on duty at
Fishkill-on-the-Hudson, October, 1777.

1891. BRIDGE, CHARLES FRANCIS,

Great-grandson of Colonel Ebenezer Bridge (1742–1823),
Colonel 27th Regiment Massachusetts Continental
Infantry, April 30, 1775; 2d Major 8th Regiment
Worcester County Militia, Colonel Abijah Stearns,
February 6, 1776; Lieutenant in Colonel Asa Whit-
comb's Massachusetts Regiment, June 3, 1775; Colo-
nel Massachusetts Militia, August 1, 1775; Member
of Massachusetts Provincial Congress, 1775.

1892. BRIDGHAM, SAMUEL WILLARD,   777

Great-grandson of Lieutenant Stephen Paine (1716
——), Lieutenant in 6th Company, Captain Loring
Peck, 4th Regiment Rhode Island Continental In-
fantry. Colonel Harry Babcock, January 18, 1776.

1892. BRIDGHAM, WILLIAM HALIBURTON,   793

Great-grandson of Lieutenant Stephen Paine (1716 ——),
Lieutenant in 6th Company, Captain Loring Peck,
4th Regiment Rhode Island Continental Infantry,
Colonel Harry Babcock, January 18, 1776.

89

Elected.

No. of
Insignia.

1888. BRIGHTMAN, HENRY JACKSON, 138

Great-grandson of Ensign John Yeomans, 4th Regi
ment Massachusetts Continental Infantry.

1891. BRINSMADE, WILLIAM BARRETT.

Great-great-grandson of Captain Abraham Brinsmade
(1726-1801), 9th Company, 4th Regiment Connecticut
Militia, Lieutenant-Colonel Jonathan Dimon, March
21, 1777.

1891. BROCKWAY, ASAHEL NORTON,

Grandson of Reverend Thomas Brockway (1745-1807),
Chaplain 4th Battalion Wadsworth's Brigade Connecticut Militia, Colonel Samuel Selden, July 15,
1776.

1889. BROKAW, JOSEPH,

Grandson of Sergeant Bergum Brokaw, 1st Battalion
Somerset County Militia, New Jersey.

1891 BROOKS, REVEREND ARTHUR, D. D.,

Great-grandson of Samuel Phillips (1752-1802), Member of Massachusetts Provincial Congress, 1775-9;
Constitutional Convention, 1779; Massachusetts Senate, 1781-1801; Justice Massachusetts Court of Common Pleas, 1781-98; Member of Andover Committee
of Safety, 1775; Representative to Massachusetts
General Court, 1775.

1891. BROOKS, FREDERICK HENRY. 608

Great-great-grandson of Lieutenant Joel Hayes (1728-
1800), Simsbury (Connecticut) Militia, "Lexington
Alarm," 1775; Lieutenant 18th Regiment Connecti-
cut Militia, August 22, 1776, served around New
York; Lieutenant Connecticut Militia, marched on
"Bennington Alarm," 1777.

90

1889. BROOME, GEORGE COCHRANE,   165

Great grandson of Lieutenant-Colonel John Broome (1738–1810), Lieutenant-Colonel 2d Regiment New York City Militia, Colonel John Jay, October 6, 1775; Chairman *pro tem.* of the New York Committee of Safety, 1775; Member of New York Provincial Congress, 1775–6; Member of Committee to superintend prisoners captured from the British, 1776.

1889. BROWN, EDWARD FLINT,

Great-grandson of Captain David Brown (—— 1802), Massachusetts Militia, served at Lexington and Concord, April 19, 1775.

1888. BROWNE, HENRY HUFFMAN,

Great-great-grandson of Quartermaster William Rodman, Pennsylvania Militia.

1891. BULL, CHARLES STEDMAN, *M. D.*,   593

Great-great-grandson of Captain Caleb Bull (1746–1797), Colonel S. B. Webb's "additional" Regiment Continental Infantry, Connecticut, January 1, 1777.

1891. BULLOCH, JOSEPH GASTON, *M. D.*,

Great-great-grandson of Governor Archibald Bulloch (1730–1777), President of Georgia Provincial Congress, 1775; Commander-in-Chief of Georgia Troops, 1776; President of Georgia, 1775-7; Member of Continental Congress, 1775.

Also, Great-great-grandson of Dr. Noble Wymberly Jones (1732-1805), Speaker of Georgia Provincial Congress, 1775; Member of Continental Congress, 1775, 1781-2.

Also, Great-grandson of John Glen (1725-1799), Chairman of Georgia Provincial Congress, 1775; Chief-Justice of Georgia, 1776 and 1778.

Also, Great-great-grandson of Private Robert Bolton (1757-1802), Georgia Militia.

Also, Great-great-great-grandson of James de Veaux (—— 1785), Member of Georgia Provincial Congress, 1775.

91

Elected. No. of Insignia.

1891. BULLOCH, ROBERT HUTCHINSON,

Great-great grandson of Governor Archibald Bulloch (1730–1777), President of Georgia Provincial Congress, 1775; Commander-in-Chief of Georgia Troops, 1776; President of Georgia, 1775–7; Member of Continental Congress, 1775.

Also, Great-great-grandson of Dr. Noble Wymberly Jones (1732–1805), Speaker of Georgia Provincial Congress, 1775; Member of Continental Congress, 1775, 1781–2.

Also, Great-grandson of John Glen (1725–1799), Chairman of Georgia Provincial Congress, 1775; Chief-Justice of Georgia, 1776 and 1778.

Also, Great-great-grandson of Private Robert Bolton (1757–1802), Georgia Militia.

Also, Great-great-great-grandson of James de Veaux (—— 1785), Member of Georgia Provincial Congress, 1775.

1886. BULLUS, ALBERT, 63

Great-grandson of Colonel Charles Rumsey (1736–1780), Member Maryland Convention, 1775; Member Maryland Council of Safety, 1776; Colonel of "Elk" Battalion Cecil County Militia, 1776; County Lieutenant Cecil County Militia, Maryland, 1777.

1891. BURGESS, EDWARD GUYRE, 506

Great-grandson of Ensign James Wands (1728–1824), 5th Regiment Albany County Militia, New York, Colonel Henry Quackenbush, April 4, 1778.

1891. BURGESS, WILLIAM EVERETT,

Great-great-grandson of Private James Proctor (1722–1776), Private in Captain David Quimby's Company, Colonel Josiah Bartlett's Regiment New Hampshire Volunteer Militia, raised to reinforce the Continental Army in Canada, July, 1776; wounded at Ticonderoga, and died from wounds on his way home.

92

1890. BURLINGHAM, ALBERT STARR,   431

Great-grandson of Lieutenant Aaron Hale (1740–1829),
Ensign in 9th Company, Captain Abraham Filer, 8th
Regiment Connecticut Continental Infantry, Colonel
Jedediah Huntington, July 6, 1775; 2d Lieutenant
in same Regiment, reorganized as 17th Continental,
1776; 1st Lieutenant in 1st Regiment Connecticut
Line, Colonel Huntington, January 1, 1777; 1st Lieu-
tenant in Captain Elisha Chapman's Company, Col-
onel Samuel McClellan's Regiment Connecticut State
Troops, 1778.

1883. BURRALL, FREDERICK AUGUSTUS, *M. D.*,

Great-grandson of Colonel Charles Burrall, Colonel of
Continental Regiment raised to serve in Northern
Department under General Schuyler, 1776; Colonel
14th Regiment Connecticut Militia, 1775–7; Member
Connecticut Assembly, 1775.

1887. BUTLER, CHARLES, *LL. D.*,   123

Son of Private Medad Butler, Connecticut Militia.

1890. BUTLER, EDWARD DEMAREST,   600

Great-grandson of Captain Samuel Demarest, Bergen
County Militia, New Jersey.

1890. BUTLER, ELLIOT L.,

Great-grandson of Private Moses Butler, Continental
Line, Massachusetts, January, 1777, to January, 1781.

1890. BUTLER, GEORGE B.,   342

Great-grandson of Colonel Beriah Norton (1734–1821),
Vineyard Regiment, Dukes County (Massachusetts)
Militia, February 1, 1776.

1889. BUTLER, GEORGE H., *M. D.*,

Great-grandson of Private Moses Butler, Continental
Line, Massachusetts, January, 1777, to January, 1781.

93

1890. BUTLER, HENRY PERCIVAL, 341

Great-grandson of Colonel Beriah Norton (1734-1821),
Vineyard Regiment, Dukes County (Massachusetts)
Militia, February 1, 1776.

1889. BUTTERFIELD, DANIEL, 375

Grandson of Private Gamaliel Olmstead, of Captain
Joseph Walker's Company, 3d Regiment Connecticut
Continental Infantry, Colonel Webb, February 1,
1778; honorably discharged February 1, 1781.

1887. BYINGTON, AARON HOMER,

Great-grandson of Private John Byington, Private 9th
Company, Captain Beardsley, 5th Regiment Connecti-
cut Militia, Colonel Waterbury, May 1, 1775; Private
Captain Abel's Company, Colonel Philip B. Bradley's
Battalion, Wadsworth's Brigade, Connecticut State
Troops, August 13, 1776.

1887. CADWALADER, JOHN LAMBERT,

Grandson of Colonel Lambert Cadwalader (1742-1823),
Lieutenant-Colonel 3d Pennsylvania Battalion, Jan-
uary 4, 1776; Colonel 4th Regiment Pennsylvania
Line, October 25, 1776; captured at Fort Washington,
November 26, 1776; Member of Provincial Congress,
1775.

1888. CANNON, HENRY WHITE, 298

Great-great-grandson of Private Joseph Enos Goodrich,
Private in Captain William Rodgers's Company in
Colonel Samuel Gerrish's Regiment Newbury (Massachusetts) Militia, "Lexington Alarm," April 19,
1775.

No. of
Insignia.

1892. CAPELL, WILLIAM BENTON,

Great-great-grandson of Private Abel Brown (——
1823), Private in Captain Abisha Brown's Company,
5th Regiment Continental Foot (Massachusetts),
Colonel Nixon, September 30, 1775; Private in Captain Nathan Rowles' Company. Colonel John Jacob's
Regiment Massachusetts Line, February 27, 1778;
Private in Captain Daniel Harrington's Company,
Colonel Jonathan Reed's Regiment of Guards, April
2, 1778.

1891. CARLETON, CHARLES A., 665

Great-grandson of Private Moses Carleton (1712-1803),
Private in Captain William Perley's Company of
Minute Men from Boxford, Essex County, Colonel
James Frye, "Lexington Alarm," April 19, 1775.

Also, Great-grandson of Captain Noadiah Leonard
(1737-1790), Captain in 25th Regiment Massachusetts
Militia, Colonel Benjamin Ruggles Woodridge, September 28, 1775.

Also, Great-grandson of Private Henry Hodge, Captain
Scott's Company, Lincoln County (Massachusetts)
Militia, Colonel Joseph North, September 10, 1777.

1891. CARLETON, GEORGE WASHINGTON,

Great-grandson of Private Moses Carleton (1712-1803),
Private in Captain William Perley's Company of
Minute Men from Boxford, Essex County, Massa-
chusetts, Colonel James Frye, "Lexington Alarm,"
April 19, 1775.

Also, Great-grandson of Captain Noadiah Leonard
(1737-1790), Captain in 25th Regiment Massachusetts
Militia, Colonel Benjamin Ruggles Woodbridge,
September 28, 1775.

Also, Great-grandson of Private Henry Hodge, Captain
Scott's Company Lincoln County (Massachusetts)
Militia, Colonel Joseph North, September 10, 1777.

95

1891. CARNES, LEWIS MORTIMER, 760

Great-grandson of Reverend John Carnes (1723-1802),
Chaplain to Colonel Edmund Phinney's Battalion
Massachusetts Bay Forces, at Fort George, December
8, 1776; Member of Massachusetts Provincial Assembly.

1889. CARPENDER, CHARLES J., 210

Great-grandson of Brigadier-General John Neilson
(1745-1833), Captain New Jersey Militia, 1775; Colonel 2d Regiment Middlesex Battalion Minute Men,
August 31, 1776; Colonel of Regiment State Troops;
Brigadier-General New Jersey Militia, February 21,
1777; also Deputy Quartermaster-General.

1888. CARPENDER, JOHN NEILSON, 27

Great-grandson of Brigadier-General John Neilson
(1745-1833), Captain New Jersey Militia, 1775; Colonel 2d Regiment Middlesex Battalion Minute Men,
August 31, 1776; Colonel of Regiment State Troops;
Brigadier-General New Jersey Militia, February 21,
1777; also Deputy Quartermaster-General.

1888. CARPENDER, WILLIAM, 28

Great-grandson of Brigadier-General John Neilson
(1745-1833), Captain New Jersey Militia, 1775; Colonel 2d Regiment Middlesex Battalion Minute Men,
August 31, 1776; Colonel of Regiment State Troops;
Brigadier-General New Jersey Militia, February 21,
1777; also Deputy Quartermaster-General.

1889. CARPENTER, CHARLES WHITNEY, 273

Great-grandson of Private John (Jacobs) Mascraft (1756-
1815), in Captain Amos Paine's Company, 11th Regiment Connecticut Militia, Colonel Ebenezer Williams,
served around New York, 1776.

1888. CARPENTER, REESE, 694

Great-grandson of Private Joseph Owen, Jr., 2d Regiment Westchester County Militia, New York, 1780-1.

96

Elected.		No. of Insignia.
1885.	CARR, WILLIAM HENRY,	261

Great-grandson of Corporal Edmund Pinnegar (1750–
1782), Private Rhode Island Militia, 1776; Private
Captain William Allen's Company, 2d Regiment
Rhode Island Continental Infantry, 1777; promoted
Corporal same Regiment, 1779; drowned from ship
"Tartar," Captain Cathcart, October, 1782.
Also, Great-grandson of Captain Caleb Carr, Colonel
Cook's Regiment Rhode Island Militia, 1776.

1886. CARROLL, EDWARD, JR., 367

Great-great-grandson of Private Joseph Lawton, South
Carolina Militia.

1890. CASE, GEORGE W., 496

Great-grandson of Private Ozias Case (1757–1820), Lieutenant Job Case's Company, 18th Regiment Connecticut Militia, on service around New York, 1776.

1887. CASEY, EDWARD P.,

Great-grandson of Private Wanton Casey (1760–1842),
Private East Greenwich (Rhode Island) Militia, "Lexington Alarm," 1775; served continuously with
Rhode Island Militia until 1779, when he retired on
account of ill health.
Also, Great-great-grandson of Captain and Brevet Major Nathan Goodale (1744–1793), Lieutenant in Colonel
David Brewer's Regiment Massachusetts Continental
Infantry, 1775; 1st Lieutenant 13th Regiment Massachusetts Continental Infantry, Colonel Joseph Read,
1776; 1st Lieutenant 25th Regiment Massachusetts
Continental Infantry, Colonel William Bond, 1776;
served around New York, 1776, in Engineers' Department, under Lieutenant-Colonel Rufus Putnam;
Captain 5th Regiment Massachusetts Continental Infantry, Colonel Rufus Putnam, 1777; "at Saratoga,"
1777; at West Point, Peekskill and White Plains,
1778; taken prisoner near Tuckahoe, August 31,
1778; exchanged 1781; brevetted Major at close of
war.

97

Elected.
No. of
Insignia.

1890. CENTER, ROBERT A., 729
Great-grandson of Captain Samuel Mansfield, 2d Corps
Continental Artillery, Colonel Lamb, Connecticut.

1891. CHAPIN, REVEREND HENRY BARTON,
Great-grandson of Colonel William Barton (1748–1831),
Colonel Rhode Island Continental Infantry, December 24, 1777: presented with a sword by the Continental Congress in recognition of his services in
capturing the British General Prescott, July 9, 1777.

1889. CHAPIN, HENRY DWIGHT, M. D.,
Great-grandson of Colonel William Barton (1748–1831),
Colonel Rhode Island Continental Infantry, December 24, 1777; presented with a sword by the Continental Congress in recognition of his services in
capturing the British General Prescott, July 9, 1777.

1888. CHAUNCEY, HENRY, JR., 86
Great-grand-nephew of Private John Chauncey, of the
1st Troop, 2d Regiment, Continental Light Dragoons,
Colonel Elisha Sheldon ; killed in a skirmish on the
Schuylkill River, Pennsylvania, December 4, 1777.

1888. CHEESMAN, TIMOTHY MATLACK, M. D. (Life Member), 77
Representative and great-grandnephew of Captain Jacob
Cheesman, 1st Regiment New York Continental In-
fantry, and Aide-de-Camp on staff of Major-General
Richard Montgomery, killed in assault on Quebec,
December 31, 1775.

1887. CHRYSTIE, JOHN ALBERT,
Great-grandson of Captain and Brevet Major James
Chrystie (1750–1807), 1st Lieutenant 2d Battalion
Pennsylvania Line, Colonel Arthur St. Clair, 1776;
served with Arnold's Expedition to Canada, 1775 6:
Captain 2d Battalion Pennsylvania Line, Colonel St.
Clair, 1776; Captain 3d Regiment Pennsylvania Line,
Colonel Joseph Wood, 1777; Captain 3d Regiment
Pennsylvania Line, Colonel Thomas Craig, 1781; Cap-
tain 2d Regiment Pennsylvania Line, Colonel Rich-
ard Humpton, 1783; Major by brevet at close of war.

98

Also, Great-grandson of Commodore James Nicholson
(1737-1804), in command of Maryland ship-of-war
"Defence," 1775; in command of Continental ship-
of-war "Virginia," 1776; Commander-in-chief of Continental Navy, 1777; in command of Continental
frigate "Trumbull," 1780.

1888. CHRYSTIE, THOMAS MACKANESS LUDLOW, *M. D.*,
Great-grandson of Captain and Brevet Major James
Chrystie (1750-1807), 1st Lieutenant 2d Battalion
Pennsylvania Line, Colonel Arthur St. Clair, 1776;
served with Arnold's Expedition to Canada, 1775-6;
Captain 2d Battalion Pennsylvania Line, Colonel St.
Clair, 1776; Captain 3d Regiment Pennsylvania Line,
Colonel Joseph Wood, 1777; Captain 3d Regiment
Pennsylvania Line, Colonel Thomas Craig, 1781; Cap-
tain 2d Regiment Pennsylvania Line, Colonel Rich-
ard Humpton, 1783; Major by brevet at close of war.
Also, Great-grandson of Commodore James Nicholson
(1737 1804), in command of Maryland ship-of-war
"Defence," 1775; in command of Continental ship-
of-war "Virginia," 1776; Commander-in-chief of Continental Navy, 1777; in command of Continental
frigate "Trumbull," 1780.

1886. *CHRYSTIE, THOMAS WITTER (died January 18, 1888).
Grandson of Captain and Brevet Major James Chrystie
(1750-1807), 1st Lieutenant 2d Battalion Pennsylvania
Line, Colonel Arthur St. Clair, 1776; served with
Arnold's Expedition to Canada, 1775-6; Captain 2d
Battalion Pennsylvania Line, Colonel St. Clair, 1776;
Captain 3d Regiment Pennsylvania Line, Colonel
Joseph Wood, 1777; Captain 3d Regiment Pennsyl-
vania Line, Colonel Thomas Craig, 1781; Captain
2d Regiment Pennsylvania Line, Colonel Richard
Humpton, 1783; Major by brevet at close of war.
Also, Grandson of Commodore James Nicholson (1737-
1804), in command of Maryland ship-of-war "De-
fence," 1775; in command of Continental ship-of-war
"Virginia," 1776; Commander-in-chief of Continen-
tal Navy, 1777; in command of Continental frigate
"Trumbull," 1780.

1892. CHURCH, ALONZO,

Great-grandson of 1st Lieutenant Reuben Church
(1757–1834), South Company, Captain Artemas How,
1st Regiment Cumberland County New York (Vermont) Militia, Lieutenant-Colonel Timothy Church
commanding, July 24, 1782.

Also, Great-great-grandson of Lieutenant-Colonel Timothy Church, 1st Regiment Cumberland County
(New York) Militia.

Also, Great-great-grandson of Lieutenant-Colonel
Joshua Porter (1730–1826), 14th Regiment Connecticut Militia, 1775; Lieutenant-Colonel in Colonel Increase Moseley's Regiment Connecticut Militia, 1777,
at "Saratoga."

1891. CHURCH, FRANCIS PHARCELLAS,

Great-grandson of Adjutant Ebenezer Conant (1743–
1783), Colonel Stearn's Regiment Massachusetts Militia, 1777; previously (1775) Lieutenant in Captain
Davis' Company, Colonel Whitcomb's Regiment
Massachusetts Continental Infantry.

1891. CHUTOWSKI, THADDEUS KOSCIUSKO,

Great-great-grandnephew and Representative of Colonel
(Count) Thaddeus Kosciusko (1736–1817), Engineer
Corps Continental Army.

Also, Great-grandson of Private William Fitch (1764–
1843), Captain Ozias Merwin's Company, Colonel
Stephen St. John's Regiment Connecticut Coast Guard
Service, 1782.

1891. CLARK, CYRUS,

Great-grandson of Private Lemuel Clark (1753–1831),
Captain Daniel Tilden's Company Connecticut Militia,
"Lexington Alarm," April 19, 1775.

100

1889.   CLARK, HIRAM,

Son of Ensign Watrous Clark, Private in Captain John
Perkins's Company Norwich Militia, "Lexington
Alarm," April, 1775; Sergeant-Major in 3d Regiment
Connecticut Militia in Continental service, Colonel
Israel Putnam, May 3, 1775, served at siege of Bos-
ton; Ensign in 20th Regiment Continental Infantry,
Colonel John Durkee, 1776.

1886.   CLARKSON, ASHTON CROSBY,

Great-great-grandson of William Floyd (1734–1821).
Signer of Declaration of Independence, and Colonel of
1st Regiment Suffolk County Militia, New York, 1775.

1889.   CLARKSON, BANYER,   187

Great-grandson of Major and Brevet Lieutenant-Colonel
Matthew Clarkson (1758–1825), Private in Colonel
Ritzema's Corps of American Fusiliers, 1775; served
with Northern Army, 1777–9; acting Aide-de-Camp
to Arnold at Saratoga; appointed Aide-de-Camp to
Major-General Lincoln in Southern Army, 1779, at
Savannah; served as Major of Light Infantry, 1780;
taken prisoner at Charleston; exchanged in 1781;
served as Aide-de-Camp to Major-General Lincoln to
close of war; Lieutenant-Colonel by brevet, 1783.

1883.   CLARKSON, FLOYD,   6

Great-grandson of William Floyd (1734–1821), Signer
of Declaration of Independence, and Colonel 1st
Regiment Suffolk County Militia, New York, 1775.

1890.   CLARKSON, FREDERICK,   355

Grandson of Major and Brevet Lieutenant-Colonel
Matthew Clarkson (1758–1825), Private in Colonel
Ritzema's Corps of American Fusiliers, 1775; served
with Northern Army, 1777–9; acting Aide-de-Camp
to Arnold at Saratoga; appointed Aide-de-Camp to
Major-General Lincoln in Southern Army, 1779, at
Savannah; served as Major of Light Infantry, 1780;
taken prisoner at Charleston; exchanged in 1781;
served as Aide-de-Camp to Major-General Lincoln to
close of war; Lieutenant-Colonel by brevet, 1783.

No. of
Insignia.

1888. CLARKSON, GEORGE TAYLOR,

Great-great-grandson of William Floyd (1734-1821),
Signer of Declaration of Independence, and Colonel
1st Regiment Suffolk County Militia, New York.
1775.

1885. CLARKSON, JOHN VAN BOSKERCK,

69

Great-great-grandson of William Floyd (1734-1821),
Signer of Declaration of Independence, and Colonel
1st Regiment Suffolk County Militia, New York.
1775.

1887. CLEARWATER, ALPHONSO TRUMPBOUR,

330

Great-great-grandson of Private Abraham Klaarwater,
Captain Philip Houghtaling's Company, Ulster
County Troop of Horse.
Also, Great-grandson of Private Thomas Klaarwater,
in Captain Cornelius E. Wynkoop's Company, Ulster
County Militia.

1890. CLINTON, ALEXANDER JAMES,

311

Great-grandson of Brigadier and Brevet Major-General James Clinton (1736-1812), Colonel 3d Regiment
New York Line, 1775; Brigadier-General Continental
Army, 1776; Major-General Continental Army by
brevet, 1783.

1891. CLINTON, SPENCER,

499

Great-grandson of Brigadier and Brevet Major-General James Clinton (1736-1812), Colonel 3d Regiment
New York Line, 1775; Brigadier-General Continental
Army, 1776; Major-General Continental Army by
brevet, 1783.

1883. COCHRANE, JOHN,

Grandson of Surgeon-General John Cochran (1730-
1807), Physician and Surgeon-General Middle Department Continental Army, April 10, 1777; Director-
General Medical Hospitals Continental Army, 1781.

LOS ANGELES MUSEUM
EXPOSITION PARK

Elected.   No. of
                                                                      Insignia.

Also, Great-grandson of Colonel James Livingston
(1747-1832), Colonel of "additional" Continental In-
fantry, March 20, 1775, to 1781, on active service in
Canada and on the Hudson; Member of New York
Provincial Congress, 1775-6; Chairman Dutchess
County Committee of Safety.

1886. COE, CHARLES A.,   223

Great-grandson of Major Godfrey Rinehart, 4th Regiment Militia, Hunterdon County, New Jersey ; also
Member of New Jersey Assembly, 1779.

1891. COGSWELL, CULLEN VAN RENSSELAER,

Great-great-grandson of Brigadier-General Robert Van
Rensselaer (1740-1802), Colonel 8th Regiment Albany
County Militia, 1776 ; Brigadier-General 2d Brigade
Albany County Militia, June 16, 1780; Member of
New York Provincial Congress, 1775.
Also, Great-great-grandson of Colonel James Bayard
(1738-1806), Major of 2d Battalion Philadelphia Mili-
tia, 1775; Colonel Philadelphia Militia, 1777; Colonel
4th Battalion Philadelphia Militia, 1779.

1890. COLE, WILLIAM MADISON,   444

Great-grandson of Private James Secor (1745-1812),
Private in Captain Francis Smith's Company New
York Militia, Colonel Odell, September 26, 1776, on
duty at Fort Montgomery; Private in Colonel Alexander McCrokey's Regiment of Militia at Ramapo,
November, 1776; served at Long Pond Wards, March,
1777; Private in Captain Archer's Company, Colonel
Gilbert Cooper's Regiment of Militia, February, 1779,
to 1781, stationed on the Hudson River.

103

Elected.

No. of
Insignia.

1891. COLLES, CHRISTOPHER JOHN, *M. D.*,

Great-great-grandson of Colonel Oliver Spencer, 1st
Major 1st Regiment Essex County (New Jersey) Mili-
tia, February 23, 1776; Lieutenant-Colonel same,
November 28, 1776; Lieutenant-Colonel New Jersey
State Troops, November 27, 1776; Colonel same, Feb-
ruary 3, 1777; Colonel of "Spencer's" Regiment New
Jersey Continental Infantry, January 15, 1777; served
to close of war.

Also, Great-grandson of Surgeon's Mate Ebenezer
Blackley (1760–1812), Volunteer Assistant Surgeon,
1776; Surgeon's Mate 10th Regiment North Carolina
Continental Infantry, 1778.

1889. COLLINS, CHARLES LEE (Lieutenant U. S. A.),   123

Great-grandson of Private Mathew Coffin, Private on
vessel "Melisha," Captain John Hall (to Machias),
August 14, 1777; Private in Captain John Hall's
Company Lincoln County Militia, Colonel Foster,
September 1, 1777, on duty at Machias.

Also, Great-great-grandson of Lieutenant Nathan
Coffin, Sergeant in Captain Tobias Fernald's Company, Colonel John Scammel's Regiment Massachusetts Continental Infantry, May 3, 1775; 1st Lieutenant in York County Militia, January 1, 1776; 1st
Lieutenant in Massachusetts Coast Guard Service,
1777.

1891. COLLINS, HOLDRIGE OZRO,   664

Great-grandson of Sergeant Walter Wooster (——
1829), Sergeant in Captain Leavenworth's Company,
6th Regiment Connecticut Line, Colonel R. J. Meigs,
March 2, 1777; wounded at Kingsbridge, New York.

Also, Great-great-grandson of Major Johannes Decker,
2d Major Goshen Regiment Orange County (New
York) Militia, Colonel William Allison, February,
1776.

Also, Great-grandson of Private Benjamin Cuddeback
(1746 ——), Private in Captain Abraham Cuddeback's
Company Orange County Militia, Colonel William
Allison, 1776.

104

Elected.   **No. of Insignia.**

Also, Great-great-grandson of William Cuddeback, Associator, Orange County, New York, 1775.

Also, Great-grandson of Anthony Van Etten, Sr., Associator, Orange County, 1775.

Also, Great-great-great-grandson of Johannus Westbrook, Associator, Orange County, 1775.

Also, Great-great-great-great-grandson of Private Harmanus Van Inwaigen, Captain Westfall's Company, Colonel Klock's Regiment Orange County Militia.

Also, Great-great-grandson of Captain Ira Beebe, Captain 27th Regiment Connecticut Militia.

1889. CONANT, GEORGE SEYMOUR, M. D.,

Great-great-grandson of Private George Conant (1723–1792), Private in Captain Jenkins's Company Massachusetts Militia, stationed at Dartmouth, 1776; Private in Captain Baker's Company, Colonel Freeman's Regiment Massachusetts Militia, 1777; later served as Private in Captain Minot's Company, Colonel Whiting's Regiment.

1887. CONSTANT, SAMUEL VICTOR,   23

Great-grandson of Corporal Jedediah Tuttle (1753 ——), Private in Captain Robert Dodge's Company, Colonel Isaac Smith's Regiment Massachusetts Militia, 1776; Private in Colonel Aaron Willard's Regiment Massachusetts Militia, on service at Ticonderoga, 1776; Private in Captain Dodge's Company Wenham Militia, at Saratoga, 1777.

1891. COON, CHARLES EDWARD,   606

Great-grandson of Major Gideon Brownson, Colonel Seth Warner's Regiment New Hampshire Continental Infantry, July 5, 1776; taken prisoner, 1779; exchanged and served to close of war.

1891. CORBIN, HENRY CLARK, Lieutenant-Colonel and Acting Adjutant-General United States Army.   688

Great-grandson of Private John Corbin, Private in 3d Regiment Virginia Line, Colonel Wheaton.

Salem   may the 10 1777

this sertifies that Stephen Tomson
Joel Terrill   Silas Lewis
apear to ~~going~~ go in the romes
of Stephen worner Enoe fist
Daniel worner who have Excused
them selves by paying their money
and giveing   notes I shold be glad
to have the money sent by the barer
to hire thes man   Ira Beehe Lu

Waterbury May 11th AD 1777
I the Subscriber the bearer of the with in Certificate
Recd of the Treasurer of the Town of Waterbury the
Sum of fifteen Pounds Lawfull money to the Paid
unto Stephen Tomson, Joel Terrell and Silas Lewis
for engaging to join the Troops at New Haven
        Recd Pr me — David Beehe

        Deliverd Pr order of Bets Johnson

Iras Beeke
Certificate

105

Elected.
No. of
Insignia.

1890. COTHEAL, ALEXANDER ISAAC, 424

Grandson of Private Isaac Cotheal (1743–1812), 4th Battalion, 2d Establishment New Jersey Line, wounded and taken prisoner at Woodbridge, New Jersey, April 19, 1777; served thirteen months in New York prison; honorably discharged May 1, 1778, on account of wounds.

1889. COTHREN, NATHANIEL,

Great-grandson of Lieutenant William Cochran (1738–1778), Private in Captain John Grannis's Company Massachusetts Militia, stationed at Tarpaulin's Cove; Corporal in same, January 4, 1776; Sergeant in same, June 1, 1776; 2d Lieutenant in Captain Elisha Nye's Company, stationed at Elizabeth Island, January 10, 1777.

1891. COURTENAY, WILLIAM, 580

Great-great-grandson of Samuel Purviance, Jr. (1728–1788), Chairman of Maryland Committee of Safety, and Purchasing Agent Continental Congress for Maryland; Member of Maryland Provincial Congress, 1776.

1891. COURTRIGHT, GEORGE ALBERT,

Great-great-grandson of Private Edmond Wood (1721–1805), Private in Captain Nathaniel Wood's Company Middleborough (Massachusetts) Minute Men, "Lexington Alarm," April 19, 1775; Private in Captain Joshua White's Company, Colonel Cushing's Regiment Massachusetts Militia, September 20, 1776.
Also, Great-grandson of Private Peter Wood (1749–1829), Private in Captain Nathaniel Wood's Company, Colonel Simon Cary's Regiment Massachusetts Militia, April 1, 1776; Private in same Company, Colonel Sprout's Regiment Massachusetts Militia, "Dartmouth Alarm," 1778; Private in Captain John Porter's Company, Colonel Cyprian Horn's Regiment, Jacobs' Brigade, in Continental Service on Rhode Island, July 30, 1780.

106

1892. COWLES, WALTER SMITH,

Grandson of Captain Ebenezer Smith (1746–1816), enlisted in Continental Army, May, 1775; Ensign in Captain Soule's Company, 6th Regiment Continental Foot (Massachusetts), Colonel Asa Whitcomb, 1776; Lieutenant in same, 1777; Captain in same, March 20, 1779; served to close of war.

1888. COYKENDALL, SAMUEL D.,   144

Great-grandson of Lieutenant Abram Shepherd, Colonel William Allison's Regiment Militia, Orange County, New York, killed in battle of Minisink, on the Delaware, July 22, 1779.

1890. CRAFT, REVEREND FRANCIS,   461

Grandson of Private William Craft (1762–1829), 2d Regiment Westchester County Militia, Colonel Thomas Thomas, September 24, 1779.

1887. CRANE, CHARLES NICOLL,   318

Great-grandson of Captain William Crane, 5th Regiment New Jersey Continental Infantry (Colonel Oliver Spencer), and Major New Jersey Militia.
Also, Great-great-grandson of Private Stephen Crane, 1st Regiment New Jersey Line, and Speaker New Jersey Assembly, 1776.

1890. CROMWELL, DAVID,   439

Great-grandson of John Cromwell (1727–1805), of Westchester County, New York, who acted as guide and teamster to the Continental Army during the war.

1888. CROSBY, HENRY A.,

Great-grandson of Surgeon Ebenezer Crosby (1753–1788), Surgeon of Washington's Life Guards, Massachusetts.
Also, Great-great-grandson of William Floyd (1734–1821), Signer of Declaration of Independence, and Colonel 1st Regiment Militia, Suffolk County, New York, 1775.

1889 CROSBY. JOHN SCHUYLER, 297

Great-grandson of Surgeon Ebenezer Crosby (1753
1788), Surgeon of Washington's Life Guards, Massachusetts.

Also, Great-grandson of Surgeon Mathias Burnet
Miller (1749–1792), Colonel David Sutherland's Regi-
ment New York State Militia, and Member of New
York Provincial Congress.

Also, Great-grandson of Colonel Stephen J. Schuyler,
6th Regiment Albany County Militia, New York.

Also, Great-great-grandson of William Floyd (1734–
1821), Signer of Declaration of Independence, and
Colonel 1st Regiment Suffolk County Militia, New
York, 1775.

1886. CROSBY. LIVINGSTON,

Great-great-grandson of Philip Livingston (1716–1778),
Signer of Declaration of Independence, New York.

Also, Great-great-grandson of William Floyd (1734–
1821). Signer of Declaration of Independence, and
Colonel 1st Regiment Militia, Suffolk County, New
York, 1775.

1890. CROSBY. STEPHEN VAN RENSSELAER,

Great-great-grandson of Surgeon Ebenezer Crosby (1753–
1788). Surgeon of Washington's Life Guards.

Also, Great-great-great-grandson of William Floyd
(1734–1821), Signer of the Declaration of Independence, and Colonel 1st Regiment Suffolk County
Militia. New York, 1775.

Also, Great-great-great-grandson of Major-General
Philip J. Schuyler (1733–1804), Major-General Continental Army, 1775; resigned 1779; Delegate to Continental Congress, 1775–7; Member New York Provincial Congress, 1778-9; Member New York State
Senate, 1781–4.

Also, Great-great-grandson of Colonel Stephen J.
Schuyler, 6th Regiment Albany County Militia,
New York.

Also. Great-great-grandson of Surgeon Mathias Burnet Miller (1749-1792), Colonel David Sutherland's Regiment New York State Militia, and Member of New York Provincial Congress.

Also, Great-great-great-grandson of Philip Livingston (1716-1778), Signer of the Declaration of Independence, New York.

1884. CROSBY, WILLIAM B.,   218

Great-grandson of Surgeon Ebenezer Crosby (1753-1788), Surgeon Washington's Life Guards. Massachusetts.

Also, Great-great-grandson of William Floyd (1734-1821), Signer of the Declaration of Independence, and Colonel 1st Regiment Militia, Suffolk County. New York, 1775.

1890. CUMMING, JAMES DUNCAN,

Grandson of Quartermaster-Sergeant William Cumming (1759-1849), entered the service under Lieutenant McAuley, Colonel Archibald Lyttle's Regiment North Carolina Militia, at "Valley Forge"; promoted Quartermaster-Sergeant 1777-8; volunteered in Colonel Ramsey's Regiment North Carolina Militia, 1780; served in Caswell's Brigade at "Camden," August 16, 1780; Quartermaster-Sergeant under Major Tatum; captured by Tarleton's Dragoons, 1781; escaped shortly afterward and served to close of war.

1890. CUMMING, JAMES DUNCAN, JR.,

Great-grandson of Quartermaster-Sergeant William Cumming (1759-1849), entered the service under Lieutenant McAuley, Colonel Archibald Lyttle's Regiment North Carolina Militia, at "Valley Forge"; promoted Quartermaster-Sergeant 1777-8; volunteered in Colonel Ramsey's Regiment North Carolina Militia, 1780; served in Caswell's Brigade at "Camden," August 16, 1780; Quartermaster-Sergeant under Major Tatum; captured by Tarleton's Dragoons, 1781; escaped shortly afterward and served to close of war.

1890. CURRIER, CHARLES GILMAN, *M. D.*,

Great-grandson of Private Benjamin Currier (1740- —),
Private in Captain Benjamin Dias's Company New
Hampshire Continental Infantry, Colonel David Gilman,
1776; Private in Captain Joseph Derburn's
Company, Colonel Moses Nichols' Regiment New
Hampshire Volunteers, August 5, 1778; joined the
Continental Army in Rhode Island, 1778.

1887. CURTIS, GEORGE E.,

Great-grandson of Lieutenant-Colonel Paul Revere,
Massachusetts Artillery, Continental Army.

1891. DANA, RICHARD STARR,   555

Great-great-grandson of Captain Josiah Keith, Lieutenant
in Captain Macy Williams' Company of Massachusetts
Minute Men, "Lexington Alarm," April 19,
1775; Captain in Colonel John Daggett's Regiment
Massachusetts Militia, December 8, 1776; Captain in
same, in Expedition to Rhode Island, August 25, 1778;
Captain in Colonel Isaac Dean's Regiment Massachusetts
Militia, in Expedition to Rhode Island, March 3,
1778; Captain in same, in Expedition to Tiverton,
Rhode Island, August 4, 1780.

1890. DARLING, CHARLES WILLIAM,

Great-grandson of Captain Robert Davis, Captain
Boston Militia, 1776; 2d Lieutenant 15th Regiment
Massachusetts Continental Infantry, Colonel John
Patterson, January, 1776; Captain 1st Regiment
Massachusetts Continental Infantry, Colonel Vose,
March 4, 1777.

1885. DARLINGTON, JOHN LACEY,

Great-grandson of Brigadier-General John Lacey (——
1814). Captain 2d Battalion Bucks County Associa-
tors, Colonel John Beatty, 1775; Lieutenant-Colonel
4th Battalion Bucks County Militia, Colonel William
Roberts, in the service of the United States. 1776;
Captain 4th Battalion Pennsylvania Line, Colonel
Anthony Wayne, served on Canadian frontier, 1776;
Brigadier-General Pennsylvania Militia. 1778; retired
from service 1781; Member of Supreme Executive
Council of Pennsylvania.

1885. DARLINGTON, WILLIAM LACEY, M. D.,

Great-grandson of Brigadier-General John Lacey (——
1814). Captain 2d Battalion Bucks County Associa-
tors, Colonel John Beatty, 1775; Lieutenant-Colonel
4th Battalion Bucks County Militia, Colonel William
Roberts, in the service of the United States, 1776;
Captain 4th Battalion Pennsylvania Line, Colonel
Anthony Wayne, served on Canadian frontier, 1776;
Brigadier-General Pennsylvania Militia, 1778; retired
from service 1781; Member of Supreme Executive
Council of Pennsylvania.

1886. DAVIDSON, GEORGE TRIMBLE,   154

Great-grandson of Surgeon Mathias Burnet Miller
(1749-1792), Colonel David Sutherland's Regiment
New York State Militia, and Member of New York
Provincial Congress.

1891. DAVIDSON, SILVANUS MILLER,

Great-grandson of Surgeon Matthias Burnet Miller
(1749-1792), Colonel David Sutherland's Regiment
New York State Militia, and Member of New York
Provincial Congress.

111

Elected.   No. of Insignia.

1891.   DAVIES, WILLIAM GILBERT,   761

> Great-grandson of Sergeant John Foote (1742-1809), Sergeant in Captain Amos Wilcox's Company, Simsbury (Connecticut) Militia, "Lexington Alarm," April, 19, 1775; Private in Captain Zacheus Case's Company, Colonel Noadiah Hooker's Regiment Connecticut Militia, May 12, 1777; Private in Captain David Olmstead's Company, Colonel Roger Enos' Regiment Connecticut Militia, June. 1778.

1889.   DAVIS, AUGUSTUS PLUMMER,   259

> Great-grandson of Lieutenant Jacob Davis (1742 1809), 1st Lieutenant in Captain Moses Whiting's Company of Roxbury (Massachusetts) Minute Men, attached to Colonel John Greaton's Regiment, April 19. 1775; served at "Bunker Hill" and Dorchester Heights. 1775; Major 5th Regiment Worcester County Militia, Colonel John Holman, February 6, 1776.

1889.   DAVIS, FELLOWES,   44

> Great-great-grandson of Colonel Aaron Davis (1709-1777) Captain of Roxbury Militia, 1775; later Colonel Massachusetts Militia; Member of Massachusetts Provincial Congress, 1774-7; Member of Massachusetts General Court, 1775-6.
>
> *Also.* Great-grandson of Major Moses Davis (1744-1823), Private in Captain Moses Whiting's Company. Colonel John Greaton's Regiment Massachusetts Militia. "Lexington Alarm," April 19, 1775.

1889.   DAVIS, HERBERT ANTHONY,

> Great-great-grandson of Lieutenant Jacob Davis (1742-1809), 1st Lieutenant in Captain Moses Whiting's Company of Roxbury (Massachusetts) Minute Men, attached to Colonel John Greaton's Regiment. April 19, 1775, served at "Bunker Hill" and Dorchester Heights, 1775; Major 5th Regiment Worcester County Militia, Colonel John Holman, February 6, 1776.

Elected.

1891. DAVIS, JOSEPH, 671

Great-great-grandson of Colonel Aaron Davis, Sr. (1709–
1777), Captain of Roxbury Militia, 1775; later
Colonel Massachusetts Militia; Member of Massa-
chusetts Provincial Congress, 1774–7: Member of
Massachusetts General Court, 1775–6.
Also, Great-grandson of Major Moses Davis (1744–1823).
Private in Captain Moses Whiting's Company, Col-
onel John Greaton's Regiment Massachusetts Militia,
"Lexington Alarm," April 19, 1775.

1889. DAYTON, CHARLES W., 49

Great-great-grandson of Colonel Andrew Adams (——
1797). Major Connecticut Militia, 1777; Lieutenant-
Colonel, 1779; Colonel 17th Regiment Connecticut
Militia, 1780: Delegate to Continental Congress,
1777–80 (Speaker 1779–80); Member Connecticut
Council of Safety.
Also, Great-great-grandson of Major John Canfield,
Adjutant Sheldon's Dragoons, 1776: Brigade-Major
in Brigadier-General Oliver Wolcott's Detachment at
"Saratoga," 1777: Member of Continental Congress.

1890. DAYTON, HAROLD CHILD,

Great-great-grandson of Colonel Andrew Adams (——
1797). Major Connecticut Militia, 1777; Lieutenant-
Colonel, 1779; Colonel 17th Regiment Connecticut
Militia, 1780; Delegate Continental Congress, 1777–80
(Speaker 1779–80); Member Connecticut Council of
Safety.
Also, Great-great-grandson of Major John Canfield,
Adjutant Sheldon's Dragoons, 1776: Brigade-Major
in Brigadier-General Oliver Wolcott's Detachment at
"Saratoga," 1777: Member of Continental Congress.

No. of
                                                                   Insignia

1889. DAYTON, WILLIAM ADAMS, *M. D.*,   242

  Great-great-grandson of Colonel Andrew Adams (——
  1797), Major Connecticut Militia, 1777; Lieutenant-
  Colonel, 1779; Colonel 17th Regiment Connecticut
  Militia, 1780; Delegate Continental Congress, 1777–80
  (Speaker 1779–80); Member Connecticut Council of
  Safety.
  Also, Great-great-grandson of Major John Canfield,
  Adjutant Sheldon's Dragoons, 1776; Brigade-Major
  in Brigadier-General Oliver Wolcott's Detachment at
  "Saratoga," 1777; Member of Continental Congress.

1889. DECHERT, YELLOTT DASHIELL,

  Great-grandson of 1st Lieutenant Robert Porter (1768-
  1842), Cadet, Proctor's Pennsylvania Artillery, January 9, 1779 ; 1st Lieutenant, July 2, 1781; 2d Lieutenant, under the arrangement of the Pennsylvania
  Artillery, January 1, 1783, Pennsylvania Line.
  Also, Great-great-grandson of Colonel Andrew Porter
  (1743–1813), Captain of Marines, June 19, 1776, serv-
  ing on frigate "Ellingham"; Captain 2d Regiment
  Continental Corps of Artillery, Colonel Lamb, Janu-
  ary 1, 1777 ; transferred January 1, 1781, to 4th
  Regiment Continental Corps of Artillery, Colonel
  Proctor; promoted Major, April 19, 1781; promoted
  Lieutenant-Colonel, December 21, 1782; promoted
  Lieutenant-Colonel Commandant, January 1, 1783.

1889. DEGRAW, CLARENCE GILBERT,

  Great-great-grandson of Captain Abraham Water-
  house, Lieutenant in 9th Company, Captain John
  Ely, 6th Regiment Connecticut Line, Colonel Parsons, May 1, 1775; Captain 10th Regiment Continental,
  Colonel Parsons, 1776; Captain 1st Regiment Connecticut Light Horse Militia, Major William Hart,
  May, 1776.

1889. DELAFIELD, ALBERT,   50

  Great-grandson of Joseph Hallett (1731 1799), Member
  of First, Second and Third Provincial Congresses,
  New York.

114

Elected.

No. of
Insignia.

1889. DELAFIELD, AUGUSTUS FLOYD,   146

Great-grandson of William Floyd (1734-1821). Signer
of the Declaration of Independence, and Colonel 1st
Regiment Suffolk County Militia, New York. 1775.

1885. DELAFIELD, CLARENCE,   82

Grandson of Major and Brevet Lieutenant-Colonel
Benjamin Tallmadge (1754-1835), Captain. 1776, Major
Sheldon's Light Dragoons; 1777, conducted "secret
service" for the Commander-in-Chief: captured Fort
George, Long Island, November 21, 1780, and
received special notice of Congress; Lieutenant-Colonel by brevet 1783.

Also, Great-grandson of William Floyd (1734-1821),
Signer of the Declaration of Independence, and Colonel 1st Regiment Suffolk County (New York) Militia, 1775.

1888. DELAFIELD, FREDERICK PRIME,

Great-great-grandson of Joseph Hallett (1731-1799),
Member of First, Second and Third Provincial Congresses, New York.

1889. DELAFIELD, FREDERICK SCHUCHARDT,

Great-great-grandson of Joseph Hallett (1731-1799),
Member of First, Second and Third Provincial Congresses, New York.

1889. DELAFIELD, HENRY PARISH,

Great-grandson of Joseph Hallett (1731-1799), Member
of First, Second and Third Provincial Congresses.
New York.

1891. DELAFIELD, MATURIN LIVINGSTON, Jr.,   576

Great-great-grandson of Joseph Hallett, Member of 1st,
2d and 3d New York Provincial Congresses.

Also, Great-great-grandson of Walter Livingston, Deputy Commissary-General, and Member of 1st Provincial Congress, New York.

Also, Great-great-grandson of Robert R. Livingston
(1746-1813), Member of Continental Congress, 1775-7;
Member of 4th New York Provincial Congress, and
Chancellor State of New York, 1777-1801.

Also, Great-great-great-grandson of Francis Lewis
(1713-1803), New York, Signer of the Declaration of
Independence.

Also, Great-great-grandson of Colonel Morgan Lewis
(1754-1844), Major 2d Regiment New York City Militia, Colonel John Jay, October 27, 1775; later, Adjutant-General on Staff of Major-General Gates.

1889. DELAFIELD, RICHARD,   68

Great-grandson of Joseph Hallett (1731-1799), Member
of First, Second and Third Provincial Congresses,
New York.

1889. DELAFIELD, RUFUS,   26

Great-great-grandson of Joseph Hallett (1731-1799),
Member of First, Second and Third Provincial Congresses, New York.

1885. DELAFIELD, TALLMADGE,   245

Grandson of Major and Brevet Lieutenant-Colonel
Benjamin Tallmadge (1754-1835), Captain, 1776, Major
Sheldon's Light Dragoons; 1777, conducted "secret
service" for the Commander-in-Chief; captured Fort
George, Long Island, November 21, 1780, and received
special notice of Congress; Lieutenant-Colonel by
brevet, 1783.

Also, Great-grandson of William Floyd (1734-1821),
Signer of the Declaration of Independence, and
Colonel 1st Regiment Suffolk County (New York)
Militia, 1775.

116

1884. DELAVAN, CHARLES H.,

Son of Captain Daniel Delavan, Captain. Lieutenant-
Colonel Albert Pawling's Regiment Westchester
County Levies, 1775; Ensign same. 1776; Lieutenant
in Colonel Morris Graham's Regiment Militia, 1778-9;
Captain in Colonel William Malcolm's Regiment
"Additional Continental," 1780; detached to 2d New
York Line until close of war.

1884. DELAVAN, CHRISTIAN S.,

Son of Captain Daniel Delavan, Captain. Lieutenant-
Colonel Albert Pawling's Regiment Westchester
County Levies, 1775; Ensign same. 1776; Lieutenant
in Colonel Morris Graham's Regiment Militia, 1778-9;
Captain in Colonel William Malcolm's Regiment
"Additional Continental," 1780; detached to 2d New
York Line until close of war.

1890. DERBY, RICHARD HENRY, M. D.,   162

Great-great-grandson of Richard Derby (1712-83), Member of Governor's Council of Massachusetts, 1774-7,
and Delegate to Massachusetts Provincial Congress,
1774-5; Chairman of Boston Committee of Safety,
1774.

1892. DESHLER, JAMES,

Great-grandson of Lieutenant-Colonel Azariah Dun-
ham (1719-1791), Muster-master of 1st, 2d and 3d
Battalions New Jersey Militia, 1775-7; Lieutenant-
Colonel 2d Middlesex (New Jersey) Battalion Militia,
1775-6 ; Chairman of Middlesex (New Jersey) Convention, 1775; Member of New Jersey Provincial
Congress, 1775-6; Member of New Jersey Committee
of Safety, 1775-6; Superintendent of Purchases of
New Jersey, 1777-83.

Elected.   No. of
                                                                                Insignia.

1891.   DEWINT, JOHN PETER HEYLIGER,   518

Great-grandson of Lieutenant-Colonel William Stephen
Smith (1755-1816), appointed Aide-de-Camp to Major-
General Sullivan, with rank of Major, August, 1776;
Lieutenant-Colonel of Massachusetts "Additional
Continental" Infantry, January 1, 1777; Inspector
and Adjutant-General to the Continental Corps of
Light Infantry under Major-General the Marquis De
Lafayette, 1779; appointed Aide-de-Camp to the Com-
mander-in-chief, July, 1781.

Also, Great-great-grandson of John Adams, Signer of
the Declaration of Independence.

1886.   *DICKERSON, EDWARD NICOLL (died December 12, 1889),

Grandson of Captain John Stotesbury, 1st Lieutenant
11th Regiment Pennsylvania Line, Colonel Richard
Humpton, 1776; 1st Lieutenant 8th Regiment
Pennsylvania Line, Colonel Mackey; wounded and
captured at "Brandywine"; prisoner in New York,
exchanged, 1780; Ensign 2d Regiment Pennsylvania
Line, Colonel Walter Stewart, 1781; Captain 6th Regiment Pennsylvania Line, Colonel Robert Magaw,
1781; served to close of war.

Also, Great-grandson of Deputy Quartermaster-General
Hugh Hughes, Continental Army, New York.

Also, Great-grandson of Captain Peter Dickerson, 3d
Battalion, 2d Establishment, New Jersey Line.

1886.   DICKERSON, EDWARD NICOLL,

Great-grandson of Captain John Stotesbury, 1st Lieutenant 11th Regiment Pennsylvania Line, Colonel
Richard Humpton, 1776; 1st Lieutenant 8th Regiment Pennsylvania Line, Colonel Mackey; wounded
and captured at "Brandywine"; prisoner in New
York, exchanged, 1780; Ensign 2d Regiment Pennsylvania Line, Colonel Walter Stewart, 1781; Captain
6th Regiment Pennsylvania Line, Colonel Robert
Magaw, 1781; served to close of war.

Also, Great-great-grandson of Deputy Quartermaster-General Hugh Hughes, Continental Army, New York.

Also, Great-great-grandson of Captain Peter Dickerson, 3d Battalion, 2d Establishment, New Jersey Line.

1886. DIEFENDORF, MENZO,

Great-grandson of Captain Henry Diefendorf (—— 1777), 1st Lieutenant, 1st Company, 3d Regiment New York Line, Colonel Gansevoort, 1776; 1st Lieutenant, 1st Company, New York Line, Colonel Van Schaick, 1777; Captain 1st Battalion Tyron County Militia, Colonel Nicholas Herkimer; killed in action at Oriskany, August 6, 1777.

1892. DIKE, CAMDEN CROSBY,

Great-grandson of Sergeant Thomas Dike (1744–1805), Captain John Green's Company, Killingly (Connecticut) Militia, "Lexington Alarm," April 19, 1775; Sergeant in Captain John Green's Company, 11th Regiment Connecticut Militia, at New York, 1776.

1891. DIKE, NORMAN STAUNTON,

Great-great-grandson of Elias Thomas (1746–1820), served as Scout under command of Lieutenant Nathan Howland, Vermont Militia, August, 1780; again under Lieutenant Abisha Samson, Vermont Militia, October, 1780; again under Captain Jesse Safford, Vermont Militia, August 10, 1781.

Also, Great-great-grandson of Sergeant Thomas Dike (1744–1805), Captain John Green's Company Killingly (Connecticut) Militia, "Lexington Alarm," April 19, 1775 ; Sergeant in Captain John Green's Company 11th Regiment Connecticut Militia at New York, 1776.

1889. DITMARS, EDWARD WILSON,

Great-grandson of 1st Lieutenant Samuel Riker (1743–1823), Captain Daniel Lawrence's Troop of Light Horse, Queens County Militia, New York, and Member Queens County Committee of Safety, 1776.

1891. DIX, REVEREND MORGAN, *D. D., D. C. L.,*   705

Grandson of Lieutenant Timothy Dix (1743-1820), 2d Lieutenant in 11th Regiment New Hampshire Militia, Colonel Thomas Stickney, March 5, 1776; marched to reinforce the Northern Army under Major-General John Sullivan at Crown Point; served thereafter at Fort Ticonderoga; honorably discharged December 1, 1776.

1890. DOMINICK, ALEXANDER,   549

Great-grandson of Captain George Dominick (1730 ——), 14th Beat Company New York City Militia, Colonel John Jay, August 29, 1775.

1890. DOMINICK, BAYARD,   533

Great-grandson of Captain George Dominick (1730 ——). 14th Beat Company, New York City Militia, Colonel John Jay, August 29, 1775.

1891. DOMINICK, GEORGE FRANCIS,   592

Great-grandson of Captain George Dominick (1730 ——), 14th Beat Company, 2d Regiment New York City Militia, Colonel John Jay, August 29, 1775.

1890. DOMINICK, HENRY BLANCHARD,   550

Great-grandson of Captain George Dominick (1730 ——). 14th Beat Company New York City Militia, Colonel John Jay, August 29, 1775.

1884. DOMINICK, MARINUS WILLETT,   263

Grandson of Captain Daniel Delavan. Captain in Lieutenant-Colonel Albert Pawling's Regiment Westchester County Levies, 1775; Ensign in same regiment, 1776; Lieutenant in Colonel Morris Graham's Regiment Militia, 1778-9; Captain in Colonel William Malcolm's Regiment "Additional Continental," 1780; detached to 2d Regiment New York Line until close of the war.

Also, Great-grandson of Captain George Dominick (1730 ——), 14th Beat Company, 2d Regiment New York City Militia, Colonel John Jay, August 29, 1775.

120

1889. DOMINICK. WILLIAM GAYER (Life Member), 122
Great-grandson of Captain George Dominick (1730 ——),
14th Beat Company, 2d Regiment New York City
Militia, Colonel John Jay, August 29, 1775.

1890. DOUBLEDAY. EDWIN THOMPSON, M. D., 410
Great-grandson of Private Nehemiah Wyman (1762-
1820), Captain Joshua Walker's Company, Colonel
David Greene, 2d Regiment Foot, Middlesex County
Militia, Massachusetts, April 19, 1775.
Also, Great-great-grandson of Private Edward Stearns
(1726-1793), Captain John Moore's Company, Bedford
Militia, Massachusetts, April 19, 1775.
Also, Great-grandson of Private Timothy Thompson
(1750-1834), Captain Wheelock's Company, Massa-
chusetts Militia, December 8, 1776.
Also, Great-grandson of Private William Calder
(1735-1802), Captain Jonathan Allen's Company,
Minute Men, "Pomeroy's" Regiment, April 19, 1775.

1887. DOUDGE. JAMES R. (Life Member), 200
Great-grandson of Lion Gardiner, Associator, 1775,
Suffolk County, New York.

1889. DOUGLAS. HARRY. 150
Great-grandson of Captain Richard Douglas, Private in
Captain Coit's Company of Volunteers from New
London, Connecticut, Lexington Alarm, April 19,
1775, at "Bunker Hill"; Ensign, 3d Company, 4th
Battalion (Wadsworth's Brigade) Connecticut Militia.
Colonel Selden, June 20, 1776; 2d Lieutenant, January
1, 1777; 1st Lieutenant, January 1, 1778; Captain-
Lieutenant, August 11, 1780; Captain, August 27,
1780, in 1st Regiment Connecticut Line, Colonel
Huntington; Captain 5th Regiment Connecticut Line,
Colonel Isaac Sherman, January 1, 1781; Captain in
Major J. P. Wylly's Regiment Light Infantry, February to November, 1781; served in Southern Army
under Lafayette; Captain 3d Regiment Connecticut
Line, Colonel S. B. Webb, January, 1783; Captain
in Colonel Heman Swift's Regiment, "final formation," June, 1783.

121

1889. DOUW, CHARLES GIBBONS.

Great-grandson of Adjutant Volckert P. Douw, Lansing's Albany County Militia, New York, and Vice-President First Provincial Congress.

1889. DOUW, JOHN DE PEYSTER.

Son of Ensign John De Peyster Douw, 4th Regiment Albany County Militia, New York, April 1, 1778.
Also, Grandson of Volckert P. Douw, Vice-President of First Provincial Congress and Adjutant of Lansing's Albany County Militia, New York.

1891. DOWD, FRANK CURTIS.

Great-great-grandson of Colonel William Douglass (1742-1777), Captain 6th Company, 1st Regiment Connecticut Militia, Colonel David Wooster, May 1, 1775: appointed Aide-de-Camp to General Wooster, June 13, 1775: Major in Colonel Andrew Ward's Regiment Connecticut Militia, 1776; Colonel 5th Battalion Wadsworth's Brigade Connecticut Militia, June 20, 1776; Colonel 6th Regiment Connecticut Line, January 1, 1777; died from effects of service, May 28, 1777; Member of Connecticut Assembly, 1776.

1887. DOWNING, SILAS.   222

Grandson of Lieutenant Benjamin Allen, 2d Lieutenant in Captain Philip Bartell's Company, 9th Regiment 2d Claverack Battalion Militia, Colonel Peter Van Ness, 1778; 1st Lieutenant same regiment, 1779.

1891. DRAPER, T. WALN-MORGAN,   695

Grandson of Private Simeon Draper (1765-1848), Private in Captain Bemis' Company, Colonel Washburn's Regiment Worcester County (Massachusetts) Militia, January 12, 1781; Private in Captain Libbeus Drew's Company, 4th Regiment Massachusetts Continental Infantry, Colonel William Shepard, June, 1781.

122

Also, Great - grandson of Private Joshua Draper
(1724–1792), Captain Ebenezer Mason's Company,
Colonel Jonathan Warren's Regiment Massachusetts
Militia, April 19, 1775, "Lexington Alarm;" Private
in Captain Benjamin Richardson's Company Colonel
Nicholas Dike's Regiment Massachusetts Militia,
September 4, 1776; Private in Captain Josiah White's
Company, Lieutenant-Colonel Benjamin Flagg's
Regiment Worcester County Militia, "Hadley
Alarm," August 21, 1777 ; Member of Worcester
County Committee of Correspondence, 1776–7.

Also, Great-grandson of Lieutenant Benjamin Bemis
(1744 ——), Private in Captain Joseph Wolcott's
Company of "Rangers" from Spencer, Massa-
chusetts, "Lexington Alarm;" Sergeant in Captain
Joel Green's Company Colonel Frye's Regiment
Massachusetts Militia, 1775; later, Lieutenant in 8th
Company Worcester County Militia and Member of
Spencer (Massachusetts) Committee of Correspond-
ence 1780.

1883. *DREXEL, JOSEPH W. (died March 25, 1888),

Grandson of Private Nicholas Hookey of Colonel James
Chambers' 1st Regiment Pennsylvania Continental
Infantry.

1890. DRIGGS, ELLIOTT FOOT,   404

Great-grandson of Ensign Sylvanus Marshall (1746–
1833), 2d Lieutenant in Captain Jesse Bell's Company,
1st Battalion Connecticut State Troops, Colonel
Whiting, 1776; Ensign in Captain Abraham Mead's
Company, 9th Regiment Connecticut Militia, Lieutenant-Colonel John Mead, August 13, 1776; Lieutenant in Captain Sylvanus Mead's Company of
Rangers, 1777; Captain of Rangers, 1781.

Also, Great-grandson of Surgeon Isaac Smith, Connecticut Militia.

Elected.

1888.   DROWNE, HENRY RUSSELL (Life Member),   538

    Great-grandson of Surgeon Solomon Drowne, M. D.,
    2d Regiment Infantry, Rhode Island State Brigade
    in Continental Service.

    Also, Great-grandson of Captain Robert Rhodes (1742-
    1821), Captain of "Alarm" Company, Warwick
    (Rhode Island) Militia, 1779; Captain of Senior Class
    Artillery Company, 1st Battalion, Kent County,
    Rhode Island, Lieutenant-Colonel Thomas Tilling-
    hast commanding, 1781-4.

    Also, Great-great-grandson of James Rhodes, Deputy
    to the Rhode Island General Azsembly, 1760-77; in
    command of Militia ordered to New Shoreham, Rhode
    Island, August, 1775.

1876.   DROWNE, HENRY THAYER,   72

    Grandson of Surgeon Solomon Drowne, M. D., 2d
    Regiment Infantry, Rhode Island State Brigade in
    Continental Service.

    Also, Great-grandson of Captain Robert Rhodes (1742-
    1821), Captain of "Alarm" Company, Warwick
    (Rhode Island) Militia, 1779; Captain of Senior Class
    Artillery Company, 1st Battalion, Kent County,
    Rhode Island, Lieutenant-Colonel Thomas Tilling-
    hast commanding, 1781-4.

    Also, Great-great-grandson of James Rhodes, Deputy
    to the Rhode Island General Assembly, 1760-77; in
    command of Militia ordered to New Shoreham, Rhode
    Island, August, 1775.

1891.   DROWNE, REV. THOMAS STAFFORD, *D. D.*,

    Grandson of Surgeon Solomon Drowne, M. D., 2d Regi-
    ment Infantry, Rhode Island State Brigade in Con-
    tinental Service.

1891.   DROWNE, THOMAS STAFFORD, JR.,

    Great-grandson of Surgeon Solomon Drowne, M. D.,
    2d Regiment Infantry, Rhode Island State Brigade
    in Continental Service.

1891.   DU BOIS, WILLIAM MAISON,   206

Great-great-grandson of Captain Louis Jonathan du Bois
(1733 ——), 3d Regiment Ulster County Militia, Colonel Levi Pawling.

1890.   DUER, WILLIAM ALEXANDER,

Great-grandson of Brigade-Major and Deputy-Adju-
tant-General William Duer (1747-1799); appointed
Brigade-Major and Deputy-Adjutant-General New
York Militia, July 27, 1775; Member of New York
Provincial Congress.
Also, Great-grandson of Major Rufus King (1755-1827).
Aide-de-Camp to Major-General Sullivan, New York.
Also, Great-great-grandson of Major-General William
Alexander, Lord Stirling (1726-1783); Colonel 1st Bat-
talion, 1st Establishment, New Jersey Line, November
7, 1775; Brigadier-General Continental Army, March
11, 1776; Major-General Continental Army, February
19, 1777; taken prisoner at battle of Long Island; twice
received the thanks of Congress for conspicuous service.
Also, Great-great-grandson of John Alsop, member of
Continental Congress from New York, 1775.
Also, Great-grandson of Lieutenant William Denning
(1740-1819), 2d Lieutenant 15th Beat Company, Captain Henry Remsen, New York "Independents,"
1775; Member of New York Provincial Congress,
1776.

1884.   EDSALL, THOMAS HENRY,   244

Great-grandson of Captain Jacobus Edsall (1724-1800),
2d Regiment Sussex County Militia, New Jersey.
Also, Great-great-grandson of Captain Benjamin Coe
(1741-1821), 1st Lieutenant Captain Abraham Remsen's
Company, South Beach Militia, Queen's County, Long
Island, March, 1776; promoted Captain, June, 1776;
Captain in Colonel Josiah Smith's Regiment, Wood-
hull's Brigade, July, 1776.

125

Also, Great-great-grandson of Sergeant Thomas Jones
(1756-1841), Captain Jonathan Barnes' Company,
Colonel Jonathan Walker's Regiment of Brookfield
(Massachusetts) Minute Men; marched to Boston on
Lexington Alarm, April 19, 1775; Sergeant Captain
Peter Harwood's Company, Colonel Ebenezer
Learned's Regiment Massachussets Militia, April 27,
1775; served at Bunker Hill, Dorchester, etc.; later
in Continental service.

Also, Great-grandson of Sergeant James Burt (1760-
1852), Private Orange County (New York) Militia,
1776; afterwards Sergeant in Captain John Min-
thorne's Company, Orange County Militia, Colonel
John Hathorn; served at Minisink, etc.

Also, Great-grandson of Lieutenant John Dunning, 2d
Lieutenant in Captain Isaiah Veal's Company, 2d
Regiment Ulster County (New York) Militia, Colonel
James Clinton; promoted 1st Lieutenant of same,
1778.

1888. ELSWORTH, EDWARD,   104

Great-great-grandson of Private Benjamin Westervelt,
2d New York Militia.

Also, Great-grandson of Private Benjamin Westervelt,
Jr., 2d New York Militia.

1891. ELY, SMITH,   677

Grandson of Private Moses Ely (1756-1838), Private
Morris County (New Jersey) Militia.

Also, Great-grandson of Private Aaron Kitchell (1744-
1820), Private Morris County (New Jersey) Militia.

1887. EMERSON, JOHN W.,   253

Great-grandson of Lieutenant Thomas Emerson, Essex
County Militia, Massachusetts; Lexington Alarm,
1775.

Also, Great-grandson of Sergeant Samuel Bradstreet,
Essex County Militia, Massachusetts; Lexington
Alarm, 1775.

1889.   EMERY, LIVINGSTON (Life Member).   316

Great-grandson of Lieutenant-Colonel William S.
Livingston (1754-1817), Lieutenant-Colonel in Colonel
S. B. Webb's Regiment "Additional Continental,"
January 1, 1777; wounded and taken prisoner on
Long Island, October 12, 1777; later Secretary and
Aide-de-Camp to his father, Governor Livingston of
New Jersey.

Also, Great-great-grandson of Governor and Brigadier-
General William Livingston (1723-1790). Brigadier-
General New Jersey Militia, October 28, 1775; Governor of New Jersey, 1776-90; also Member of Continental Congress.

1891.   ENOS, FRANK,   701

Great-great-grandson of Private Samuel Trask (1720-
1790), Private in Captain John Hall's Company, Colonel Palmer's Regiment Massachusetts Militia, March
4, 1776; Private in Captain Andrew Elliott's Company, Colonel Jonathan Holman's Regiment Massachusetts Militia, December 10, 1776; later, Private in
Captain Miles Greenwood's Company Massachusetts
Militia, Colonel Jacob Gerrish.

1889.   ERVING, JOHN LANGDON.

Great-great-grandson of John Langdon (1739-1819),
Member Continental Congress, 1775-6 and 1783; in
command of company of volunteers at Bennington.
Saratoga and Rhode Island; Speaker of New Hampshire Assembly; Judge of Court of Common Pleas.
1776-7; Continental Agent in New Hampshire, 1779.

Also, Great-great-great-grandson of Philip Livingston
(1716-1778), Signer of the Declaration of Independence, New York.

Also, Great-great-grandson of William Paterson, Delegate and Secretary First Provincial Congress, New
Jersey; Member Continental Congress and of the
Convention for Adoption of Constitution, and Attor-
ney-General of New Jersey, 1776-86.

Elected.

1889.   ESTEY. JULIUS J..

>   Great-grandson of Private Joshua Kendall, Framing-
>   ham Militia. Massachusetts.

1885.   EVANS, THOMAS GRIER,

>   Great-grandson of Major Thomas DeWitt, 1st Lieu-
>   tenant 3d Regiment New York Line, Colonel James
>   Clinton. 1775: Captain 2d Company, 3d Battalion
>   New York Line. Colonel Gansevoort, 1779; resigned
>   January 7, 1780; Major in Lieutenant-Colonel Albert
>   Pawling's Regiment New York Levies, 1780; Major
>   in Lieutenant-Colonel Marinus Willett's Regiment
>   New York Levies, 1782.
>   *Also*, Great-great-grandson of Brigadier-General Ja-
>   cobus Swartwout (1734-1824), appointed by Provin-
>   cial Congress Muster-Master New York Troops, 1775;
>   Colonel 1st Regiment Dutchess County Militia, 1776:
>   Colonel Charlotte County (New York) Militia, 1778;
>   Brigadier-General Dutchess County Militia, 1780.
>   *Also*, Great-grandson of Colonel John Seward (1730-
>   ——), Captain, Lieutenant-Colonel and Colonel Sus-
>   sex County Militia, New Jersey.

1887.   FAIRCHILD. BENJAMIN T.,

202

>   Great-grandson of Private John Curtis Fairchild, 2d
>   Company, Captain Samuel Whiting, 5th Regiment
>   Connecticut Line, Colonel David Waterbury, 1775.
>   *Also*, Great-grandson of Lieutenant Thomas Elwood,
>   Private in Captain David Dimon's Company of
>   Minute Men that marched from Fairfield to the relief
>   of Boston, on Lexington Alarm, April 19, 1775;
>   Private in Captain Dimon's Company, 5th Regiment
>   Connecticut Line, Colonel David Waterbury, May
>   10, 1775: Lieutenant of Marines on frigate "Alliance,"
>   32 guns, Captain Peter Landais, afterwards Captain
>   Barry, August 24, 1778; retired from service, May 1,
>   1783.

1887. FAIRCHILD, SAMUEL W.,   137

Great-grandson of Private John Curtis Fairchild, 2d
Company. Captain Samuel Whiting, 5th Regiment
Connecticut Line, Colonel David Waterbury, 1775.
Also, Great-grandson of Lieutenant Thomas Elwood.
Private in Captain David Dimon's Company of Min-
ute Men, that marched from Fairfield to the relief of
Boston on Lexington Alarm, April 19, 1775; Private
in Captain Dimon's Company, 5th Regiment Connect-
icut Line, Colonel David Waterbury. May 10, 1775;
Lieutenant of Marines on frigate "Alliance," 32 guns,
Captain Peter Landais, afterwards Captain Barry,
August 24, 1778; retired from service May 1, 1783.

1887. FAIRCHILD, THOMAS B.,

Grandson of Lieutenant Thomas Elwood. Private in
Captain David Dimon's Company of Minute Men,
that marched from Fairfield to the relief of Boston
on Lexington Alarm, April 19, 1775; Private in Captain Dimon's Company, 5th Regiment Connecticut
Line, Colonel David Waterbury, May 10, 1775; Lieutenant of Marines on frigate "Alliance," 32 guns,
Captain Peter Landais, afterwards Captain Barry,
August 24, 1778; retired from service May 1. 1783.

1886. FARLEY, GUSTAVUS, JR.,   148

Great-grandson of Major-General Michael Farley (1719-
1789), Quartermaster Massachusetts Militia, Colonel
Gerrish, 1775; 2d Lieutenant and Quartermaster 26th
Regiment Massachusetts Continental Infantry. Col-
onel Laomi Baldwin, 1776; Brigadier-General Essex
County Militia, 1776; 3d Major-General Massachusetts
Militia, 1777; 2d Major-General same, 1778; Member
Massachusetts Bay Committee, 1775; Member Mas-
sachusetts Provincial Congress, 1775-80.
Also, Grandson of Private Robert Farley, Captain Asa
Prince's Company, Colonel Danforth Keyes' Regi-
ment Massachusetts Militia; captured and confined
11 months in prison ship "Jersey."

1891. FARNAM, ELBERT ELI,

Great-grandson of Lieutenant Charles Dix (1730 1810), Colonel Samuel Canfield's Regiment Connecticut Militia; served at West Point, 1781.
Also, Great-grandson of Private John Foreman (1739–1792), Captain Timothy Barrow's Company, Colonel Timothy Bedel's Regiment New Hampshire Militia, raised for defence of the frontiers, April 16, 1778.

1888. FARRAND, OLIVER M.,

Great-grandson of Private Bethuel Farrand, Morris County Militia, New Jersey.

1886. FEETER, JACOB W.,

Grandson of Private William Feeter, Tryon County Militia, New York.

1888. FERRIS, MORRIS PATTERSON, 255

Great-grandson of Private Cornelius Van Wyck, 5th Regiment Dutchess County Militia, Colonel James Vanderburgh, New York.
Also, Great-grandson of Gregarius Storm, Associator, Dutchess County, New York.

1891. *FERRY, JEDEDIAH BALDWIN (died July 28, 1891),

Great-grandson of Corporal Solomon Ferry (1744–1810), Captain Jonathan Wales' Company Hampshire County (Massachusetts) Militia, Colonel Dickinson, September 22, 1777; previously (August 17, 1777) Corporal in same.

1888. *FINCKE, CHARLES LOUIS (died November 11, 1890),

Great-grandson of Captain Andrew Fincke (—— 1820), 1st New York Line (Colonel Van Schaick), and Major and Inspector of Bounty Regiments, New York.

1892. FINDLEY, WILLIAM LUTHER, 779

Great-grandson of Deputy Quartermaster-General William Amberson (1752–1835), 1st Lieutenant in 8th Regiment Pennsylvania Line, Colonel Eneas Mackey, 1776 9; Deputy Quartermaster-General, 1779.

130

1890. ℱ Finney, Robert Spencer,

Great-grandson of Lieutenant Lazarus Finney (1751–1833), 2d Lieutenant in 4th Company, 2d Battalion Chester County (Pennsylvania) Associators, Colonel Evan Evans, May 5, 1777; 1st Lieutenant in same, 1778.

1891. Fitch, Benjamin, 578

Great-grandson of Colonel Nathaniel Rochester (1752–1831), Paymaster, with rank of Major, North Carolina Line, August, 1775; Paymaster 7th Regiment North Carolina Militia, 1776 ; Lieutenant-Colonel Orange County (North Carolina) Militia, April 22, 1776; promoted Colonel of same, 1777; Deputy Commissary-General of military and other stores in North Carolina, May 10, 1776; Member of Orange County (North Carolina) Committee of Safety, 1775 ; Member of North Carolina Provincial Congress, 1776.

1889. Fitch, Francis Emory, 142

Great-grandson of Lieutenant William Wordin (1728–1808), Lieutenant in Captain Sterling's Company, 4th Regiment Connecticut Militia, Lieutenant-Colonel Jonathan Dimon, October 5, 1777; Private in 2d Regiment, Continental Corps of Artillery, Colonel Lamb, 1780.

Also, Great-grandson of Reverend Thomas Brockway (1745–1807), Chaplain 4th Battalion Wadsworth's Brigade Connecticut Militia, Colonel Samuel Seldon, July 15, 1776.

1885. *Fitch, John (died September 1, 1889),

Great-grandson of Captain and Brevet Major Andrew Fitch, Clerk of Captain Clark's Company, Connecticut Militia, Lexington Alarm, 1775; Lieutenant 6th Company, 3d Regiment Connecticut Militia, Colonel Putnam, 1775; Lieutenant in Colonel Ward's Regiment Connecticut Line, 1776; Captain 4th Regiment Connecticut Line, Colonel John Durkee (1777–81); retired by consolidation with brevet of Major.

1885. FLOYD, AUGUSTUS,

Great-grandson of William Floyd (1734-1821). Signer
of the Declaration of Independence, and Colonel 1st
Regiment Suffolk County Militia, New York. 1775.

1886. FLOYD, JOHN G.,   551

Great-grandson of William Floyd (1734-1821). Signer
of the Declaration of Independence, and Colonel 1st
Regiment Suffolk County Militia, New York. 1775.

1888. FLOYD, NICOLL, JR.,

Great-great-grandson of William Floyd (1734-1821),
Signer of the Declaration of Independence, and Colonel 1st Regiment Suffolk County Militia, New York.
1775.

1889. FLOYD-JONES, DE LANCEY, Colonel U. S. A., retired
(Life Member),   160
Great-grandson of Hendrick Onderdonck, Member of
Committee of Safety, Queens County, New York.

1885. FLOYD-JONES, GEORGE STANTON,   149·

Great-great-grandson of Hendrick Onderdonck, Member
of Committee of Safety, Queens County, New York.

1890. FOOTE, GEORGE BENTON.

Great-great-grandson of Captain Cornelius Van Wyck,
5th Regiment Dutchess County Militia, Colonel
Abraham Brinckerhoff, killed at White Plains, Octo-
ber 31, 1776.
Also, Great-great-grandson of Private Aaron Hall
(1760-1839), Captain Stephen Hall's Company, 7th
Regiment Connecticut Continental Infantry, Colonel
Heman Swift, May 15, 1780.

1890. FOOTE, GILBERT FLAGLER,

Great-great-grandson of Captain Cornelius Van Wyck,
5th Regiment Dutchess County Militia, Colonel
Abraham Brinckerhoff, killed at White Plains, October 31. 1776.

132

No. of
Insignia.

Also. Great - great - grandson of Private Aaron Hall
(1760–1839), Captain Stephen Hall's Company 7th
Regiment Connecticut Continental Infantry, Colonel
Heman Swift, May 15, 1780.

1889. FOOTE, MORRIS COOPER (Captain U. S. A.),   267
Great-grandson of Major Jacob Morris (1755–1844),
Major in Westchester County (New York) Militia,
Colonel Dubois, December 14, 1776; Aide-de-Camp to
Major-General Charles Lee, 1776; Aide-de-Camp to
Major-General Nathaniel Greene, 1778.
Also, Great-great-grandson of Lewis Morris (1726–1798),
Brigadier-General of Westchester County Militia,
1776; Delegate to Continental Congress, 1774-7;
Signer of the Declaration of Independence.

1891. FORBES, FRANK HERBERT.   523
Great-grandson of Private James Hall (1752–1780), Captain Daniel Hand's Company, Colonel Talcott's Regiment Connecticut Militia, May 22, 1776; died on
prison ship at New York, January 16, 1780.

1891. FORBES, HENRY HALL, *M. D.*,
Great-great-grandson of Private James Hall (1752–
1780), Captain Daniel Hand's Company, Colonel Talcott's Regiment Connecticut Militia, died on prison
ship at New York, January 16, 1780; commissioned
May 22, 1776.

1891. FORD, JAMES DUFF.
Grandson of Lieutenant Chilion Ford (1757–1800), 2d
Regiment Continental Corps of Artillery (New
Jersey), Colonel John Lamb, April 10, 1777; Quarter-
master same Regiment, August 1, 1779).
Also, Grandson of Sergeant John Burnham (1758–
1837), Captain Charles Whiting's Company, Colonel
S. B. Webb's Regiment, "additional Continental,"
May 15, 1777; Seaman on Continental frigate
"Trumbull," Commander Saltonstall, February,
1777; taken prisoner 1778; confined in New York
"Sugar House," thence to prison ship "Good In-
tent;" exchanged and subsequently served on a
privateer under Captain Bulkley.

Elected.

1892. FORD, JAMES E.,

Great-grandson of Lieutenant-Colonel Jacob Ford (1744-1837), Captain of 4th Company, 9th Regiment Albany County Militia, Colonel Peter Van Ness, October 20, 1775; promoted 1st Major same; Lieutenant-Colonel same, May 28, 1778.

1890. FORD, PAUL LEICESTER,

Great-great-grandson of Captain Noah Webster (1722-1813), Connecticut Militia, on duty on Hudson River, 1777.

1889. FORD, WILLIAM H.,   32

Great-grandson of Private Abijah Ford, Private in Captain Benjamin Hoppin's Company, 4th Regiment Rhode Island Continental Infantry, Colonel Christopher Lippitt, served at Trenton and Princeton; honorably discharged at Morristown, 1777; Private Captain William Humphrey's Company, 2d Regiment Rhode Island Continental Infantry, Colonel Israel Angell, 1777; transferred to 1st Regiment Rhode Island Continental Infantry, Colonel Christopher Greene, January 1, 1781; honorably discharged, November 3, 1783.

1891. FORD, WORTHINGTON CHAUNCEY,

Great-great-grandson of Captain Noah Webster (1722-1813), Connecticut Militia, on duty on Hudson River. 1777.

1887. *FOSTER, JAMES A. (died March 10, 1888),

Great-grandson of Brevet Major-General James Clinton (1736-1812), Colonel 3d Regiment New York Line, 1775; Brigadier-General Continental Army, 1776; Major-General Continental Army, by brevet, 1783.

134

1891. FOWLER, EDWARD SIDNEY,   650

Great-grandson of Private Abel Belknap (1739-1804),
Private in Captain Samuel Clark's Company, Col-
onel Jonathan Hasbrouck's Regiment Ulster County
Militia, 4th Brigade, 1776.

1888. FOWLER, ROBERT LUDLOW,

Great-great-grandson of Colonel Charles Rumsey (1736-
1780), County Lieutenant Cecil County Militia, Maryland, 1777; Colonel of "Elk" Battalion Cecil County
Militia, 1776; Member Maryland Convention, 1775;
Member Maryland Council of Safety, 1776.

1888. FOWLER, THOMAS POWELL,   240

Great-great-grandson of Colonel Charles Rumsey (1736-
1780), County Lieutenant Cecil County Militia, Maryland, 1777; Colonel of "Elk" Battalion Cecil County
Militia, 1776; Member Maryland Convention, 1775;
Member Maryland Council of Safety, 1776.

1891. FRELINGHUYSEN, JOSEPH SHERMAN,

Great-grandson of Colonel Frederick Frelinghuysen
(—— 1804), 1st Major of Colonel Stewart's Battalion
New Jersey Minute Men, February 15, 1776; Captain
Eastern Company of Artillery, New Jersey State
Troops, March 1, 1776; Colonel 1st Battalion Somerset
County Militia, February 28, 1778; Member of New
Jersey Provincial Congress, 1775-8; Member of Con-
tinental Congress, 1778, and 1782-3.

1889. FRENCH, REVEREND LOUIS,

Grandson of Lieutenant William Glenney (1743-1791),
Private in Captain McGregier's Company, 4th Regi-
ment Connecticut Line, Colonel John Durkee, Janu-
ary 16, 1776; Sergeant in same, January 1, 1777;
Ensign in same, May 20, 1779; Lieutenant in 1st
Regiment Connecticut Line, Colonel Durkee, Janu-
ary 1, 1781; Ensign 1st Regiment Connecticut Line,
Colonel Zebulon Butler, January, 1783; Lieutenant in
Colonel Heman Swift's Regiment, "final formation,"
June, 1783.

135

1889.   FRENCH, LOUIS MARDENBROUGH,   302

Great-grandson of Lieutenant William Glenney (1743–
1791), Private in Captain McGregier's Company, 4th
Regiment Connecticut Line, Colonel John Durkee,
January 16, 1776; Sergeant in same, January 1, 1777;
Ensign in same, May 20, 1779; Lieutenant in 1st
Regiment Connecticut Line, Colonel Durkee, January
1, 1781; Ensign 1st Regiment Connecticut Line, Col-
onel Zebulon Butler, January, 1783; Lieutenant in
Colonel Heman Swift's Regiment, "final formation,"
June, 1783.

Also, Great-grandson of Midshipman Samuel Stowe
(1758–1830), Midshipman on the Continental frigate
"Trumbull," Commander Saltonstall, December 15,
1776; Midshipman on man-of-war "Oliver Cromwell,"
Captain Coit, January 20, 1778.

Also, Great-great-grandson of Stephen Stowe, who
volunteered as nurse to the Continental soldiers confined in the prison-ships, and died of a contagious
disease while on such service.

1889.   FRENCH, WILLIAM FREEMAN, M. D.,   238

Great-grandson of Lieutenant William Glenney (1743–
1791), Private in Captain McGregier's Company, 4th
Regiment Connecticut Line, Colonel John Durkee,
January 16, 1776; Sergeant in same, January 1, 1777;
Ensign in same, May 20, 1779; Lieutenant in 1st
Regiment Connecticut Line, Colonel Durkee, January
1, 1781; Ensign 1st Regiment Connecticut Line, Col-
onel Zebulon Butler, January, 1783; Lieutenant in
Colonel Heman Swift's Regiment, "final formation,"
June, 1783.

Also, Great-grandson of Midshipman Samuel Stowe
(1758–1830), Midshipman on the Continental frigate
"Trumbull," Commander Saltonstall, December 15,
1776; Midshipman on man-of-war "Oliver Cromwell,"
Captain Coit, January 20, 1778.

Also, Great-great-grandson of Stephen Stowe, who
volunteered as nurse to the Continental soldiers confined in the prison-ships, and died of a contagious
disease while on such service.

136

1889. FREY, AUGUSTUS BEARDSLEE,

Great-grandson of Brigade-Major John Frey (1740-1833), Tryon County (New York) Militia, Colonel Marinus Willett, August 6, 1777.

1890. FROTHINGHAM, SAMUEL,

Great-great-grandson of Nathaniel Frothingham (1722-1791), one of the "Boston Tea Party," and member of the Boston Committee of Correspondence.

1887. FRY, GEORGE GARDINER.

Great-great-grandson of Captain Benjamin Fry, 4th Regiment Rhode Island State Troops.
Also, Great-great-grandson of Colonel Amos Atwell, Rhode Island Militia.

1889. FULLER, LEVI K.,   127

Great-grandson of Private Jacob Constantine, Colonel Whitcomb's Regiment, Massachusetts Line.

1891. GADSDEN, GEORGE MORRALL,

Great-great-grandson of Brigadier-General Christopher Gadsden (1724-1805), Continental Army; Delegate 1st Continental Congress; Colonel 1st Regiment South Carolina Militia, 1775; Colonel 3d Regiment South Carolina Militia, 1775; Member Continental Naval Committee, 1776; Brigadier-General Continental Army, 1776; Member Constitutional Convention, South Carolina; Lieutenant-Governor, South Carolina, 1780; Member South Carolina Assembly, 1782; elected Governor of South Carolina, 1782; was prisoner at St. Augustine, July, 1780, to June, 1781.

1883. GALLUP, C. VAN EVERSDYK,

Great-great-grandson of Major-General William Heath, Continental Army, Massachusetts.

137

1876.   GARDINER, ASA BIRD, *LL. D.*,   83

Great-grandson of Ensign Reuben Willard (1755-1823),
Volunteer in Captain Jonathan Davis' Company of
Minute Men, " Lexington Alarm," April 19, 1775;
enlisted in 24th Regiment Continental Infantry,
Colonel Ephraim Doolittle, April 28, 1775; promoted
Ensign in same, November 27, 1775; honorably re-
tired on reorganization of the main Continental
Army, January 1, 1776; 2d Lieutenant 2d Regiment
Massachusetts Volunteer Infantry, Colonel Jonathan
Holman, Brigadier-General John Fellows' Brigade,
June 25 to December 1, 1776; volunteered in Captain
Jonathan Davis' Company, Colonel Samuel Denny's
Regiment Massachusetts Volunteer Infantry, June
25, 1779, appointed Sergeant-Major; promoted Lieu-
tenant in same, August 12, 1779; honorably dis-
charged March 25, 1780.

Also, Great-great-grandson of Lieutenant Othaniel Gardiner (1743-1777), Associator, 1775; Lieutenant in 14th
Regiment Albany County (New York) Militia, Colonel John Knickerbacker, October 20, 1775, at " Bennington "; died in service December, 1777.

Also, Great-grandson of Sergeant Jacob Rosenbergh
(1756-1828), Sergeant in Captain John Tater's Company, Colonel Cornelius Dota's Regiment Vermont
Militia; served at Battle of Bennington: honorably
discharged October 23, 1781.

Also, Representative of Lieutenant Jonathan Willard
(1744-1832), Sergeant in Captain Samuel Wetherbee's
Company, 2d Regiment New Hampshire Volunteer
Infantry, Colonel Isaac Wyman, for " Canadian
service," July 16, 1776; 1st Sergeant in same, August
6, 1776; Ensign in 1st Regiment New Hampshire
Continental Infantry, Colonel John Stark, November 8, 1776; 2d Lieutenant in same, January 10, 1778;
1st Lieutenant in same, August 24, 1779; appointed
Regimental Quartermaster, July 20, 1780; honorably
discharged May 10, 1782.

138

1889. GARDINER, GEORGE NORMAN.   273

Great-grandson of Ensign Reuben Willard (1755-1823).
Volunteer in Captain Jonathan Davis' Company of
Minute Men, "Lexington Alarm," April 19, 1775;
enlisted in 24th Regiment Continental Infantry,
Colonel Ephraim Doolittle, April 28, 1775; promoted
Ensign in same, November 27, 1775; honorably re-
tired on reorganization of the main Continental
Army, January 1, 1776; 2d Lieutenant 2d Regiment
Massachusetts Volunteer Infantry, Colonel Jonathan
Holman, Brigadier-General John Fellows' Brigade,
June 25 to December 1, 1776; volunteered in Captain
Jonathan Davis' Company, Colonel Samuel Denny's
Regiment Massachusetts Volunteer Infantry, June
25, 1779, appointed Sergeant-Major; promoted Lieu-
tenant in same, August 12, 1779; honorably dis-
charged March 25, 1780.

Also, Great-great-grandson of Lieutenant Othaniel Gardiner (1743-1777), Associator, 1775; Lieutenant in 14th
Regiment Albany County (New York) Militia. Colonel John Knickerbacker, October 20, 1775, at "Bennington"; died in service December, 1777.

Also, Great-grandson of Sergeant Jacob Rosenbergh
(1756-1828), Sergeant in Captain John Tater's Company, Colonel Cornelius Dota's Regiment Vermont
Militia; served at Battle of Bennington; honorably
discharged October 23, 1781.

1889. GARRISON, WILLIAM DOMINICK.   532

Great-grandson of Captain George Dominick (1730 ——),
14th Beat Company, 2d Regiment New York City
Militia, Colonel John Jay, August 29, 1775.

1887. GAWTRY, E. HARRISON,

Great-grandson of Wagonmaster Zadock Hedden, Continental Wagonmaster-General's Department, New
Jersey.

1887. GEDNEY, FREDERICK G.,   67

Great-grandson of Private Phineas Mapes, Additional
Regiment Continental Infantry, Colonel William
Malcolm.

130

1889. GEER, FREDERIC MILLS,

Grandson of Corporal Samuel Frederick Mills (1759-
1857), Private Fairfield County Militia, Lexington
Alarm, April 19, 1775; Private Captain Tomlinson's
Company, 4th Regiment Connecticut Militia, Lieu-
tenant-Colonel Ichabod Lewis, August, 1776, served
around New York; Private in Captain Blackman's
Company, Colonel Whiting's Regiment Connecticut
Militia, November, 1776, served in Westchester County,
New York; served in Westchester County, February,
1777; at Ridgefield, Connecticut, April 27, 1777; served
at the Sawpits, under Colonel Deming, June 1, 1777;
Private in Captain John Yates' Company, Connecti-
cut Militia, September, 1777, served at Fishkill, New
York; Private in Captain Pettibone's Company,
Colonel Canfield's Regiment Connecticut Militia,
December, 1777, served at Kingsbridge, New York;
Private in Captain Leavenworth's Company, Colonel
Whiting's Regiment Connecticut Militia, at Fairfield,
May, 1778; Corporal in Captain John Yates' Com-
pany, Connecticut Militia, at Horse Neck, July, 1779.

1885. GENET, ALBERT RIVERS,

Great-great-grandson of Brigadier and Brevet Major-
General George Clinton (1739-1812), Brigadier-Gen-
eral Continental Army, 1776; Member of Continental
Congress, 1775; Governor of New York, 1777-95;
Major-General by brevet.

1883. GENET, GEORGE CLINTON,   95

Grandson of Brigade-Major Samuel Osgood, Private in Captain Peter Talbot's Company, Colonel
Lemuel Robinson's Regiment Massachusetts Militia,
marched from Stoughton, on Lexington Alarm,
April 19, 1775; Brigade-Major Massachusetts Militia,
1775; Member of Massachusetts Provincial Congress,
1775-6; Aide-de-Camp to General Ward, 1775-7;
Representative to Massachusetts General Court, 1776,
1779-84; Member Massachusetts Senate, 1780; member Continental Congress, 1781.

1889. GERRY, ALLSTON,   236

Great-grandson of Private Humphrey H. Richards,
Private in Captain Mighell's Company. Massachusetts
Militia, from Rowley, April, 1775.

Also, Great-grandson of Sergeant Reuben Gary. Private
in Captain Thomas Gates' Company, Lancaster Militia.
Lexington Alarm, 1775; Private in Captain Samuel
Sawyer's Company, Colonel Dike's Regiment, January
1. 1777; Sergeant in Captain John White's Company,
Colonel Job Cushing's Regiment, Bennington Alarm,
July 28, 1777.

Also. Great-grandson of Commander Ephraim Lombard,
Privateer Service, Massachusetts, 1778.

1885. GERRY, ELBRIDGE T. (Life Member),

Grandson of Elbridge Gerry, Signer of the Declaration
of Independence, Massachusetts.

1887. GIBSON, GEORGE RUTLEDGE,   186

Great-grandson of Edward Rutledge (1749–1800). Signer
of the Declaration of Independence, South Carolina.

1887. *GIBSON, JAMES RENWICK, JR. (died March 5, 1890).

Great-great-grandson of Ensign Mathew Van Keuren,
2d Regiment Dutchess County Minute Men, New York.

1888. GIBSON, ROBERT RENWICK,

Great-great-great-grandson of Ensign Mathew Van Keuren, 2d Regiment Dutchess County Minute Men. New
York.

Also, Great-great-grandson of Governor Richard How-
ley, Member Georgia Legislature, 1779; Governor of
Georgia, 1780; Member of Continental Congress,
1780–81.

1888. GOODWIN, JAMES JUNIUS,   225

Great-grandson of Captain Lemuel Roberts. Captain of
Simsbury Militia that marched in the Lexington
Alarm, April, 1775; also in the Commissary's Depart-
ment; Captain 18th Regiment Connecticut Militia.
August 24. 1776, in service around New York. 1776.

141

1890. GOODRICH, LE ROY LIVINGSTON,   331

Great-grandson of Sergeant William Johnson (1758-1851), Private in Captain Watson's Company, 9th Regiment Massachusetts Continental Infantry, Colonel Wesson, January 1, 1777; Sergeant in Captain North's Company, Colonel Henry Jackson's Regiment Massachusetts Continental Infantry, March, 1781; afterwards transferred to Captain White's Company of Light Infantry.

1886. GOOLD, CLARENCE WINFIELD,   _152

Great-grandson of Ensign Josiah Moody, Corporal in Captain Henry Dearborn's Company, Colonel John Stark's Regiment New Hampshire Militia, 1775; Ensign 5th Regiment New Hampshire Continental Infantry, Colonel John Waldron, 1776.

1891. GRAHAM, MALCOLM,

Great-grandson of Private Andrew Graham (1728-1785), Captain John Hinman's Company 13th Regiment Connecticut Militia, Colonel Benjamin Hinman, August 18, 1776; served around New York, 1776; later Surgeon in same Regiment.

1891. GRANT, WILLIAM DANIEL,   646

Great-grandson of Lieutenant-Colonel James Jackson (1757-1806), Lieutenant, promoted Captain, Georgia Militia, 1775-6; Major in Colonel Baker's Regiment Georgia Militia, 1779; Brigade-Major of General Andrew Pickens' Brigade, January, 1781; Lieutenant-Colonel Georgia Militia, 1781; received the formal surrender of Savannah, 1782.

Also, Great-grandson of Ensign Thomas Grant (1757-1828), Ensign in 6th Regiment North Carolina Continental Infantry, April 16, 1776.

Also, Great-great-grandson of William Young (1743-1776), Speaker of Georgia Assembly 1775, and Member of 1st Georgia Provincial Congress.

142

1891.   GREEN, WILLIAM,   632

Grandson of Captain James Green (1751–1837), Captain
Winthorn Adams' Company New Hampshire Continental Infantry, Colonel Enoch Poor.
Also, Grandson of John McKinley (1751–1811), enlisted
at Danbury, Connecticut, 1778, for two years' service
as Artillery Artificer.

1888.   GREEN, WILLIAM WEBB,

Grandson of Captain James Green, 2d Regiment Con-
necticut Militia Light Horse, Major Elijah Hyde, at
"Saratoga."
Also, Grandson of "Landman" William Webb, Con-
tinental Frigate "Trumbull."
Also, Great-grandson of Ebenezer Webb, Associator,
Suffolk County, New York.

1891.   GREENE, CHARLES ARTHUR,   638

Great-great-grandson of Ensign John Greene (1745–
1830), Ensign of 2d Company Charleston (Rhode
Island) Militia, 1780.

1890.   GREENE, EDWARD,   364

Great-grandson of Colonel Christopher Greene (1727–
1781), Major in Colonel J. M. Varnum's Regiment,
Rhode Island, May, 1775; Colonel of 1st Regiment
Rhode Island Continental Infantry, May, 1777;
voted a sword for gallant services at Red Bank,
New Jersey; killed in Westchester County, New
York, May 13, 1781.

1888.   GREENE, RICHARD HENRY,   92

Great-grandson of Captain James Green, 2d Regiment
Connecticut Militia Light Horse, Major Elijah Hyde,
at "Saratoga."
Also, Great-grandson of "Landman" William Webb,
Continental Frigate "Trumbull."
Also, Great-great-grandson of Ebenezer Webb, Associ-
ator, Suffolk County, New York.

143

Elected.

No. of
Insignia.

1890. GREENE, JOHN WYNANTZ, *M. D.* (Life Member).   519
Great-grandson of Captain Benjamin Winans, 1st Regiment Essex County Militia, New Jersey.

1890. GREENWOOD, ISAAC JOHN,   333
Grandson of Fife-Major John Greenwood (1760–1790), Fifer in Captain Theo. T. Bliss's Company, Massachusetts Militia, May, 1775, and appointed Fife-Major in Colonel Patterson's Regiment Lenox Militia, serving to close of 1776; Fifer in Captain John Hinckley's Company, Lieutenant-Colonel Symond's Detachment of Guards in Boston, February 13, 1778; Midshipman on privateer "Cumberland," Commander John Manly, January, 1779; captured, and prisoner some months, at Barbadoes; Master-at-Arms on privateer "Tartar," Captain David Porter, November, 1779; served on brigantine "General Lincoln," Captain John Carnes, captured and carried to New York, 1780; served on letter-of-marque "Aurora," Captain Porter, October, 1780; 2d Mate on letter-of-marque "Race Horse," Captain Thayer, 1781; in active naval service to close of war.

1890. GREENWOOD, LANGDON,   338
Grandson of Fife-Major John Greenwood (1760–1790), Fifer in Captain Theo. T. Bliss's Company, Massachusetts Militia, May, 1775, and appointed Fife-Major in Colonel Patterson's Regiment Lenox Militia, serving to close of 1776; Fifer in Captain John Hinckley's Company, Lieutenant-Colonel Symond's Detachment of Guards in Boston, February 13, 1778; Midshipman on privateer "Cumberland," Commander John Manly, January, 1779; captured, and prisoner some months, at Barbadoes; Master-at-Arms on privateer "Tartar," Captain David Porter, November, 1779; served on brigantine "General Lincoln," Captain John Carnes, captured and carried to New York, 1780; served on letter-of-marque "Aurora," Captain Porter, October, 1780; 2d Mate on letter-of-marque "Race Horse," Captain Thayer, 1781; in active naval service to close of war.

144

1890. GREENWOOD, LANGDON, JR., 356

Great-grandson of Fife-Major John Greenwood (1760–1790), Fifer in Captain Theo. T. Bliss's Company, Massachusetts Militia, May, 1775, and appointed Fife-Major in Colonel Patterson's Regiment Lenox Militia, serving to close of 1776; Fifer in Captain John Hinckley's Company, Lieutenant-Colonel Symond's Detachment of Guards in Boston, February 13, 1778; Midshipman on privateer "Cumberland," Commander John Manly, 1779; captured, and prisoner some months, at Barbadoes; Master-at-Arms on privateer "Tartar," Captain David Porter, November, 1779; served on brigantine "General Lincoln," Captain John Carnes, captured and carried to New York, 1780; served on letter-of-marque "Aurora," Captain Porter, October, 1780; 2d Mate on letter-of-marque "Race Horse," Captain Thayer, 1781; in active naval service to close of war.

1891. GREGG, LEVI LAERTES, 662

Great-grandson of Captain James Gregg, 2d Lieutenant 3d Regiment New York Line, July 21, 1775; 2d Lieutenant 4th Regiment New York Line, February 28, 1776; 1st Lieutenant 3d Regiment New York Line, June 26, 1776; Captain 6th Company 3d Regiment New York Line, Colonel Peter Gansevoort, November 21, 1776; was shot through the body, tomahawked, and scalped, at Fort Schuyler, June 25, 1777; recovered, and served to close of war.

1888. GRIFFIN, FRANCIS B., 217

Great-grandson of Colonel Zebulon Butler (1731–1795), Lieutenant-Colonel 3d Regiment Connecticut Line, January 1, 1777; Colonel 2d Regiment Connecticut Line, November 15, 1778; on duty at Wyoming Massacre, July 3, 1778; with Sullivan's Expedition, 1779; Colonel 4th Regiment Connecticut Line, 1781; Colonel 1st Regiment Connecticut Line, "final formation," 1783.

1887. GRISWOLD, CHESTER.

Great-grandson of Private Simeon Griswold (1753-1813).
Private in Captain Thomas Pitkin's Company, Connecticut Militia; marched to Boston, on Lexington
Alarm, 1775; Private Captain Solomon Willes' Company, 2d Regiment Connecticut Line, Colonel Spencer,
1777.

Also, Great-great-grandson of Lieutenant-Colonel Ste-
phen Moulton, Lieutenant-Colonel (Stafford, Con-
necticut) Militia, Lexington Alarm, 1775; Lieutenant-
Colonel 22d Regiment Connecticut Militia, Colonel
Samuel Chapman; taken prisoner at New York,
September 15, 1776, exchanged March 2, 1777.

1888. GRUBB, EDWARD BURD.

Great-grandson of Captain Peter Grubb, 3d Lieutenant.
Captain George Nagel's Company of Riflemen, at
Cambridge, July 17, 1775; Captain in Colonel Sam-
uel Miles' "Rifles," March 12, 1776; Captain in Col-
onel John Patton's Regiment (Pennsylvania)
"Additional Continental," 1777.

1888. GUERNSEY, EGBERT, *M. D.*,

Great-grandson of Chauncey Garnsey, Litchfield
County Militia, Connecticut.

1884. GUILD, FREDERICK AUGUSTUS,   105

Great-grandson of Captain Joseph Guild. Captain
of Company Dedham Minute Men "Lexington
Alarm," 1775; Captain 24th Regiment Continental
Infantry, Colonel John Greaton, served in Canada
under General Montgomery, 1775; Member Massachusetts Provincial Congress, 1776; Member of Massachusetts Committee of Safety, Correspondence, and
Inspection, 1775-81.

146

1884. HACKLEY, CALEB BREWSTER,   21

Grandson of Captain-Lieutenant Caleb Brewster (——
1827), 2d Lieutenant Suffolk County Militia, 1776;
Ensign 2d Company, Captain John Davis, 4th Regiment New York Line, Colonel Henry B. Livingston,
1776; 1st Lieutenant 2d Regiment Continental Corps
of Artillery, Colonel John Lamb, 1777; promoted
Captain-Lieutenant of same, 1780; honorably discharged at close of war.   Also Associator Suffolk
County, New York, 1775.

1887. HACKSTAFF, WILLIAM G.,   272

Grandson of William Hallock, Associator, Suffolk
County, New York.

1889. HAIGHT, FREDERICK EVEREST,   531

Great-great-great-grandson of Lieutenant-Colonel Isaac
Cook, Jr. (1739-1810), 1st Regiment 7th Company, 1st
Regiment Connecticut Continental Infantry, Colonel
David Wooster, May 1, 1775; Major 10th Regiment
Connecticut Militia, Colonel James Wadsworth, Jan-
uary 10, 1780; promoted Lieutenant-Colonel, June,
1783.

Also, Great-great-great-grandson of Captain Isaac Cook,
Sr. (1711-1790), Captain of Wallingford (Connecticut)
Militia "Lexington Alarm," April 19, 1775; served
around Boston.

Also, Great-great-grandson of Private Aaron Betts
(1757-1833), Private in Captain Aaron Rowley's Company, Colonel John Brown's Detachment Massachusetts Militia, at Ticonderoga, June 30, 1777; Private
in Captain Amos Rathbun's Company, same Regiment, September 21, 1777; Private in Captain James
Raymond's Company, Colonel Rossiter's Regiment
Hampshire County Militia, Fellowes Brigade, October 14, 1780, at "Saratoga."

Also, Great-great-grandson of Private Daniel Everest
(1752-1825), Private in Captain John Stevens' Company, Connecticut Continental Infantry, Colonel
Charles Burrall, February 21, 1776; served in the
Northern Department under General Schuyler.

Also, Great-great-great-grandson of Captain Stephen
Hall (1724 1783), 1st Lieutenant 2d Company, Captain Andrew Ward, 1st Regiment Connecticut Continental Infantry, Colonel David Wooster, May 1,
1775; Captain in Colonel Heman Swift's Battalion
Connecticut State Troops, July, 1776; Captain 7th
Regiment Connecticut Line, Colonel Heman Swift,
January 1, 1777; retired by consolidation, January 1,
1781.

1891   HALE, JOSEPH, Captain U. S. A.,   714

Great-grandson of Private Richard Downing (1757–
1790), Private in Captain Joseph Whipple's Company
Essex County (Massachusetts) Militia, raised for de
fense of the seacoast, July 13, 1775, to December 31,
1775; Matross in 2d Company, Captain Joseph Mel-
vill, Colonel Craft's Battalion Massachusetts Artillery, May 29, 1776, to May 8, 1777.

1887   HALE, MATTHEW,

Grandson of Colonel Nathan Hale, Captain in command
of Company of New Hampshire Militia, marched to
Lexington and Cambridge on "Lexington Alarm,"
April, 1775; appointed Major in Colonel Reed's Regiment New Hampshire Continental Infantry, June,
1775; Lieutenant-Colonel 2d Battalion (Continental),
1776; promoted Colonel, 1777; taken prisoner on
Long Island, and died there while a prisoner, September 23, 1780.

1888.   HALL, FREDERICK J.,

Great-great-grandson of Private James M. Hall, in Captain Joseph Chapin's Company of Massachusetts
Minute Men, that marched from Uxbridge on "Lexington Alarm," April 19, 1775.

1888   HALL, HENRY,   308
Great-grandson of Private William Hall, Connecticut
Militia.

148

No. of
insignia.

1889. HALSEY, GEORGE A.,   76

Great-grandson of Private Jonathan Osborn, Captain
Peter Hallock's Company, Suffolk County Militia,
New York.

1890. HAMERSLEY, ANDREW S., JR.,   522

Great-great-grandson of Governor and Brigadier-General William Livingston (1723-1790), Brigadier-General New Jersey Militia, October 28, 1775; Governor
of New Jersey, 1776-90; also Member of Continental
Congress.

1890. HAMILTON, REVEREND ALEXANDER,

Great-grandson of Brevet Colonel Alexander Hamilton
(1757-1804), Captain of New York Provincial Artillery, 1776; Lieutenant-Colonel and Aide-de-Camp to
the Commander-in-Chief, 1777; Colonel by brevet at
close of war.
Also, Great-great-grandson of Major-General Philip
Schuyler (1733-1804), Major-General Continental
Army, 1775; resigned 1779; Delegate to Continental
Congress, 1775-7; Member New York Provincial
Congress, 1778-9; Member New York State Senate,
1781-84.

1886. *HAMILTON, ROBERT RAY (died August 23, 1890),

Great-grandson of Brevet Colonel Alexander Hamilton
(1757-1804), Captain of New York Provincial Artillery, 1776; Lieutenant-Colonel and Aide-de-Camp to
the Commander-in-Chief, 1777; Colonel by brevet at
close of war.
Also, Great-great-grandson of Major-General Philip
Schuyler (1733-1804), Major-General Continental
Army, 1775; resigned 1779; Delegate to Continental
Congress, 1775-7; Member New York Provincial
Congress, 1778-9; Member of New York Senate,
1781-4.

1888. HAMILTON, SCHUYLER,   353

> Grandson of Brevet Colonel Alexander Hamilton
> (1757–1804), Captain of New York Provincial Artil-
> lery, 1776; Lieutenant-Colonel and Aide-de-Camp to
> the Commander-in-Chief, 1777; Colonel by brevet at
> close of war.
> *Also*, Great-grandson of Major-General Philip Schuyler
> (1733–1804), Major-General Continental Army, 1775;
> resigned 1779; Delegate to Continental Congress,
> 1775 7: Member New York Provincial Congress,
> 1778 9; Member New York State Senate, 1781–4.

1886. HAMILTON, WILLIAM GASTON,   13

> Grandson of Brevet Colonel Alexander Hamilton
> (1757–1804), Captain of New York Provincial Artil-
> lery, 1776; Lieutenant-Colonel and Aide-de-Camp to
> the Commander-in-Chief, 1777; Colonel by brevet at
> close of war.
> *Also*, Great-grandson of Major-General Philip Schuyler
> (1733–1804), Major-General Continental Army, 1775;
> resigned 1779; Delegate to Continental Congress,
> 1775–7; Member New York Provincial Congress,
> 1778–9: Member New York State Senate, 1781–4.

1892. HAMILTON, WILLIAM PIERSON,   805

> Great-grandson of Brevet Colonel Alexander Hamilton
> (1757–1804), Captain of New York Provincial Artil-
> lery, 1776: Lieutenant-Colonel and Aide-de-Camp to
> the Commander-in-Chief, 1777; Colonel by brevet at
> close of war.
> *Also*, Great-great-grandson of Major-General Philip
> Schuyler (1733–1804), Major-General Continental
> Army, 1775; resigned 1779; Delegate to Continental
> Congress, 1775–7; Member New York Provincial
> Congress, 1778–9; Member New York State Senate,
> 1781–4.

150

Elected.   No. of Insignia.

1892. HAMMOND, ANDREW GOODRICH, Lieutenant U. S. A.,   794

Great-great-grandson of Lieutenant Colonel John Barrett (1731-1806), Captain in Colonel Seth Warner's Regiment, Vermont Militia, 1775; Lieutenant-Colonel Upper Regiment Cumberland County New York (Vermont) Militia, November 21, 1775.

1892. HAMMOND, GRAEME MONROE, M. D.,

Great-great-grandson of Rezin Hammond (1706-1781), Member of the Maryland Constitutional Convention, 1776.

1890. HARDEN, WILLIAM,   436

Great-grandson of Colonel John Baker, Commanding Liberty County Militia, Georgia.

1887. HARPER, FRANKLIN,   299

Great-great-grandson of Peter Lyon (1744-1824), Member of Committee of Safety, Westchester County, New York.

1892. HARRIMAN, FRANCIS COTTENET,   796

Great-great-great-grandson of Josiah Hornblower, Speaker of Lower House (Assembly) Provincial Congress, New Jersey, 1780; Member of Upper House (Council), 1781-4.

1892. HARRIMAN, WILLIAM EDWARD,   795

Great-great-great-grandson of Josiah Hornblower, Speaker of Lower House (Assembly) Provincial Congress, New Jersey, 1780; Member of Upper House (Council), 1781-4.

1890. HARRISON, RUSSELL B.,   448

Great-great-grandson of Benjamin Harrison of Virginia (1730-1791), Member of Virginia Conventions; Member of Continental Congress; Signer of the Declaration of Independence; Chairman of the Continental Board of War; and Governor of Virginia, 1782.

Also, Great-great-grandson of Colonel John Cleves Symmes (1742-1814), 3d Battalion Sussex County Militia, resigned, May 23, 1777, to accept the appointment of Justice of the Supreme Court of New Jersey.

Also, Great-great-great-grandson of Governor and Brigadier-General William Livingson (1723-1790), Brigadier-General New Jersey Militia, October 28, 1775; Member of Continental Congress; and Governor of New Jersey, 1776-90.

1891. HARRISON, WILLIAM HENRY,   674

Great-grandson of Private John Woolsey, Jr. (1752-1815), Private in Captain Marcus Moseman's Company 2d Regiment Westchester County Militia, Colonel Thomas Thomas, 1778.

Also, Great-great-grandson of Private John Woolsey, Sr. (1727-1805), Private in Captain Marcus Moseman's Company 2d Regiment Westchester County Militia, Colonel Thomas Thomas, 1778.

1891. HARVEY, LEON FERDINAND,   747

Great-grandson of Orderly-Sergeant John Sherwood (1754-1841), Orderly-Sergeant in Captain Thomas De Witt's Company, 3d Regiment New York Line, Colonel Gansevoort, May 14, 1778; discharged on account of ill-health, November, 1778.

1889. HARVEY, RICHARD S.,

Great-grandson of Colonel Samuel Selden (1723-1776), Major 3d Regiment Connecticut Militia, Colonel Saltonstall, 1775; Colonel 4th Battalion Wadsworth's Brigade Connecticut Militia, June 20, 1776; taken prisoner at New York, September 15, 1776; died while a prisoner in New York, October 11, 1776; Member of Connecticut Assembly, 1776.

152

1885. HATCH, ARTHUR MELVIN,   3

   Great-great-grandson of the Rev. Nathanael Taylor (1722–1800), of New Milford, Connecticut, contributed one year's salary to the cause, as shown by Parish records, April, 1779.

   Also, Great-grandson of Private Joseph Hatch, Captain Turner's Company, Colonel John Cushing's Regiment, Massachusetts Militia.

1889. HATCH, HENRY PRESCOTT,   250

   Great-great-grandson of the Rev. Nathanael Taylor (1722–1800), of New Milford, Connecticut, contributed one year's salary to the cause, as shown by Parish records, April, 1779.

   Also, Great-grandson of Private Joseph Hatch, Captain Turner's Company, Colonel John Cushing's Regiment, Massachusetts Militia.

1886. *HATCH, NATHANIEL W. T. (died May 8, 1888),

   Great-great grandson of the Rev. Nathanael Taylor (1722–1800), of New Milford, Connecticut, contributed one year's salary to the cause, as shown by Parish records, April, 1779.

   Also, Great-grandson of Private Joseph Hatch, Captain Turner's Company, Colonel John Cushing's Regiment, Massachusetts Militia.

1884. HAWES, GILBERT RAY,

   Great-grandson of Lieutenant Joseph Hawes (1727–1818), Captain Fairbanks' Company Massachusetts Militia, and representative to General Court, 1778–81.

1891. HAWKINS, RUSH CHRISTOPHER,

   Grandson of Private Dexter Hawkins (1761–1830), 3d Regiment Rhode Island Infantry, Colonel Archibald Cary, December, 1776.

153

1890.   HAY, HENRY LUDLOW,

Grandson of Lieutenant-Colonel Samuel Hay (—— 1783),
Captain 6th Pennsylvania Battalion, Colonel William
Irvine, January 9, 1776; Captain 7th Regiment
Pennsylvania Line, Colonel William Irvine, October
5, 1776; Major in same, March 12, 1777; Lieutenant-
Colonel in same, and Lieutenant-Colonel 10th Regi-
ment Pennsylvania Line, February 21, 1778; wound-
ed in attack on Stony Point.

1890.   HAY, JAMES RICHARDS,

Grandson of Lieutenant-Colonel Samuel Hay (—— 1783),
Captain 6th Pennsylvania Battalion, Colonel William
Irvine, January 9, 1776; Captain 7th Regiment
Pennsylvania Line, Colonel William Irvine, October
5, 1776; Major in same, March 12, 1777; Lieutenant-
Colonel in same, and Lieutenant-Colonel 10th Regi-
ment Pennsylvania Line, February 21, 1778; wounded
in attack on Stony Point.

1890.   HAY, SILAS CONDIT,

Grandson of Lieutenant-Colonel Samuel Hay (—— 1783),
Captain 6th Pennsylvania Battalion, Colonel William
Irvine, January 9, 1776; Captain 7th Regiment
Pennsylvania Line, Colonel William Irvine, October
5, 1776; Major in same, March 12, 1777; Lieutenant-
Colonel in same, and Lieutenant-Colonel 10th Regi-
ment Pennsylvania Line, February 21, 1778; wound-
ed in attack on Stony Point.

1886.   HAYES, RICHARD SOMERS,   135

Great-grandnephew and representative of Captain
John Barry (1745-1803), Captain of ship "Lexington," 1776; served for a short time with the army in
New Jersey, 1777; in command of Continental frigate "Raleigh," 32 guns, 1778; in command of the
"Alliance," conveying United States Ambassador
to the Court of France, 1781.

Elected.

No. of
Insignia.

1885. HEALEY, WARREN M., 15·

Great-grandson of Private James Thayer, Captain John
Vinton's Independent Company, Massachusetts
Militia.

1888. HECKER, GEORGE F.,

Great-grandson of Private Jonah Winslow Wentworth,
enlisted in Continental Infantry from Rhoton Hill,
near Old Well, Connecticut; drew pension for services.

1885. HEDDEN, EDWARD L.,

Grandson of Wagonmaster Zadock Hedden. Continental Wagonmaster-General's Department, New
Jersey.

1887. HEDDEN, JOSIAH, 194

Great-grandson of Wagonmaster Zadock Hedden, Continental Wagonmaster-General's Department, New
Jersey.

1889. HEILNER, GEORGE CORSON, 156

Great-grandson of Colonel Zebulon Butler (1731-1795).
Lieutenant-Colonel 3d Regiment Connecticut Line,
January 1, 1777; Colonel 2d Regiment Connecticut
Line, November 15, 1778; on duty at Wyoming Mas-
sacre, July 3, 1778; with Sullivan's Expedition, 1779;
Colonel 4th Regiment Connecticut Line, 1781; Col
onel 1st Regiment Connecticut Line, "final forma-
tion," 1783.

1889. HERRICK, JOHN VAN BOSKERCK,

Great-great-grandson of Lieutenant-Colonel Rufus
Herrick, Captain 4th Regiment Dutchess County
(New York) Militia, Colonel Holmes, June 28, 1775;
Lieutenant-Colonel in Colonel Zephaniah Platt's
Regiment New York Associated Exempt Volunteer
Infantry, October 19, 1779.

155

1889. HIGGINS, EUGENE,   190

Great-grandson of Captain Daniel Baldwin, 1st Lieutenant in Captain Morris' Company, 1st Battalion 1st Establishment New Jersey Line, November 8, 1775; Captain 1st Battalion 2d Establishment, November 29, 1776; severely wounded, lost a leg in battle of Germantown, October 4, 1777; honorably discharged, March 1, 1779.

1885. HILL, JOHN L.,

Son of Sergeant Nicholas Hill (1766-1856), attached to 3d Company, Captain Benjamin Hicks, 1st Regiment New York Continental Infantry, Colonel Goose Van Schaick, 1777; Musician same, 1778; honorably discharged with rank of Sergeant, June 8, 1783.

1891. HILL, WILLIAM SQUIRE,

Great-grandson of Captain Squire Hill (1747-1830), Sergeant in Captain Thomas Knowlton's Company of Ashford (Connecticut) Militia, "Lexington Alarm," April 19, 1775; Ensign in Captain Knowlton's Company 3d Regiment Connecticut Continental Infantry, Colonel Israel Putnam, May 1, 1775, at "Bunker Hill;" 1st Lieutenant in Captain Amaziah Wright's Company, Colonel Roger Enos' Regiment Connecticut State Troops, 1776-7; Captain in Colonel Samuel McClellan's Regiment Connecticut State Troops, March 1, 1778; served in Tyler's Brigade, under General Sullivan, in Rhode Island, September, 1778.

1889. HINE, FRANCIS L.,   260

Great-grandson of Private Stephen Hine, of Brigadier-General Oliver Wolcott's Detachment Volunteers, Connecticut Militia, at "Saratoga" in 1777.

1890. HINMAN, EDWARD,   313.

Great-great-grandson of Colonel Benjamin Hinman (1720-1810), Colonel 13th Regiment Connecticut Militia, 1775; Colonel 4th Regiment Connecticut Continental Infantry, May 1, 1775; Member of Connecticut General Assembly, 1757-98.

156

1890.   HINMAN, MATTHEW,

Great-great-grandson of Colonel Benjamin Hinman
(1720-1810), Colonel 13th Regiment Connecticut
Militia, 1775; Colonel 4th Regiment Connecticut
Continental Infantry, May 1, 1775; Member of Connecticut General Assembly, 1757–98.

1889.   HOADLEY, JAMES H.,   20

Grandson of Captain Andrew Hillyer (1743-1828),
mustered a company of Militia, marched to
Boston, "Lexington Alarm," April, 1775; Lieutenant in Captain Elihu Humphrey's 8th Regiment Connecticut Militia, Colonel Jedediah Huntington, July,
1775; Adjutant same, 1776; Adjutant in Colonel
Pettibone's Regiment of Militia, at Turtle Bay, New
York, 1776; Ensign 2d Company, Captain Wylly's
6th Battalion Wadsworth's Brigade, Colonel Chester,
June, 1776; served in New York and on Long Isl-
and; Captain of Connecticut Militia at Horse Neck,
1779; Captain 5th Regiment Connecticut Light Horse,
Colonel Elisha Sheldon, May, 1776.

1889.   HODGES, ALFRED,   134

Great-grandson of Colonel John Hathorn, "Florida
and Warwick" Regiment, Orange County Militia,
New York, February 28, 1776; called out on the
"Alarm of Minisink," July, 1777; Chairman of
Goshen Committee of Safety.

1889.   HOES, REV. ROSWELL RANDALL, U. S. N.,

Great-grandson of Ensign Peter Swart, 15th Regiment
(Schoharie and Duanesburgh) Militia, New York,
Colonel Peter Vrooman, February 20, 1778.

1891.   HOLLAND, JOHN BUTTERFEILD,   698

Great-grandson of Lieutenant Ivory Holland (1740-
1820), 5th Regiment Massachusetts Continental Infantry, Colonel Rufus Putnam, November 11, 1778.

1891. HOLLISTER, HENRY HUTCHINSON,   738

Grandson of Captain John Hutchinson Buell (1753–
1813), Sergeant in Captain Daniel Tilden's Company,
Lebanon (Connecticut) Militia, "Lexington Alarm,"
April 19, 1775; Captain in 1st Regiment Connecticut
Line, Colonel John Durkee, 1777–83; honorably dis-
charged, November 3, 1783.

1885. HOLT, GEORGE C.,   88

Grandson of Sergeant Nehemiah Holt (1756 1824), of
Captain Thomas Dyer's Company 20th Regiment Con-
tinental Foot (4th Connecticut, Colonel John Durkee)
in 1776–7, and 1st Sergeant, 7th August, 1780, of 5th
Company in Colonel Hezekiah Wylly's Regiment
Connecticut Volunteer Infantry, garrisoning New
London Harbor.

Also, Great-grandson of Captain James Stedman
(1726–1788), Colonel Andrew Ward's Regiment Connecticut Continental Infantry, 1776–7; and "Lexington Alarm," April, 1775.

1890. HONE, JOHN, JR.,   363

Great-grandson of Christopher Raymond Perry (1761–
1818), served on the "Mifflin," Commander Babcock;
captured, confined in prison ship "Jersey"; escaped
after three months' confinement; subsequently served
as Midshipman on Continental frigate "Trumbull,"
Captain James Nicholson.

1891. HONE, JOHN, 3d,

Great-great-grandson of Christopher Raymond Perry
(1761–1818), served on the "Mifflin," Commander
Babcock; captured, confined in prison ship "Jersey"; escaped after three months' confinement; subsequently served as Midshipman on Continental
frigate "Trumbull," Captain James Nicholson.

158

1891. HOPKINS, HENRY REED,

Grandson of Sergeant James Hopkins (1761-1843), Private in Captain Joseph Finley's Company of New Hampshire Volunteers, from Londonderry. New Hampshire, October 10, 1776; Sergeant in Captain James Aikin's Company, Colonel Thomas Bartlett's Regiment New Hampshire Volunteers in Continental service, July 6, 1780, at West Point.

Also, Great-grandson of Captain James Aikin (1731-1817), Captain in Colonel Moses Kelley's Regiment New Hampshire Volunteers, served with Continental Army in Rhode Island, August 7, 1778; Captain in Colonel Thomas Bartlett's Regiment New Hampshire Volunteers in Continental service, June 29, 1780.

1892. HOPPIN, FRANCIS LAURENS VINTON,

Great-grandson of Benjamin Hoppin (1747-1809), Lieutenant Rhode Island Militia. 1776; Captain Rhode Island State Troops, 1776; Captain 2d Regiment Rhode Island State Troops.

Also, Great-grandson of Captain William Jones (1755-1822), Colonel Christopher Lippitt's Regiment Rhode Island Continental Infantry 1776; later Captain of Marines on frigate "Providence;" taken prisoner at Charleston, South Carolina, and on parole to close of war.

1890. HOPPIN, WILLIAM WARNER,   360

Great-grandson of Captain Benjamin Hoppin (1747-1809). Lieutenant Rhode Island Militia. 1776; Captain Rhode Island State Troops. 1776; Captain 2d Regiment Rhode Island Continental Infantry.

1889. HOPSON, FRANCIS JOHNSTONE,

Great-grandson of Captain John Williamson. 1st Regiment South Carolina Continental Infantry.

159

No. of Insignia.

1890. HORNBLOWER, WILLIAM BUTLER, 416

Great-grandson of Josiah Hornblower, Speaker of Lower House (Assembly), Provincial Congress, New Jersey, 1780; member of Upper House (Council), 1781–1784.

Also, Great-grandson of Major Augustine Pease (1757–1791), Aide-de-Camp to Major-General Spencer.

Also, Great-great-grandson of Surgeon-General William Burnet (1730–1791), Surgeon 1st Battalion, 1st Establishment, New Jersey Line, December 8, 1775; Surgeon 1st Battalion, 2d Establishment, November 28, 1776; Surgeon 1st Regiment; resigned, and appointed Surgeon-General for Eastern District Continental Army, 1781–1783.

Also, Great-great-grandson of Captain Joseph Alling, Essex County Militia, New Jersey, 1776.

1889. HOSMER, JAMES RAY, 332

Great-grandson of Titus Hosmer (1736–1780), Speaker of Connecticut Assembly, 1773–80; Member of Continental Congress, 1776–7; Judge United States Maritime Court of Appeals, 1780, but died before entering upon his duties.

Also, Great-grandson of Major-General Samuel Holden Parsons (—— 1787), Colonel 10th Regiment Connecticut Continental Infantry, 1776; Brigadier-General Connecticut Army, 1776; Major-General Connecticut Army, 1780; retired, on account of ill health, 1782; in continuous active service from 1776 to 1782.

Also, Great-grandson of Lieutenant Joseph Hawes, Captain Fairbanks' Company Massachusetts Militia, and representative to General Court, 1778–81.

'1889. HOTCHKISS, HENRY D.,

Great-grandson of Private Caleb Hotchkiss, Connecticut Militia, under General Spencer, in Rhode Island; killed in action at New Haven, July 5, 1779.

1889. HOTCHKISS, JAMES F., 164

Great-grandson of Private Caleb Hotchkiss, Connecticut Militia, under General Spencer, in Rhode Island; killed in action at New Haven, July 5, 1779.

160

1891. HOTCHKISS, THOMAS WOODWARD,

Great-great-grandson of Private Caleb Hotchkiss, Connecticut Militia, killed in action at New Haven, July 5, 1779; previously Private in Connecticut Militia, under General Spencer, in Rhode Island.

1891. HOUGH, ALFRED LACEY, Lieutenant-Colonel U. S. A. (retired), 727

Grandson of Brigadier-General John Lacey (1755–1814), Captain 4th Regiment Pennsylvania Line, Colonel Wayne, January 5, 1776, served in Canada; Lieutenant-Colonel Bucks County (Pennsylvania) Militia, May 6, 1777; Brigadier-General Pennsylvania Militia, January, 1778; Member of Supreme Executive Council of Pennsylvania, 1779–83.

Also, Great-grandson of Colonel Thomas Reynolds (1729–1803), Colonel Burlington County (New Jersey) Militia, June 6, 1777; prisoner of war; paroled and exchanged for Colonel Simcoe, British Foot.

1876. *HOUGHTON, GEORGE WASHINGTON WRIGHT (died April 1, 1891),

Great-grandson of Lieutenant Jonathan Houghton, Colonel Asa Whitcomb's Regiment Massachusetts Militia.

1887. HOWELL, FRANCIS B.,

Great-grandson of Captain Joseph Howell, Captain in Colonel S. J. Atlee's Pennsylvania Musketry Battalion, March 15, 1776; captured at Battle of Long Island, August 27, 1776; exchanged December 9, 1776, for Captain Livingston; Captain 2d Regiment Pennsylvania Continental Infantry, Colonel De Haas, 1777; Paymaster in same, August 27, 1778; Paymaster-General Continental Army, 1778.

1887. HOWELL, HENRY W.,

Grandson of Captain Joseph Howell, Captain in Colouel S. J. Atlee's Pennsylvania Musketry Battalion, March 15, 1776; captured at Battle of Long Island, August 27, 1776; exchanged December 9, 1776, for Captain Livingston; Captain 2d Regiment Pennsylvania Continental Infantry, Colonel De Haas, 1777; Paymaster in same, August 27, 1778; Paymaster-General Continental Army, 1778.

1887. HOWELL, HENRY W., JR.,

Great-grandson of Captain Joseph Howell. Captain in Colonel S. J. Atlee's Pennsylvania Musketry Battalion, March 15, 1776; captured at Battle of Long Island, August 27, 1776; exchanged December 9, 1776, for Captain Livingston; Captain 2d Regiment Pennsylvania Continental Infantry, Colonel De Haas, 1777; Paymaster in same, August 27, 1778; Paymaster-General Continental Army, 1778.

1891. HOWELL, RICHARD LEWIS,

Great-grandson of Major Richard Howell. Captain 5th Company 2d Battalion, 1st Establishment New Jersey Line, 1775; Brigade-Major, 1776; Major 2d Battalion 2d Establishment New Jersey Line, 1776; Major 2d Regiment New Jersey Line, 1777; resigned April 7, 1779.

1885. HOWELL, RICHARD STOCKTON,   556

Grandson of Major Richard Howell. Captain 5th Company, 2d Battalion, 1st Establishment, New Jersey Line, 1775; Brigade-Major, 1776; Major 2d Battalion, 2d Establishment, New Jersey Line, 1776; Major 2d Regiment New Jersey Line, 1777; resigned, April 7, 1779.

1891. HOWLAND, ELIJAH ALVORD,

Great-grandson of Private Jonathan Fisher (1743–1777), Captain Jonathan Wales' Company Hampshire County (Massachusetts) Militia; died in service at Morristown, New Jersey, 1777.

1891. HOWLAND, HENRY RAYMOND,

Great-grandson of Private Jonathan Fisher (1743-1777),
Captain Jonathan Wales' Company, Hampshire
County (Mass.) Militia, died in service at Morristown,
N. J., 1777.

1885. HUBBARD, GROSVENOR SILLIMAN,

Great-grandson of Brigadier-General Gold Selleck Silliman (1732-1790), Colonel 4th Regiment Connecticut
Militia, 1775; Colonel 1st Regiment Connecticut
Militia, Wadsworth's Brigade, 1776; Colonel Connecticut Light Horse Militia, 1776; Brigadier-General
4th Brigade Connecticut Militia, 1776; resigned January, 1781, but served continuously on alarms to
close of war; captured, 1779; held prisoner on Long
Island until exchanged for the Loyalist Judge Jones,
January, 1782.

Also, Great-great-grandson of Governor Jonathan
Trumbull, LL. D. (1710-1785), Governor of Connecticut, 1770-84.

1890. HUBBELL, CHARLES BULKLEY,   528

Great-grandson of Lieutenant-Colonel David Rossiter
(1732-1810), Captain in Colonel John Patterson's
Regiment Berkshire County (Massachusetts) Militia,
April, 1775; Lieutenant-Colonel in 2d Regiment
Berkshire County Militia, Colonel Simonds.

1891. HULL, GEORGE HUNTINGTON,   628

Great-grandson of Private Solomon Lord (—— 1815),
4th Regiment Connecticut Line, Colonel John Durkee, July 12, 1780.

Also, Grandson of Titus Hull (1751 ——), Private in
Connecticut Volunteer Militia, 1776.

1887. HUMPHREYS, A. W.,

Great-grandson of Captain William Humphreys, Ad-
jutant in Colonel Samuel Ashley's Regiment, New
Hampshire, raised to relieve Ticonderoga, 1776;
Captain 3d Regiment New Hampshire Continental
Volunteer Infantry, Colonel Joshua Wingate, raised
for Canadian service, 1776.

163

1888. HUMPHREYS, REV. FRANK LANDON, *Mus. D.*,   62

Great-grandson of Private Asher Humphreys (1759-
1826), Captain Abel Pettibone's Company, Colonel
Thomas Belden's Regiment, Connecticut Militia, in
service under Major-General Alexander McDougall
in New York, in 1777.

1890. HUNGERFORD, WILLIAM ALLYN,   415

Great-grandson of Corporal Christopher Merriam (1752-
1838), 2d Regiment Connecticut Line, Colonel Charles
Webb, July 27, 1780.

1883. HUNTINGTON, AUSTIN,   8

Great-great-grandson of Major-General Jabez Huntington (1719-1786), Member Connecticut Assembly,
1775-7; 2d Major-General Connecticut Militia, 1776;
1st Major-General Connecticut Militia, 1777; retired
1779, on account of ill health.

1883. HUNTINGTON, FREDERICK JABEZ,

Great-great-grandson of Governor Jonathan Trumbull,
LL. D. (1710-1785), Connecticut.
Also, Great-great-grandson of Brigadier-General Jed-
ediah Huntington (1745-1818), Colonel Connecticut
Militia, 1775; Colonel 8th Regiment Connecticut
Militia, 1775; Colonel 17th Regiment Connecticut
Line, 1776; Colonel 1st Regiment Connecticut Line,
1777; Brigadier-General Continental Army, 1777; in
command of Connecticut Line throughout the war;
retired with disbandment of the army, 1783,
Also Great-great-grandson of Major-General Jabez
Huntington (1719-1786), Member Connecticut Assembly, 1775-7; 2d Major-General Connecticut Militia,
1776; 1st Major-General Connecticut Militia, 1777;
retired 1779, on account of ill-health.

1892. HUNTINGTON, HENRY,

Great-grandson of Benjamin Huntington (1736-1800),
Member of Connecticut Committee of Safety, 1775;
Member of New Haven Convention for Regulating the
Army, 1778; Member of Continental Congress, 1780-4.

164

1885.   HURLBURT, PERCY DAKIN,   189

Great-great-grandson of Lieutenant Samuel Farrer
(1731-1783), Massachusetts Minute Men under Captain William Smith, Colonel Abijah Pierce, "Lexington Alarm," April 19, 1775; Member Massachusetts Provincial Congress, 1775.

Also, Great-great-grandson of Quartermaster Frederick
Manson, Sergeant in Captain Prentice's Company,
Colonel Thomas Marshall's Regiment Massachusetts
Militia, 1776; Sergeant-Major Captain Joseph Fuller's
Company, Colonel Samuel Bullard's Regiment Mas-
sachusetts Militia, 1777; Quartermaster Colonel Ab-
ner Perry's Regiment Massachusetts Militia, in
service in Rhode Island, 1780.

Also, Great-great-grandson of Captain Daniel Shays
(1740-1825), Ensign Colonel Abijah Brown's Regiment Massachusetts Continental Infantry, 1775;
Captain in 5th Regiment Massachusetts Continental
Infantry, Colonel Rufus Putnam, 1777.

1891.   HYATT, A. JACKSON,   520

Grandson of Lieutenant Abram Hyatt (1750-1821), 2d
Lieutenant 4th Regiment New York Line, Colonel
H. B. Livingston, November 21, 1776; 2d Lieutenant
6th Company 2d Regiment New York Minute Men,
Colonel Jacobus Swartwout, March 11, 1776; 1st
Lieutenant 8th Company, Captain Jonathan Titus,
4th Regiment New York Line, Colonel Livingston,
November 9, 1777; Acting Adjutant, 1780.

1891.   HYATT, ABRAM MARSHALL,

Great-great-grandson of Lieutenant Abram Hyatt (1750-
1821), 2d Lieutenant 4th Regiment New York Line,
Colonel H. B. Livingston, November 21. 1776; 2d
Lieutenant 6th Company, 2d Regiment New York
Minute Men, Colonel Jacobus Swartwout, March 11,
1776; 1st Lieutenant 8th Company, Captain Jonathan Titus, 4th Regiment New York Line, Colonel
Livingston, November 9, 1777; Acting Adjutant,
1780.

1886. IMLAY. WESSEL TEN BROECK STOUT,

Great-grandson of Lieutenant and Brevet Captain Wessel Ten Broeck Stout, 2d Lieutenant 4th Battalion 2d Establishment New Jersey Line, 1777; transferred to 3d Battalion; Ensign 3d Regiment New Jersey Line; Lieutenant ditto, 1782; Lieutenant 1st Regiment New Jersey Line; discharged at close of war; Captain by brevet.

1886. INGERSOLL, REV. EDWARD P., *D. D.*,

Great-grandson of Sylvanus Dimmick, Privateersman, Falmouth, Massachusetts.

1884. IRELAND, JOHN BUSTEED, 9

Great-grandson of Brigade-Major Jonathan Lawrence, Brigade-Major Queens County Militia, New York, 1775; Lieutenant in Colonel William Malcolm's Regiment "Additional Continental," 1777; Captain in Lieutenant-Colonel H. K. Van Rensselaer's Regiment New York Levies, 1779; Captain in Colonel John Harper's Regiment New York Levies, in service of United States, 1780; Member New York Provincial Congress, 1776.

Also, Great-grandson of William Floyd (1734-1821), Signer of the Declaration of Independence, Colonel 1st Regiment Suffolk County Militia, New York, 1775.

1888. IRELAND, JOHN DE COURCY,

Great-great-grandson of Brigade-Major Jonathan Lawrence, Brigade-Major Queens County Militia, New York, 1775; Lieutenant in Colonel William Malcolm's Regiment "Additional Continental," 1777; Captain in Lieutenant-Colonel H. K. Van Rensselaer's Regiment New York Levies, 1779; Captain in Colonel John Harper's Regiment New York Levies, in service of United States, 1780; Member New York Provincial Congress, 1776.

Also, Great-great-grandson of William Floyd (1734-1821), Signer of the Declaration of Independence, and Colonel 1st Regiment Suffolk County Militia, New York, 1775.

Elected.

Also, Great-great-grandson of Lieutenant-Colonel Robert Troup, Continental Army, New York.

1888. IRELAND, ROBERT LIVINGSTON,

Great-great-grandson of Brigade-Major Jonathan Lawrence, Brigade-Major Queens County Militia, New York, 1775; Lieutenant in Colonel William Malcolm's Regiment "Additional Continental," 1777; Captain in Lieutenant-Colonel H. K. Van Rensselaer's Regiment New York Levies, 1779; Captain in Colonel John Harper's Regiment New York Levies, in service of United States, 1780; Member New York Provincial Congress, 1776.

Also, Great-great-grandson of William Floyd (1734-1821), Signer of the Declaration of Independence, and Colonel 1st Regiment Suffolk County Militia, New York, 1775.

Also, Great-great-grandson of Lieutenant-Colonel Robert Troup, Continental Army, New York.

1892. IRVING, ALEXANDER DUER,

Great-grandson of Brigade-Major and Deputy Adjutant-General William Duer (1747-1799), appointed Brigade-Major and Deputy Adjutant-General New York Militia, July 27, 1775; Member of New York Provincial Congress.

Also, Great-great-grandson of Major-General William Alexander (Lord Stirling), (1726-1783); Colonel 1st Battalion, 1st Establishment, New Jersey Line, November 7, 1775; Brigadier-General Continental Army, March 11, 1776; Major-General Continental Army, February 19, 1777; taken prisoner at Battle of Long Island; twice received the thanks of Congress for conspicuous service.

1890. ISHAM, CHARLES,   403

Great-grandson of Commissary Samuel Isham (1752-1827), Connecticut.

Also, Great-great-grandson of Sergeant Cornelius Burhans (1746-1827), Captain Van Beuren's Company, Colonel Wynkoop's Regiment New York Line.

167

1888. JACKSON, ERNEST HENRY, 205

Great-grandson of Captain Stephen Jackson, New
Jersey Militia.
Also, Great-great-grandson of Private Enos Beach,
New Jersey Militia.

1890. JACKSON, FRANK WATSON, M. D.,

Great-grandson of Reverend Joseph Wheeler (1735–
1793), Private in Captain Samuel Stone's Company,
Colonel William Prescott's Regiment Massachusetts
Militia, Lexington Alarm, April 19, 1775; Member
of Massachusetts Provincial Congress.

1890. JACKSON, FREDERIC WENDELL,

Great-grandson of Reverend Joseph Wheeler (1735–
1793), Private in Captain Samuel Stone's Company,
Colonel William Prescott's Regiment Massachusetts
Militia, Lexington Alarm, April 19, 1775; Member of
Massachusetts Provincial Congress.

1890. JACKSON, JOHN DAY,

Great-great-grandson of Major-General Oliver Wolcott
(1726–1797), Colonel 17th Regiment Connecticut Militia, 1775–6; Brigadier-General of 6th Brigade Connecticut Militia, 1776; marched with Volunteers to
reinforce General Gates at Saratoga, 1777; appointed
Major-General Connecticut Militia, May, 1779; in
service to close of war; Member of Council of State,
1774–86; Member of Continental Congress, 1776–86;
Signer of Declaration of Independence.

1888. JACKSON, JOSEPH C.,

Grandson of Major-General Oliver Wolcott (1726–1797),
Colonel 17th Regiment Connecticut Militia, 1775–6;
Brigadier-General of 6th Brigade Connecticut Militia,
1776; marched with Volunteers to reinforce General
Gates at Saratoga, 1777; appointed Major-General
Connecticut Militia, May, 1779; in service to close of
war; Member of Council of State, 1774–86; Member of
Continental Congress, 1776–86; Signer of Declara-
tion of Independence.

168

No. of
Insignia.

1889. JACKSON, JOSEPH C., JR.,   42

Great-grandson of Major-General Oliver Wolcott (1726–
1797), Colonel 17th Regiment Connecticut Militia,
1775–6; Brigadier-General of 6th Brigade Connecticut
Militia, 1776; marched with Volunteers to reinforce
General Gates at Saratoga, 1777; appointed Major-
General Connecticut Militia, May, 1779; in service to
close of war; Member of Council of State, 1774–86;
Member of Continental Congress, 1776–86; Signer of
Declaration of Independence.

1891. JACKSON, OSWALD,   750

Great-great-grandson of Charles Carroll of Carrollton
(1737–1832), of Maryland, Signer of the Declaration
of Independence.
Also, Great-great-grandson of Major Thomas Lloyd
Moore (1759–1819), 1st Lieutenant in Captain Ru-
dolph Bunner's Company, 2d Battalion Pennsylvania
Continental Infantry, Colonel Arthur St. Clair; Cap-
tain 3d Regiment Pennsylvania Line, Colonel Joseph
Wood, May 21, 1776; Major 9th Regiment Pennsyl-
vania Line, Colonel Irvine, May 12, 1779; Major 5th
Regiment Pennsylvania Line, Colonel Richard But-
ler, January 17, 1781, to January 1, 1783.
Also, Great-great-great-grandson of William Moore
(—— 1793), Member of Pennsylvania Council of
Safety, 1776; Member of Pennsylvania Council of
War, 1777; Vice-President of Supreme Executive
Council of Pennsylvania, 1779–80; President, Captain General and Commander-in-Chief of the Com-
monwealth of Pennsylvania, 1781; Judge of the
Court of Appeals, 1783.
Also, Great-great-grandson of Thomas Willing (1731–
1821), President of Pennsylvania Provincial Congress,
1774; Member of Continental Congress, 1775–6.

1886. JACKSON, WILLIAM H.,   362

Great-grandson of Sergeant Lewis Covenhoven, Light
Horse Monmouth County Militia, New Jersey.

169

No. of
Insignia

1890. JACKSON, WILLIAM HENRY, 414

Great-grandson of Reverend Joseph Wheeler (1735–1793), Private in Captain Samuel Stone's Company, Colonel William Prescott's Regiment Massachusetts Militia, Lexington Alarm, April 19, 1775; Member of Massachusetts Provincial Congress.

1891. JAFFRAY, ROBERT, JR., 692

Great-great-grandson of Dr. Samuel Mather, of Connecticut, in medical service Connecticut Militia in New Jersey, 1776; also Captain Connecticut Militia, 1776.

1886. JAY, JOHN CLARKSON, M. D., 10

Great-grandson of John Jay (1745–1829), Member of Continental Congress, and President of same three years; prepared draft of Constitution of New York, 1777, and appointed first Chief Justice under it; Chairman of New York Council of Safety; Member of New York Provincial Congress; appointed Colonel of 2d Regiment New York City Militia, October 27, 1775.

1887. JAY, WILLIAM,

Great-grandson of John Jay (1745–1829), Member of Continental Congress, and President of same three years; prepared draft of Constitution of New York, 1777, and appointed first Chief Justice under it; Chairman of New York Council of Safety; Member of New York Provincial Congress; appointed Colonel of 2d Regiment New York City Militia, October 27, 1775.

1891. JENKINS, EDMUND FELLOWS, 739

Great-grandson of Brigadier-General John Fellows (1733–1808), Colonel of Berkshire County (Massachusetts) Minute Men, 1775; Brigadier-General Massachusetts Militia, June 25, 1776.

1892. JENNINGS, ALBERT GOULD, 791

Great-great-grandson of Lieutenant Colonel Abraham Gould (1732–1777), Captain Connecticut Militia, 1775; Lieutenant-Colonel Connecticut Militia, 1777; killed in action at "Danbury Raid," April 25, 1777.

1889. JOHNSON, ALEXANDER BRYAN,

Great-grandson of Adjutant Volckert P. Douw, Lansing's Albany County Militia, and Vice-President First Provincial Congress.

1889. JOHNSON, BRADISH, JR.,   300

Great-great-grandson of Brigade-Major Jonathan Lawrence, Brigade-Major Queens County Militia, 1775; Lieutenant in Colonel William Malcolm's Regiment "Additional Continental," 1777; Captain in Lieutenant-Colonel H. K. Van Rensselaer's Regiment New York Levies, 1779; Captain in Colonel John Harper's Regiment New York Levies, in service of United States, 1780; Member New York Provincial Congress, 1776.

1889. JOHNSON, FRANCIS LEWIS,

Great-grandson of Francis Lewis (1713-1803), Signer of the Declaration of Independence, New York.

1891. JOHNSON, JAMES LEWIS,   691

Great-grandson of Colonel James Johnson (1736-1809), Colonel of 2d Battalion Frederick County (Maryland) Militia, January 6, 1776.

1891. JOHNSON, JOHN QUINCY ADAMS,

Great-great-grandson of John Adams, of Massachusetts (1735-1826), Signer of the Declaration of Independence.

1890. JONES, MEREDITH LEWIS,

Great-grandson of Ensign John Benedict (1747-1810), Captain John Minthorn's Company (Florida and Warwick), Orange County Militia, Colonel John Hathorn, February 19, 1778.

1888. JORDAN, JOHN POWERS,

Great-great-grandson of Private William Jordan, Westchester County Militia, New York.

1892. KEELER, DAVID BRADLEY, JR.,

Great-grandson of Colonel Philip Burr Bradley (1738–1821), Lieutenant-Colonel in Colonel Waterbury's Regiment Connecticut State Troops, February, 1776; Colonel of Battalion Connecticut State Troops, Wadsworth's Brigade, May, 1776; Colonel of 5th Regiment Connecticut Line, January 1, 1777; retired by consolidation, January, 1781.

1889. KELLEY, FRANK MUMFORD, 305

Great-grandson of Captain George Dominick (1730 ——), 14th Beat Company, 2d Regiment New York City Militia, Colonel John Jay, August 29, 1775.

1889. KELLOGG, CHARLES, 201

Great-grandson of Captain Roger Welles (1751 ——), 2d Lieutenant in Colonel S. B. Webb's Regiment "Additional Continental," January 1, 1777; 1st Lieutenant same, May 16, 1778; Captain same, April 8, 1780; Captain 3d Regiment Connecticut Line, 1781; wounded at Yorktown, October 14; Captain in Colonel S. B. Webb's Regiment, January, 1783; Captain in Colonel Heman Swift's Regiment, "final formation," June, 1783.

1891. KELSO, JAMES SINCLAIR, JR.,

Great-grandson of Private Leonard Fisher (—— 1835), 1st Battalion New York City Militia, Colonel John Lasher, 1776.

1892. KENNEDY, MCPHERSON,

Great-grandson of Lieutenant John McPherson (1760–1829). Maryland Line.

1887. KENT, EDWARD HENRY, 220

Great-grandson of Private Augustus Kent (1754 ——), Private ,in Captain Elihu Kent's Company Suffield (Connecticut) Militia; marched to Boston, on "Lexington Alarm," at "Bunker Hill," and siege of Boston, 1775; Private in Captain Simeon Sheldon's Company Connecticut Militia, "New Haven Alarm," 1779.

Elected.

1888. KING, JOHN ALSOP, 120-

Grandson of Major Rufus King (1755-1827), Aide-de-
Camp to General Sullivan, New York.
Also, Great-grandson of John Alsop. Member of Conti-
nental Congress, New York.

1891. KING, LANDRETH HEZEKIAH,

Great-grandson of Private Lemuel King (1765-1827),
Lieutenant-Colonel Levi Wells' Regiment Connecticut
Militia, wounded at Horse Neck, December 10, 1780.

1891. KING, RUFUS,

Grandson of Private Abraham Odell (1760-1820), Captain Honeywell's Company Westchester County
(New York) Militia, Colonel Van Bergen.

1891. KNAPP, H. K.,

Great-grandson of Reverend Samuel Spring, D. D.
(1746-1819), joined the Continental Army as Chap-
lain, 1775; accompanied the Expedition (Arnold's) to
Quebec, and served through the Northern campaign.
Also, Great-grandson of Ensign Jonathan Knapp (1754
——), Captain Gabriel Requa's Company, Colonel
Joseph Drake's Regiment Westchester County Mili-
itia, General Lewis Morris' Brigade, January 1, 1776.

1887. KNAPP, SHEPHERD (Life Member), 243

Great-grandson of Rev. Samuel Spring, D. D. (1746-
1819), joined the Continental Army as Chaplain,
1775; accompanied the Expedition (Arnold's) to Quebec, and served through the Northern Campaign.
Also, Great-grandson of Ensign Jonathan Knapp (1754
——), Captain Gabriel Requa's Company, Colonel
Joseph Drake's Regiment Westchester County Militia, General Lewis Morris' Brigade, January 1, 1776.

1886. KNICKERBACKER, HENRY, 79

Grandson of Colonel John Knickerbacker (1723-1802),
14th Regiment Albany County Militia, New York.

1887. KNIGHT, CHARLES HUNTOON, M. D., 158

Great-grandson of Private Josiah Huntoon, Colonel
Bellows' Regiment, New Hampshire.

173

1889. LAIMBEER, FRANCIS EFFINGHAM,

Grandson of Private William Pinto, Connecticut Militia.
" New Haven Alarm," 1781.

1889. LAIMBEER, JOHN, JR.,

Grandson of Private William Pinto, Connecticut Militia.
" New Haven Alarm," 1781.

1890. LAMBERTON, CHARLES LYTLE,   595

Grandson of Ensign William Harkness (1739–1822),
Captain John Mateer's Company 3d Battalion Cum-
berland County (Pennsylvania) Militia, Colonel
William Chalmers, July 3, 1777.

1889. LANE, EDWARD VAN ZANDT,

Great-grandson of Private Jonathan Lane, Private
in Captain Joshua Hayward's Company, Colonel
David Gilman's New Hampshire Regiment, raised to
reinforce the Continental Army at New York, December 16, 1776; Private in Captain Goe's Company of
Militia at Portsmouth, New Hampshire, 1779; Private
in Captain Nute's Company New Hampshire Militia,
Colonel Wentworth, September 27, 1779; Private in
Captain Moses Leavitt's Company, Colonel Thomas
Bartlett's Regiment New Hampshire Militia, July,
1780.

1889. LANE, FRANCIS T. LUQUEER,

Great-grandson of Private Jonathan Lane, Private
in Captain Joshua Hayward's Company, Colonel
David Gilman's New Hampshire Regiment, raised to
reinforce the Continental Army at New York, December 16, 1776; Private in Captain Goe's Company of
Militia at Portsmouth, New Hampshire, 1779; Private
in Captain Nute's Company New Hampshire Militia,
Colonel Wentworth, September 27, 1779; Private in
Captain Moses Leavitt's Company, Colonel Thomas
Bartlett's Regiment New Hampshire Militia, July,
1780.

1889. LANE, PETER VAN ZANDT,

> Grandson of Private Jonathan Lane, Private in Captain Joshua Hayward's Company, Colonel David Gilman's New Hampshire Regiment, raised to reinforce the Continental Army at New York, December 16, 1776; Private in Captain Goe's Company of Militia at Portsmouth, New Hampshire, 1779; Private in Captain Nute's Company New Hampshire Militia, Colonel Wentworth, September 27, 1779; Private in Captain Moses Leavitt's Company, Colonel Thomas Bartlett's Regiment New Hampshire Militia, July, 1780.

1890. LARNED, EDWIN CHANNING,   443

> Great-great-grandson of Governor William Greene (1731–1809), of Rhode Island.
> *Also,* Great-grandson of Major William Larned (1752–1828), Rhode Island Militia.

1886. LATHROP, FRANCIS,   140

> Great-grandson of Major-General Samuel Holden Parsons (—— 1787), Colonel 10th Regiment Connecticut Continental Infantry, 1776; Brigadier-General Connecticut Army, 1776; Major-General Connecticut Army, 1780; retired on account of ill health, 1782; in continuous active service from 1776 to 1782.

1889. *LATHROP, FRANCIS H. (died November 15, 1891).

> Great-grandson of Governor Richard Howley, Member Georgia Legislature, 1779; Governor of Georgia, 1780; Member of Continental Congress, 1780–1.

1886. LATHROP, GEORGE PARSONS,   328

> Great-grandson of Major-General Samuel Holden Parsons (—— 1787), Colonel 10th Regiment Connecticut Continental Infantry, 1776; Brigadier-General Connecticut Army, 1776; Major-General Connecticut Army, 1780; retired on account of ill health, 1782; in continuous active service from 1776 to 1782.

175

1891. LATTING, CHARLES PERCY,   512

> Great-grandson of Rev. Daniel Hopkins, D. D. (1734-
> 1814), Chaplain 1st Massachusetts, Member 3d
> Massachusetts Provincial Congress, and Member
> Massachusetts Conventional Government. 1778.

1890. LAWRANCE, JOHN FISHER,

> Great-great-grandson of Brigade-Major Jonathan Law-
> rence, Brigade-Major Queens County Militia, New
> York, 1775; Lieutenant in Colonel William Malcolm's
> Regiment "Additional Continental," 1777; Cap-
> tain in Lieutenant-Colonel H. K. Van Rensselaer's
> Regiment New York Levies, 1779; Captain in Colonel
> John Harper's Regiment New York Levies, in service
> of United States, 1780; Member New York Provincial
> Congress, 1776.
> *Also*, Great-grandson of Private Theophilus Morgan
> (1732-1788), Captain John Williams' Company, Con-
> necticut Militia; on duty at Fort Griswold, July 11,
> 1779.

1890. LAWRENCE, JOHN,   336

> Great-grandson of Captain John Lawrence (1755-1844),
> 4th Regiment Continental Establishment (New York),
> Colonel James Holmes, 1776; Company Paymaster,
> 1777.

1891. LEAMING, JAMES ROSEBRUGH, *M. D.*,   615

> Great-grandson of Reverend James Rosebrugh (1714-
> 1777); Chaplain 3d Regiment Northampton County
> (Pennsylvania) Militia, Colonel George Taylor, 1776;
> killed in action at Trenton, New Jersey, January 2,
> 1777.

1889. LEE, BENJAMIN FRANKLIN,

> Great-grandson of Captain William Lawrence, New-
> town Militia, New York.
> *Also*, Great-grandson of Lieutenant Samuel Riker (1743-
> 1823), of Captain Daniel Lawrence's Troop of Light
> Horse, Queens County Militia, New York, and Mem-
> ber Queens County Council of Safety, 1776.

Elected.

1891. LEE, CHARLES CARROLL, *M. D.*,

Grandson of Governor Thomas Sim Lee (1745-1819),
Member of Governor's Council and Maryland Legis-
lature, 1777, and Governor of Maryland, 1779-1782;
Major of Lower Battalion Prince George's County
Militia, 1776 ; Member of Maryland Convention,
1775-6.

Also, Great-grandson of Charles Carroll of Carrollton
(1757-1832), of Maryland, Signer of the Declaration
of Independence.

1889. LEE, WILLIAM HENRY LAWRENCE,

Great-grandson of Captain William Lawrence, New-
town Militia, New York.

Also, Great-grandson of Lieutenant Samuel Riker (1743-
1823), of Captain Daniel Lawrence's Troop of Light
Horse, Queens County Militia, New York, and Member Queens County Council of Safety, 1776.

1885. LE ROY, HENRY WYCKOFF.   5

Great-great-grandson of Captain John Nicoll, Colonel
James Clinton's 2d Ulster County Regiment, New
York.

1891. LE ROY, JACOB RUTGERS,

Great-grandson of Captain Abraham George Claypoole
(1756-1827), Ensign in 3d Battalion Philadelphia Associators, July 8, 1776; 1st Lieutenant in Lieutenant-
Colonel John Patton's Regiment, January 14, 1777;
Captain 11th Regiment Pennsylvania Line, June 10,
1778; Captain 3d Regiment Pennsylvania Line,
March 22, 1781.

1890. LE ROY, OTIS,

Great-great-grandson of Captain Shubal Downs (1741-
1796), Massachusetts Militia, 1781.

1891. LEONARD, CLARENCE ETTIÉNNE,   673

Great-great-grandson of Brigadier-General George God-
frey (1721-1793), Brigadier-General Bristol County
(Massachusetts) Militia, February 8, 1776; Member of
Bristol County Committee of Safety.

Also, Great-grandson of Private John Godfrey (1754–1829), Private in Captain James Williams' Company Taunton Militia, April 20, 1775; Ensign in Captain Joshua Wilbore's Company, Colonel Ebenezer France's Regiment Massachusetts Militia, 1776; Ensign same, September 23, 1776; 2d Lieutenant in Captain Matthew Randall's Company, Colonel John Daggett's Regiment Massachusetts Militia, January 1, 1778; Private in 3d Company, Colonel Mitchell's Regiment Bristol County (Massachusetts) Militia, August 12, 1780.

Also, Great-great-grandson of Lieutenant Abijah Hodges, Jr., Lieutenant in 2d Company, Captain Jonathan Shaw, 3d Regiment Massachusetts Militia, December, 1776; Sergeant in Captain Josiah Crocker's Company, Colonel Thomas Carpenter's Regiment Massachusetts Militia, July, 1778, and August 2, 1780; served in Rhode Island.

Also, Great-great-grandson of 1st Lieutenant Philip Leonard (—— 1785), 1st Lieutenant of 1st Company Plymouth County (Massachusetts) Militia, June 6, 1766; 1st Lieutenant 1st Regiment Plymouth County Militia, October 28, 1776.

Also, Great-great-grandson of Sergeant Abner Pratt, Private in 3d Company Marshfield Militia, Captain Amos Wade, "Lexington Alarm," April 19, 1775; Private same Company, under Colonel Cotton, October 7, 1775; Private in Captain Elisha Mitchell's Company, Colonel James Cary's Regiment Massachusetts Militia, April 12, 1776; Private in Captain Abram Washburn's Company, Colonel Edward Mitchell's Regiment Massachusetts Militia, to Bristol, Rhode Island, December 8, 1776; Private in Captain Joseph Keith's Company, Colonel Cotton's Regiment Militia, to Tiverton, Rhode Island, January 25, 1777; Corporal in Captain William Tupper's Company, Colonel Ebenezer Sprout's Regiment Militia, "Dartmouth Alarm," May and September, 1778; Sergeant in same Company, under Colonel Ebenezer White, to Rhode Island, July 22, 1780.

Also, Great-great-grandson of Private Ebenezer Wood (1735-1802), Private in Captain William Tupper's Company, Colonel Sprout's Regiment Massachusetts Militia, to Rhode Island, December 8. 1776; Private same. "Dartmouth Alarm," May and September, 1778; Private in Captain Ebenezer Battelle's Company, Lieutenant-Colonel Samuel Pierce's Regiment Massachusetts Militia, to Rhode Island. May 24, 1779.

1889. LIVINGSTONE, DUNCAN MACRA,

Great-great-grandson of Walter Livingston. Deputy-Commissary-General and Member of 1st Provincial Congress, New York.

Also, Great-great-grandson of Admiral Count de Grasse (—— 1788), of France, appointed to command the French Fleet to co-operate with the American Army, 1781.

1883. LIVINGSTON, JAMES DUANE,

Great-great-grandson of Robert Livingston ; gave the use of his foundry to the Continental Congress, New York.

1891. LIVINGSTON, LEWIS HOWARD,   500

Great-great-grandson of Francis Lewis (1713-1803), Signer of the Declaration of Independence. New York.

1887. LIVINGSTON, PHILIP LIVINGSTON,   772

Great-great-grandson of Philip Livingston (1716-1778), Signer of the Declaration of Independence, New York.

1868. LOCKE, REVEREND JESSE ALBERT,

Great-grandson of Private Simon Locke (—— 1831), Colonel Senter's Rhode Island Regiment, August, 1777.

Also. Great-great-grandson of Private Joseph Coolidge (1730-1775), Captain Barnard's Company of Watertown (Massachusetts) Militia; killed in action at Lexington, April 19, 1775.

1883. LOCKWOOD, HOWARD, 183

Great-grandson of Lieutenant Simon Ingersoll, 4th
Company, 1st Battalion Connecticut Militia, Colonel
Silliman, raised to reinforce the Army at New York,
1776.

1888. LOCKWOOD, ISAAC FERRIS,

Great-grandson of Rev. William Lockwood (—— 1828),
Chaplain 1st Regiment Massachusetts Continental
Infantry, Colonel Patterson.

1884. LOCKWOOD, JAMES BETTS, 128

Great-grandson of Major Ebenezer Lockwood (1737
——), Major 2d Regiment Westchester County (New
York) Militia, Colonel Thomas Thomas, 1775, re-
appointed, 1778; Member 2d and 3d New York Provincial Congress; Delegate Constitutional Convention, 1777; and Member New York Assembly, 1778-9.

1891. LOCKWOOD, WILLIAM TOMPKINS,

Great-grandson of Captain Joseph Lockwood, Jr.
(1731-1792), 2d Regiment Westchester County Militia,
Colonel Thomas Thomas, September 13, 1775.

1892. LORD, DANIEL, JR., 780

Great-great-grandson of Ensign Daniel Lord (1739-
1796), Captain Joseph Jewett's Company Lyme (Connecticut) Militia, "Lexington Alarm," April 19, 1775.

1892. LORD, FRANKLIN BUTLER,

Great-great-grandson of Ensign Daniel Lord (1739-
1796), Captain Joseph Jewett's Company Lyme (Connecticut) Militia, "Lexington Alarm," April 19, 1775.

1889. LOVE, HENRY MORRIS, 239

Great-great-grandson of Private Robert Love, Rhode
Island Militia.

1885. LUCKEY, CHARLES CLARENCE,

Great-grandson of Private Jacob Hartshorn, Rhode
Island Militia.

Elected.   No. of
                                                                                 Insignia.
1888. LUMMIS, CHARLES A.,   97
    Great-grandson of Captain John Maxwell, 2d Regiment
    Hunterdon County Militia, New Jersey.

1890. LUMMIS, WILLIAM,   354
    Great-grandson of Captain John Maxwell, 2d Regiment
    Hunterdon County Militia, New Jersey.

1890. LYNCH, EUGENE TILLOTSON, JR.,
    Great-grandson of Surgeon Thomas Tillotson, Mary-
    land Line, and 1st Lieutenant Queen Anne County
    Militia, Captain Kent, February 3, 1776.

1889. LYON, WILLIAM SCOTT,   157
    Great-grandson of Daniel Hand (1744–1841). Associ-
    ator, Suffolk County, New York.

1889. LYONS, CROSSMAN,   38
    Grandson of Corporal Jedediah Lyons, 1st Regiment
    Line, New Jersey.

1890. MCCLELLAN, GEORGE BRINTON,   488
    Great-great-grandson of Colonel Samuel McClellan
    (1730–1807), Major 11th Regiment Connecticut Militia,
    October 15, 1775; Lieutenant-Colonel of Connecticut
    Militia, December 2, 1776; Lieutenant-Colonel 11th
    Regiment Connecticut Militia, December 27, 1776;
    Colonel of a Battalion Connecticut Militia, Septem-
    ber 25, 1777; Colonel 11th Regiment Connecticut
    Militia, January 23, 1779.

1890. MCCLURE, WILLIAM,
    Great-grandson of Colonel George Gibson (1738-1791),
    Captain of 1st Battalion Virginia Militia, February
    2, 1776; later Colonel Virginia Continental Infantry.

No. of
Elected.   Insignia.

1891. McGAW, JOHN WOODBURY, M. D.,

Great-great-great-grandson of Colonel Matthew Thornton (1714–1803), Colonel New Hampshire Militia, 1775,
to close of war; President of New Hampshire Provincial Congress, 1775; Chairman of New Hampshire
Committee of Safety, 1775–80; Chief-Justice of New
Hampshire Court of Common Pleas, 1775–80; Member of Continental Congress, and Signer of the Declaration of Independence.

Also, Great-great-grandson of Private Peter Woodbury, Private in Captain Benjamin Taylor's Company
New Hampshire Militia, raised to reinforce Continental Army at Winter Hill, December 8, 1775.

Also, Great-great-great-grandson of Private Josiah
Woodbury, Private in Captain Dodge's Company
Massachusetts Minute Men, "Lexington Alarm,"
April 19, 1775.

1891. McKEAN, WILLIAM CHAMBERS,

Great-grandson of Colonel David Chambers (1748–
1842), Colonel of 3d Regiment Hunterdon County
(New Jersey) Militia, June 19, 1776; Colonel of Battalion State Troops, November 27, 1776; Colonel 2d
Regiment Hunterdon County Militia, September 9,
1777; resigned May 28, 1779.

1889. McKESSON, GEORGE CLINTON,   25

Great-grandson of Lieutenant-Colonel William Hull,
Captain-Lieutenant 2d Company 7th Regiment Con-
necticut Line, Colonel Webb, July 6, 1775; promoted
Captain in same, October 9, 1775; Captain 19th Regi-
ment Continental Infantry, Colonel Charles Webb,
1776; promoted Major 8th Regiment Massachusetts
Continental Infantry, January 1, 1777; Lieutenant-
Colonel of same, 1779.

1891. McLENAHAN, GEORGE WILLIAM,   689

Great-great-grandson of Major-General James Potter
(1729–1789), Colonel Pennsylvania Militia, 1775;
Brigadier-General Pennsylvania Militia, April 5, 1777;
Major-General, 1782; Member of Pennsylvania Convention, 1776; Vice-President of Pennsylvania, 1781.

182

Elected.   Insignia.

1889.   MACDONALD, PIERRE FLEMING,   252

Great-grandson of Major William Popham (1752-1847),
entered the service as Lieutenant of Minute Men before the formal organization of the regiments for
the war; served in the Battle of Long Island; appointed Aide-de-Camp to General James Clinton,
1777; served with the Sullivan Expedition, 1779;
subsequently transferred to the staff of Baron Steu-
ben, with rank of Major.

1891.   MACDONOUGH, GEORGE HACKSTAFF,   746

Great-grandson of Major Thomas Macdonough (——
1795), Major Delaware Continental Infantry, April,
1776.
Also, Great-great-grandson of Lieutenant William
Denning (1740-1819), 2d Lieutenant 15th Beat Company, Captain Henry Remsen, New York "Independents," 1775; Member of New York Provincial
Congress, 1776.

1886.   MALCOLM, PHILIP SCHUYLER.

Great-grandson of Colonel William Malcolm (1732-
1792), Major 2d Battalion New York City Militia,
1776; Colonel 2d Regiment New York Volunteer
Infantry, 1776; Colonel "Additional" Regiment
Continental Infantry, 1777-9; Continental Adjutant-
General of the Northern Department, 1780; Colonel
1st Regiment New York Volunteer Infantry Levies,
1780-1; and Member New York Provincial Congress,
1776.
Also, Great-grandson of Major-General Philip Schuyler
(1733-1804), Major-General Continental Army, 1775;
resigned, 1779; Delegate to Continental Congress,
1775-7; Member New York Provincial Congress,
1778-9; Member New York State Senate, 1781-4.

1890. MANDEVILLE, HENRY.

Son of Private Henry H. Mandeville (1760-1847). Private New Jersey Militia under Captain Jonas Ward, November, 1776; Private in Captain Ogden's Company New Jersey Militia, January, 1777; Private in Lieutenant Anthony Mandeville's Company New Jersey Militia, December, 1778; Private in Captain Minard's Company New Jersey Militia, 1779; also served in New Jersey Militia, 1779-81.

1890. MANDEVILLE, HENRY CLAY. 597

Grandson of Private Henry H. Mandeville (1760-1847), Private New Jersey Militia under Captain Jonas Ward, November, 1776; Private in Captain Ogden's Company New Jersey Militia, January 17, 1777; Private in Lieutenant Anthony Mandeville's Company New Jersey Militia, December, 1778; Private in Captain Minard's Company New Jersey Militia, 1779; also served in New Jersey Militia, 1779-81.

1889. MANN, SAMUEL VERNON.

Great-great-grandson of William Vernon (1719-1806), President of Naval Board, Rhode Island.

1691. MANSON, THOMAS LINCOLN, JR.,

Great-grandson of Private Nehemiah Manson (1761-1832), Private in Capain Heyward Purvis' Company, Colonel Theophilus Cotton's Regiment Massachusetts Militia, on Expedition to Rhode Island, September, 1777; Seaman on ship "Warren," Commander Saltonstall, on the Penobscot, June, 1779; served under Captain Calvin Curtiss at Warren and Bristol Ferry, 1779; volunteered for six months under Captain Jonathan Turner, on duty around New York, 1780; served under Captain William Barker at Butt's Hill, Rhode Island, 1781; volunteered for three years under Captain Jonathan Turner, in Colonel Tupper's Continental Regiment, November, 1781; transferred to Colonel Marshall's Massachusetts Regiment; afterwards detailed for service in the Commander-in-Chief's barges; honorably discharged, December, 1783.

184

1883. MARSH, CHARLES BAUMANN.

Great-grandson of Major and Brevet Lieutenant-Colonel
Sebastian Bauman (—— 1803). 2d Regiment Continental Corps of Artillery, Colonel Lamb.

1891. MARSHALL, HENRY RUTGERS.

Great-great-grandson of Colonel Charles DeWitt
(1727–1787), Colonel Northern Regiment of Minute
Men Ulster County, December 27, 1775; Chairman
of Ulster County Convention, 1775; Member of New
York Provincial Congress, 1775–7; Member of New
York State Assembly, 1781–5.

Also, Great-grandson of Lieutenant Peter Tappan,
2d Lieutenant 2d Regiment Continental Corps of
Artillery, Colonel Lamb, August 21, 1781.

Also, Great-great-grandson of Major Christopher Tappan, Northern Regiment Minute Men, Ulster County,
New York, Colonel Charles DeWitt, December 21, 1775,
and Member of New York Provincial Congress, 1775.

1891. MARSHALL, HOWARD.

Great-great-grandson of Ensign Sylvanus Marshall
(1746–1833), 2d Lieutenant in Captain Jesse Bell's
Company, 1st Battalion Connecticut State Troops,
Colonel Whiting. 1776; Ensign in Captain Abraham
Mead's Company, 9th Regiment Connecticut Militia,
Lieutenant-Colonel John Mead, August 13, 1776;
Lieutenant in Captain Sylvanus Mead's Company of
Rangers. 1777; Captain of Rangers, 1781.

Also, Great-great-grandson of Surgeon Isaac Smith,
Connecticut Militia.

1890. MARSHALL, JOHN GILBERT. 329

Great-grandson of Ensign Sylvanus Marshall (1746–
1833), 2d Lieutenant in Captain Jesse Bell's Company, 1st Battalion Connecticut State Troops, Colonel
Whiting, 1776; Ensign in Captain Abraham Mead's
Company, 9th Regiment Connecticut Militia, Lieutenant-Colonel John Mead, August 13, 1776; Lieutenant in Captain Sylvanus Mead's Company of
Rangers, 1777; Captain of Rangers, 1781.

Also, Great-grandson of Surgeon Isaac Smith, Connecticut Militia.

1889. MARTIN, CHARLES BOMAN,

> Great-grandson of Lieutenant Joseph Vail, 2d Lieu-
> tenant in Colonel Drake's and Van Cortlandt's Regi-
> ment (3d or Manor of Van Cortlandt), in active ser-
> vice from August 15, 1778, to November 20, 1781.
> *Also,* Great-great-grandson of Private Gilbert T. Vail,
> Orange County Militia, killed at Minisink Massacre,
> July 22, 1779.

1889. MARTIN, WILLIAM IRWIN,   89

> Great-grandson of Private William Martin (1757-1824),
> Private Middlesex County (New Jersey) Militia, 1776;
> Private Captain Abraham Lyons' Company, 4th
> Battalion, 2d Establishment, New Jersey Line, Feb-
> ruary, 1777; transferred to Captain Richard Cox's
> Company, 3d Battalion; served also in 1st Battalion,
> New Jersey Line; assigned for duty in the "Com-
> mander-in-Chief's Guard," 1780, where he remained
> until close of the war.

1888. MARTIN, WILLIAM VAIL,   155

> Great-grandson of Lieutenant Joseph Vail, 2d Lieu-
> tenant in Colonel Drake's and Van Cortlandt's Regi-
> ment (3d or Manor of Van Cortlandt), in active ser-
> vice from August 15, 1778, to November 20, 1781.
> *Also,* Great-great-grandson of Private Gilbert T. Vail,
> Orange County Militia, killed at Minisink Massacre,
> July 22, 1779.

1891. MATHEWSON, ARTHUR, *M. D.*,   539

> Great-grandson of William Williams (1731-1811) of
> Connecticut, Signer of the Declaration of Independ-
> ence, and Colonel 12th Regiment Connecticut Militia,
> May, 1775.
> *Also,* Great-grandson of Colonel Samuel McClellan
> (1730-1807), Major 11th Regiment Connecticut Militia,
> October 15, 1775; Lieutenant-Colonel of Connecticut
> Militia, December 2, 1776; Lieutenant-Colonel 11th
> Regiment Connecticut Militia, December 27, 1776:
> Colonel of a Battalion Connecticut Militia, September
> 25, 1777; Colonel 11th Regiment Connecticut Militia,
> January 23, 1779.

Also, Great-great-grandson of Governor Jonathan
Trumbull, LL. D. (1710-1785), Connecticut.

·4

1890. MAYNARD, GEORGE WILLOUGHBY,   423

Great-grandson of Corporal Lemuel Maynard (1739-
1808), Captain James Horsley's Company, Colonel
William Prescott's Regiment Massachusetts Militia,
"Lexington Alarm," April 19, 1775.
Also, Grandson of Fifer Moses Doty (1758-1823), Fifer
in Captain Billings' Company, Colonel Learned's
Regiment Massachusetts Militia, October 7, 1775;
Fifer in Captain Morse's Company, Massachusetts
Continental Infantry, Colonel Putnam, March 1, 1777.

1890. MEAD, WALTER H. (Life Member),   484

Great-great-grandson of Lieutenant-Colonel Matthew
Mead, Captain 5th Company, 5th Regiment Connecti-
cut Line, Colonel David Waterbury, May 1, 1775;
served in Canada, and wounded near St. Johns,
September 6, 1775; Major 1st Battalion Connecticut
Militia, Colonel Silliman, June 20, 1776; Captain 9th
Regiment Connecticut Militia, Lieutenant-Colonel
John Mead, August 16, 1776; Lieutenant-Colonel 5th
Regiment Connecticut Line, Colonel Philip B. Brad-
ley, January 1, 1777.

1888. MEIGS, CHARLES A.,

Grandson of Lieutenant John Meigs, Ensign in Colonel
S. B. Webb's Regiment "Additional Continental,"
January 1, 1777; Adjutant same, April 22, 1778; Lieu-
tenant same, May 16, 1778; Adjutant 3d Regiment
Connecticut Line, Colonel S. B. Webb, January,
1781; served to close of war.

1891. MELVILLE, HENRY,

Great-grandson of Private Josiah (Melville) Melvin, Jr.
(1758-1818), Private in Captain Hancock's Company
of 15th Division Six Months' Men, Concord Militia;
served with Continental Army in New York, July 14,
1780.

187

Also, Great-great-grandson of Private Josiah Melvin (1727–1809). Private in Concord Militia at Ticonderoga, 1776; Private in Captain Abisha Brown's Company Concord Militia, 1777.

Also, Great-great-grandson of Captain Jonas Minot, Concord Minute Men, eight months' service, 1775.

Also, Great-great-grandson of Private James Nesmith, Jr. (1718–1793). Private in Captain John Reid's Company, Colonel John Stark's Regiment New Hampshire Militia, May 4, 1775; Private in Captain Samuel McConnel's Company, Colonel David Gilman's Regiment New Hampshire Militia in Continental Service, December 16, 1776; Private in 8th Regiment New Hampshire Continental Infantry, 1778.

Also, Great-great-great-grandson of Sergeant Adam Dickey (1722 —). Private in Captain Daniel Reynolds' Company, Colonel Moses Nichol's Regiment, Stark's Brigade New Hampshire Militia, "Bennington Campaign," July 14 to September 29, 1780; Sergeant in Captain William Boyes' Company, Colonel Daniel Reynolds' Regiment New Hampshire Militia, September 15, 1781.

Also, Great-grandson of Private Reuben Gregg (1756–1840). Private in Captain Peter Clark's Company, Colonel Stickney's Regiment, Stark's Brigade New Hampshire Militia, 1777; Private in Captain William Boyes' Company, Colonel Moses Kelley's Regiment New Hampshire Militia, 1778; served in Expedition to Rhode Island.

Also, Great-great-grandson of Private Hugh Gregg, Private in Captain Philip Thomas' Company, Colonel James Reed's Regiment New Hampshire Militia, 1775; Private in Captain Joseph Parker's Company, Colonel Enoch Hale's Regiment New Hampshire Militia, 1776; joined the Northern Army at Ticonderoga; Private in Captain John Taggart's Company, Colonel Thomas Heald's Regiment New Hampshire Volunteers for relief of Ticonderoga, 1777.

Also, Great-grandson of Private Josiah Whitney, Jr. (1753 —). Private in Minute Men from Harvard, "Lexington Alarm," April 19, 1775; Private in Captain Manasseh Sawyer's Company, Colonel Dikes' Regiment Massachusetts Militia, 1776.

188

Also. Great-great-grandson of Brigadier-General Josiah
Whitney, Sr. (1730-1806), one of the "Boston Tea
Party." December 16, 1773; at "Concord," April 19,
1775; Lieutenant-Colonel in Colonel Asa Whitcomb's
Regiment Massachusetts Militia, at "Bunker Hill"
and seige of Boston, April to December, 1775; Col-
onel of Massachusetts Militia, January to April,
1776; Colonel of "Colony" Regiment, raised to for-
tify the town and harbor of Boston, April, 1776, to
January, 1777; Colonel of 2d Regiment Worcester
County Militia, on "Rhode Island Alarm," July,
1777; "Bennington Alarm," August, 1777; at "Saratoga," September and October, 1777; later Brigadier-
General of Massachusetts Militia; Member of
Massachusetts General Court, 1780; Member of
Massachusetts Constitutional Convention, 1778.

1883. *MERCHANT, JOHN (died July 7, 1886).

Great-grandson of John Hicks, Massachusetts Minute
Men, killed in action at Lexington, April 19, 1775.
Also. Grandson of Private Abel Merchant, Dutchess
County Militia, New York.

1890. MEREDITH, WILLIAM TUCKEY,

Great-great-grandson of Brigadier-General John Morin
Scott (1730-1784). Brigadier-General New York
Militia, June, 1776; Member New York Provincial
Congress, 1776; Secretary of State for New York;
Member of New York Constitutional Convention;
Member of Continental Congress, 1782-3.

1892. MERRITT, CHARLES.   800

Grandson of Private Ebenezer Merritt (1764-1826),
served four months in team service under Captain
Samuel Taylor, Connecticut Militia, 1778; Private in
Captain Eliphalet Thorp's Company, Colonel Samuel
Whiting's Regiment Connecticut Militia, April 1,
1779; later Private in Captain Paul Brigham's Com-
pany, 8th Regiment Connecticut Line, Colonel Giles
Russell.

189

Elected.
1891. MERRITT, DOUGLASS,

No. of
Insignia
571

Great-great-grandson of Major Aza Douglass (1715-
1792), Captain 1st Company 17th Regiment Albany
County (New York) Militia, Colonel Bradford Whiting; promoted 1st Major in same, June 16, 1778.
Also, Great-great-grandson of Colonel David Sutherland (1722-1794), Colonel 6th Regiment, Charlotte
Precinct, Dutchess County (New York) Militia, October 17, 1775.
Also, Great-great-grandson of Private Ezra Thompson
(1738-1816), Captain Brinckerhoff's Company, 2d
Regiment Dutchess County Militia, 1776.

1888. MERWIN, AUGUSTUS W.,

129

Great-grandson of Captain Timothy Taylor, Sergeant
9th Company, Captain Beardsley, 5th Regiment Connecticut Militia, Colonel Waterbury, May 9 to December 11, 1775; Ensign Captain Noble Benedict's Company, Bradley's Battalion, Wadsworth's Brigade, Connecticut Militia, May, 1776; captured at Fort Washington, November 16, 1776; Lieutenant 2d Regiment
Connecticut Line, Colonel Charles Webb, September
1, 1777; 2d Lieutenant in Meigs' Light Infantry, 2d
Battalion, July, 1779, engaged at Stony Point; Captain 3d Regiment Connecticut Line, Colonel S. B.
Webb, December 17, 1781; Captain 2d Regiment Connecticut Line, Colonel Heman Swift, January, 1783;
Captain in Colonel Heman Swift's Regiment, "final
formation," June, 1783.

1891. MERWIN, BERKLEY R.,

743

Great-grandson of Private Thomas Painter, 5th Company, Captain Jonas Prentice, 5th Battalion, Colonel
William Douglass, Wadsworth's Brigade Connecticut
State Troops, raised to reinforce Washington's Army
at New York, 1776.

No, of
Elected.   Insignia.

1888.   *MERWIN, REV. SAMUEL J. M. (died September 12. 1888),
        Grandson of Captain Timothy Taylor, Sergeant 9th
        Company, Captain Beardsley, 5th Regiment Con-
        necticut Militia, Colonel Waterbury, May 9 to Decem-
        ber 11, 1775; Ensign Captain Noble Benedict's Com-
        pany, Bradley's Battalion, Wadsworth's Brigade,
        Connecticut Militia, May, 1776; captured at Fort
        Washington, November 16, 1776; Lieutenant 2d Regi-
        ment Connecticut Line, Colonel Charles Webb, Sep-
        tember 1, 1777; 2d Lieutenant Meigs' Light Infantry,
        2d Battalion, July, 1779, engaged at Stony Point;
        Captain 3d Regiment Connecticut Line, Colonel S.
        B. Webb, December 17, 1781; Captain 2d Regiment
        Connecticut Line, Colonel Heman Swift, January,
        1783; Captain in Colonel Heman Swift's Regiment,
        "final formation," June, 1783.

1891.   METCALF, JAMES BETTS,   728
        Great-great-grandson of Lieutenant-Colonel James Met-
        calf (1729–1803), 2d Major of West Regiment Massa-
        setts Minute Men, April 19, 1775, at "Lexington;"
        Captain 13th Regiment Continental Foot, Colonel
        Joseph Read, January 30, 1776, at siege of Boston;
        1st Major 4th Regiment Suffolk County (Massachu-
        setts) Militia, Colonel Ephraim Wheelock, February
        10, 1776; Major commanding 4th Regiment Suffolk
        County Militia, December 8, 1776, served in Rhode
        Island; Lieutenant-Colonel same, 1779; served to
        close of war.

        Also, Great-grandson of Sergeant James Metcalf, Jr.
        (1757–1843), Bombardier in 9th Company, Captain
        Perez Cushing, Colonel Thomas Craft's Regiment
        Massachusetts State Artillery, September 9. 1776, in
        Continental service in Boston Harbor and sea coast
        defences; Private in Captain Asa Fairbank's Com-
        pany, Colonel Benjamin Hawes' Regiment Massa-
        chusetts Volunteer Infantry, September 30, 1777;
        served in Rhode Island under Major-General Spen-
        cer; Sergeant in Captain John Metcalf's Company,
        4th Regiment Suffolk County Militia, Colonel Seth
        Bullard, January 27, 1780; served in Rhode Island
        under Major-General J. M. Varnum.

Also, Great-grandson of Private Uriah Betts (1761-1841), Captain Nathan Gilbert's Company, Colonel Samuel Whiting's Regiment Connecticut Militia, October 5, 1777; served with Continental Army on the Hudson.

Also, Great-grandson of Captain Selah Benton (1740-1812), Private 9th Company, 7th Regiment Connecticut Continental Infantry, July 10, 1775; 2d Sergeant 9th Company, 7th Regiment Connecticut Continental Infantry, October 30, 1775; Ensign 19th Regiment Connecticut Continental Infantry, Colonel Charles Webb, January 1, 1776; 2d Lieutenant in same, August 10, 1776; served at Boston and around New York; 2d Lieutenant 8th Regiment Connecticut Line, Colonel John Chandler, January 1, 1777; 1st Lieutenant in same, January 16, 1778; Captain in same, October 28, 1779; Captain in 5th Regiment Connecticut Line, Lieutenant-Colonel Isaac Sherman, January 1, 1781; Captain in 1st Regiment Connecticut Line, Colonel Zebulon Butler, January 1, 1783; served to close of war.

1889. MIDDLEBROOK, GEORGE STANLEY.   296

Great-great-grandson of Lieutenant Ephraim Middlebrook (1736-77), Connecticut Militia, killed in action at Ridgefield, Connecticut, April 27, 1777, while in command of his company; also served in the New York campaign, 1776.

1888. MILLER, CHARLES BENJAMIN,

Great-grandson of Fifer James Miller (——1788), Artillery Regiment (Colonel Robert Elliott), Rhode Island State Brigade in Continental Service.

Also, Great-grandson of Private Asa Todd (1756-1847), Captain Phineas Porter's Company, 1st Regiment Connecticut Line, Colonel David Wooster.

Also, Great-great-grandson of Lieutenant Thomas Weeks (1735-1817), Captain Josiah Smith's Company, Colonel Whitney's Regiment Massachusetts Militia, and Adjutant Massachusetts Line, Colonel David Brewer.

192

1890.   MILLER, EDWARD CLARENCE,

Great-grandson of Fifer James Miller (——— 1788),
Captain Pittman's Company, Colonel Elliott's Regiment Artillery, Rhode Island State Troops.

Also, Great-grandson of Private Asa Todd (1756-1847),
Captain Phineas Porter's Company, 1st Regiment
Connecticut Line, Colonel David Wooster.

Also, Great-great-grandson of Lieutenant Thomas
Weeks (1735-1817), Captain Josiah Smith's Company,
Colonel Whitney's Regiment Massachusetts Militia,
and Adjutant Massachusetts Line, Colonel David
Brewer.

1888.   MILLER, GEORGE ERNEST,

Great-grandson of Fifer James Miller (——— 1788),
Artillery Regiment (Colonel Robert Elliott), Rhode
Island State Brigade in Continental Service.

Also, Great-grandson of Private Asa Todd (1756-1847),
Captain Phineas Porter's Company, 1st Regiment
Connecticut Line, Colonel Daniel Wooster.

Also, Great-great-grandson of Lieutenant Thomas
Weeks (1735-1817), Captain Josiah Smith's Company,
Colonel Whitney's Regiment Massachusetts Militia,
and Adjutant Massachusetts Line, Colonel David
Brewer.

1891.   MILLER, GEORGE PERKINS (Life Member),   651

Great-great-grandson of Surgeon Matthias Burnet Miller (1749-1792), Colonel David Sutherland's Regiment
New York State Militia, and Member of New York
Provincial Congress.

Also, Great-great-grandson of Lieutenant-Colonel Jonathan Forman, 1st Lieutenant in Captain Burrowes'
Company, 1st Regiment Monmouth County (New
Jersey) Militia, 1776; promoted Captain same Regiment, June 16, 1776; Captain 4th Battalion 2d Establishment, New Jersey Line, November 23, 1776;
Captain 1st Regiment New Jersey Line, Colonel
Matthias Ogden, September 26, 1780; Major 3d Regiment New Jersey Line, November 21, 1781; Lieutenant-Colonel 2d Regiment New Jersey Line, February
11, 1783.

193

Also, Great-great-grandson of Captain Moses Seymour, Captain 5th Regiment Connecticut Light Horse Militia, Major Elisha Sheldon, 1776; Captain Connecticut Militia, serving under General Gates to the Northward, 1777; Captain Connecticut Light Dragoons, " New Haven Alarm," July, 1779.

1883. MILLER, J. BLEECKER,   241

Great-great-grandson of James Duane, Member of Continental Congress, New York.

1890. MILLER, THOMAS PORTER.

Grandson of Fifer James Miller (—— 1788), Artillery Regiment, Colonel Robert Elliott, Rhode Island State Brigade in Continental service.

Also, Grandson of Private Asa Todd (1756-1847), Captain Phineas Porter's Company, 1st Regiment Connecticut Line, Colonel David Wooster.

Also, Great-grandson of Lieutenant Thomas Weeks (1735-1817), Captain Josiah Smith's Company, Colonel Whitney's Regiment Massachusetts Militia, and Adjutant Massachusetts Line, Colonel David Brewer.

1891. MILLS, CHARLES HOOD,

Great-grandson of Private George Mills (1754-1826), Captain Hubbard's Company Massachusetts Militia, 1776: went with Arnold's Expedition to Quebec: captured; exchanged 1777; later, Private Captain Webster's Company, Colonel Fellows' Regiment Massachusetts Militia.

1891. MILLS, ISAAC NEWTON,

Great-grandson of Private Nathaniel Mills (1742-1814), Private in Lieutenant Paine Converse's Company, 11th Regiment Connecticut Militia, 1776.

1889. MITCHELL, WILLIAM ANDERSON,   269

Great-great-grandson of Rev. Josiah Sherman (—— 1789), Chaplain of 7th Regiment Connecticut Continental Infantry, Colonel Heman Swift, January 1, 1777.

1889.   MIX, JAMES B.,   227

Great-great-great-grandson of Lieutenant Timothy Mix,
Private in Captain Hooker's Company, 2d Regiment
Connecticut Militia, Colonel Joseph Spencer, May 6.
1775, served during seige of Boston and on Arnold's
expedition to Quebec ; Sergeant 2d Regiment Continental Corps of Artillery, Colonel Lamb, April 19.
1777 ; promoted 2d Lieutenant same, September 12,
1778.

1791.   MONTAGUE, FRANK L.,   702

Great-great-grandson of Captain Caleb Montague
(1731-1782), Sergeant in Captain Noadiah Leonard's
Company, Colonel Benjamin Ruggles Woodbridge's
Regiment Massachusetts Militia, "Lexington Alarm,"
April 19, 1775; Captain in Hampshire County Militia,
Lieutenant-Colonel Samuel Williams, May 10, 1776.

1890.   MONTGOMERY, HENRY EGLINTON,

Great-grandson of Surgeon Thomas Tillotson, Maryland Line, and 1st Lieutenant Queen Anne County
Militia, Captain Kent, February 3, 1776.

1890.   MONTGOMERY, JAMES LYNCH,

Great-grandson of Surgeon Thomas Tillotson, Maryland Line, and 1st Lieutenant Queen Anne County
Militia, Captain Kent, February 3, 1776.

1883.   MONTGOMERY, JAMES MORTIMER,   2

Great-great-grandson of Colonel William Malcolm,
(1732-1792), Major 2d Battalion New York City
Militia, 1776; Colonel 2d Regiment New York Vol-
unteer Infantry, 1776; Colonel "Additional" Regi-
ment Continental Infantry, 1777-9 ; Continental
Adjutant General of the Northern Department, 1780;
Colonel 1st Regiment New York Volunteer Infantry
Levies, 1780-1 ; and Member New York Provincial
Congress 1776.

Also, Great-great-great-grandson of Colonel William
Henry (1727-1793), County Lieutenant, Philadelphia
County, Pennsylvania, 1777-90.

Also, Great-great-grandson of Commissary George
Henry (1751-1790), Continental Navy, Pennsylvania,
and Member of Philadelphia Troop of Light Horse.

1886. MONTGOMERY, RICHARD MALCOLM,   75

Great-great-grandson of Colonel William Malcolm
(1732-1792), Major 2d Battalion New York City Militia, 1776; Colonel 2d Regiment New York Volunteer
Infantry, 1776; Colonel "Additional" Regiment Continental Infantry, 1777-9; Continental Adjutant-
General of the Northern Department, 1780; Colonel
1st Regiment New York Volunteer Infantry Levies,
1780-1; and Member New York Provincial Congress,
1776.

Also, Great-great-great-grandson of Colonel William
Henry (1727-1793), County-Lieutenant, Philadelphia
County, Pennsylvania, 1777-90.

Also, Great-great-grandson of Commissary George
Henry (1751-1790), Continental Navy, Pennsylvania,
and Member of Philadelphia Troop of Light Horse.

1889. MOODY, EDWARD FRANCIS (of Massachusetts).   130

Great-grandson of Sergeant Paul Moody (1743-1842),
Captain Jacob Gerrish's Company, Colonel Moses
Little's Regiment, Massachusetts State Troops, "Lexington Alarm," April 19, 1775; wounded at the Battle of Bunker Hill.

1891. MOORHEAD, HORACE R.,   700

Great-grandson of Captain Fergus Moorhead (1742-
1821), Captain Westmoreland County (Pennsylvania)
Militia, 1777; taken prisoner at Blanket Hill: confined at Quebec eleven months.

1891. MOORHEAD, JOHN, JR.,   675

Great-grandson of Captain Fergus Moorhead (1742-
1821), Captain Westmoreland County (Pennsylvania)
Militia, 1777; taken prisoner at Blanket Hill; confined at Quebec eleven months.

Grandson of Lieutenant Henry Morfit (—— 1794), 1st
Lieutenant 7th Company Bucks County (Pennsylvania) Militia, 5th Battalion, Colonel Joseph McIl-
vaine, May 6, 1777; later Lieutenant Pennsylvania
Line; taken prisoner February 19, 1778, and released at close of war.

1890. MORGAN, APPLETON,   401

Grandson of Major Abner Morgan (1748-1837). Major
in Colonel Elisha Porter's Regiment of Berkshire
and Hampshire Counties, Massachussets, raised to
reinforce the Continental Army in Canada, January
9, 1776; and Chairman of Massachusetts Committee
of Safety; Member of Massachusetts General Court,
1775.

Also, Great-grandson of Private David Morgan (1745
——), Private in Captain Joseph Hoar's Company,
Colonel Gideon Burt's Regiment Massachusetts Mili-
tia, June 16, 1782.

1886. MORGAN, REVEREND BROCKHOLST,   12

Great-great-grandson of Governor and Brigadier-General William Livingston (1723-1790), Brigadier-General New Jersey Militia, October 28, 1775; Governor
of New Jersey, 1776-90; also Member of Continental
Congress.

Also. Great-grandson of Colonel Jacob Morgan, Jr.
(1742-1802), Major 1st Battalion Philadelphia Associators, 1775; Colonel of same, 1777; Colonel 2d Battalion Philadelphia County Militia, 1777.

Also, Great-great-grandson of Colonel Jacob Morgan,
Sr. (1716-1792). Member of Provincial Congress,
1776; Member of the Council of Safety of Pennsyl-
vania; Member of Pennsylvania Supreme Executive
Council; Assistant Forage Master Pennsylvania
Militia, April, 1780.

1891. MORGAN, EDWIN DENISON,   504

Great-great-grandson of Corporal William Avery
Morgan (1754-1842), Corporal in Captain Spicer's
Company 6th Regiment Connecticut Militia, Colonel
S. H. Parsons, May 9, 1775; Corporal in Captain Gal-
lup's Company 8th Regiment Connecticut Militia,
Lieutenant-Colonel Oliver Smith, September 8, 1776.
Also, Great-great-great-grandson of Sergeant Christo-
pher Avery, 27th Regiment Connecticut Militia,
killed in action at Fort Griswold, Connecticut, Sep-
tember 6, 1781.

1889. MORGAN, JAMES HENRY.   90

Great-grandson of Corporal William Avery Morgan
(1754-1842), Corporal in Captain Spicer's Company
6th Regiment Connecticut Militia, Colonel S. H.
Parsons, May 9, 1775; Corporal in Captain Gallup's
Company 8th Regiment Connecticut Militia, Lieuten-
ant-Colonel Oliver Smith, September 8, 1776.
Also, Great-grandson of Private Jonathan Gardner,
Captain Nehemiah Waterman's Company, 20th Regiment Connecticut Militia, Major Benjamin Leffingwell.
Also, Great-great-grandson of Sergeant Christopher
Avery, 27th Regiment Connecticut Militia, killed
in action at Fort Griswold, Connecticut, September
6, 1781.
Also, Great-great-grandson of Captain Joseph Church-
ill (1734 ——), Captain 8th Company, 3d Battalion,
Colonel Comfort Sage, Wadsworth's Brigade Con-
necticut State Troops, June, 1776, to December 25,
1776; served with the Continental Army in New
York City and on Long Island.

1891. MORGAN, JUNIUS SPENCER,   599

Great-great-grandson of Corporal William Avery Morgan (1754-1842), Corporal in Captain Spicer's Company, 6th Regiment Connecticut Militia, Colonel S.
H. Parsons, May 9, 1775; Corporal in Captain Gallup's Company, 8th Regiment Connecticut Militia,
Lieutenant-Colonel Oliver Smith, September 8, 1776.

198

Elected.

Also, Great-great-great-great-grandson of Sergeant
Christopher Avery, 27th Regiment Connecticut Militia, killed in action at Fort Griswold, Connecticut,
September 6, 1781.

1888. MORRIS, DWIGHT,

Son of Captain and Brevet Major James Morris, Ensign
5th Company 2d Regiment, Colonel Fisher Gay,
Connecticut Militia, June, 1776; 1st Lieutenant 5th
Regiment Connecticut Line, Colonel Philip B. Bradley, January 1, 1777; taken prisoner at Germantown, October 4, 1777; exchanged January 3, 1781;
promoted Captain-Lieutenant, July 29, 1780; promoted Captain, August 22, 1780; Captain 2d Regiment Connecticut Line, Colonel Heman Swift, 1781;
Captain in Colonel Scammell's Regiment Connecticut
Continental Light Infantry, 1781; served with
Southern Army.

1884. MORRIS, GOUVERNEUR,

Great-great-grandson of Brigadier-General Lewis Morris
(1726–1798), Brigadier-General Westchester County
Militia, 1776; Delegate to Continental Congress,
1774–7; Signer of the Declaration of Independence.

1890. MORRIS, GOUVERNEUR WILLIAM,   406

Grandson of Lieutenant William Walton Morris, 2d
Continental Corps of Artillery, Colonel Lamb, August 21, 1785.
Also, Great-grandson of Brigadier-General Lewis
Morris (1726–1798), Brigadier-General Westchester
County Militia, 1776; Delegate to Continental Congress, 1774–7; Signer of the Declaration of Independence.

1890. MORRIS, LEWIS RUTHERFURD, *M. D.,*   195

Great-grandson of Major Jacob Morris (1755–1844),
Major in Westchester County (New York) Militia,
Colonel Dubois, December 14, 1776; Aide-de-Camp to
Major-General Charles Lee, 1776; Aide-de-Camp to
Major-General Nathaniel Greene, 1778.

Elected.

Also, Great-great-grandson of Brigadier-General Lewis Morris (1726–1798), Brigadier-General Westchester County Militia, 1776; Delegate to Continental Congress, 1774–7: Signer of the Declaration of Independence.

1889. MORRIS, NEWBOLD,

Great-great-grandson of Brigadier-General Lewis Morris (1726–1798), Brigadier-General Westchester County Militia, 1776 ; Delegate to Continental Congress, 1774 7: Signer of the Declaration of Independence.

1891. MORRIS, ROBERT CLARK,

Grandson of Brevet-Major and Captain James Morris, Ensign 5th Company 2d Regiment, Colonel Fisher Gay, Connecticut Militia, June, 1776; 1st Lieutenant 5th Regiment Connecticut Line, Colonel Philip B. Bradley, January 1, 1777; taken prisoner at Germantown, October 4, 1777; exchanged January 3, 1781; promoted Captain-Lieutenant, July 29, 1780; promoted Captain, August 22, 1780; Captain 2d Regiment Connecticut Line, Colonel Heman Swift, 1781: Captain in Colonel Scammell's Regiment Connecticut Continental Light Infantry, 1781; served with Southern Army.

1891. MORRIS, ROBERT TUTTLE, *M. D.*,

Great-grandson of Ensign Lucius Tuttle (1749–1846), Captain Bezaleel Ives' Company, Lieutenant-Colonel J. Baldwin's Regiment Connecticut Militia, on duty at Fishkill, New York, October, 1777.

1890. MORRIS, SAMUEL FISHER,

Great-grandson of Robert Morris (1734–1806), Member and Vice-President of the Pennsylvania Committee of Safety; Member of Continental Congress; Signer of the Declaration of Independence; appointed Superintendent of Finance of the United States, 1781.

1889.   MORSE, WALDO GRANT,   81

Great-grandson of Lieutenant Christopher Grant, Jr.
(1743 ——), Lieutenant in Captain Abner Craft's Com-
pany, Colonel Gardner's Regiment Massachusetts
Militia, 1775, at seige of Boston.
Also, Great-great-grandson of Private Christopher
Grant, Sr., Private in Captain Samuel Barnard's
Company, Watertown (Massachusetts) Militia, Lex-
ington Alarm, April 19, 1775.

1889.   MORTON, HENRY HOLDICK,   275

Great-grandson of Lieutenant Shepard Kollock, 2d Regiment Continental Corps of Artillery, Colonel Lamb,
Captain by brevet.

1890.   MUNSON, HENRY THEODORE,   306

Grandson of Private Joseph Munson (1765-1841), Drum-
mer, Captain Birdseye's Company, 4th Connecticut
Militia, October 5, 1777.
Also, Great-great-grandson of Private Marshall Alling,
Captain Prentice's Company, 5th Battalion Connect-
icut Militia, Colonel William Douglass.
Also, Great-grandson of Private Hartham Ramsdell,
Massachusetts Militia.

1885.   MURRAY, CHARLES H.,   207

Great-grandson of Captain Elihu Murray (1752-1835),
Private Captain Chapin's Company, Colonel John
Fellows' Regiment Massachusetts Continental Infantry, 1775; on expiration of service, commissioned
Captain in Colonel Joseph Reed's Regiment;
transferred to Quartermaster-General's Department,
under General James Wadsworth, and served to close
of war.
Also, Great-grandson of Ensign Daniel Billings (1750-
1801), Sergeant 3d Company, Captain Samuel Prentice, 6th Regiment Connecticut Militia, Colonel S.
H. Parsons, 1775; Ensign 10th Regiment Connecticut Line, Colonel S. H. Parsons, 1775.

Also, Great-great-grandson of Ensign Charles Eldridge
(1743-1798), Connecticut Militia; wounded in action
at Groton Heights, Connecticut, September 6, 1781.
Also, Great-grandson of Private Hezekiah Seymour,
Captain Prior's Company, Colonel Erastus Wolcott's
Regiment Connecticut State Troops, 1776; Private
Captain Uriah Seymour's Company Connecticut
Light Horse, Major Sheldon, 1776.

1887. MURRAY, LOGAN C.,   84

Great-grandson of Colonel Benjamin Logan, Kentucky
Militia; erected Logan's Fort at Stanford, Kentucky,
1774; served in Dunmore's Expedition, 1775, and at
Blue Licks, August 19, 1782.

1888. MURRAY, RUSSELL,

Great-great-grandson of Lieutenant-Colonel Henry
Wisner, Major Florida and Warwick Regiment
Orange County Militia, 1776; Lieutenant-Colonel
same Regiment (Colonel John Hathorn), February
19, 1778; Member New York Provincial Congress,
1775; Member of Continental Congress, 1776.

1887. MYER, ALBERT J.,

Great-grandson of Private Ebenezer Walden, Private
Captain Porter's Company Massachusetts Militia,
from Becket, 1777; Private Lieutenant Chamberlin's
Company, Colonel John Brown's Regiment Massachusetts Militia at "Bennington," 1777.

1891. MYER, ISAAC,   534

Grandson of Private Benjamin Myer (1764——). Essex County (New Jersey) Militia, served at Springfield, New Jersey.
Also, Great-grandson of Joseph Riggs (1720-1799), Associator, Essex County, New Jersey, Member of New
Jersey Committee of Correspondence, 1775.

Elected.

1888. MYGATT, JOHN TRACEY,

Great-great-grandson of Lieutenant-Colonel Eli Mygatt, Major 16th Regiment Connecticut Militia, Colonel Joseph Platt Cooke, May, 1777; promoted Lieutenant-Colonel same, February 12, 1778.

1889. MYGATT, LEMUEL CARRINGTON,   265

Great-grandson of Lieutenant-Colonel Eli Mygatt, Major 16th Regiment Connecticut Militia, Colonel Joseph Platt Cooke, May, 1777; promoted Lieutenant-Colonel same, February 12, 1778.

1890. NEILSON, HENRY AUGUSTUS,

Great-grandson of Brigadier-General John Neilson (1745-1833), Captain New Jersey Militia, 1775; Colonel 2d Regiment Middlesex Battalion Minute Men, August 31, 1776; Colonel of Regiment State Troops; Brigadier-General New Jersey Militia, February 21, 1777; also Deputy Quartermaster-General.

1891. NELLIS, WILLIAM JACOB, M. D.,   513

Great-grandson of Private Peter Nellis (1760-1813), Captain Zeely's Company 2d Regiment Tryon County (New York) Militia, Colonel Jacob Klock, February 18, 1779.

1889. NEWKIRK, WARREN B.,   145

Great-great-grandson of Major and Brevet Lieutenant-Colonel Sebastian Bauman, 2d Regiment Continental Corps of Artillery.

1891. NEWMAN, JOHN LUDLOW,

Great-grandson of Lieutenant James Lyman (1748-1804), Captain Seth Peirce's Company, Colonel Murray's Regiment Hampshire County (Massachusetts) Militia, served on the Hudson, 1780; previously (May 10, 1777), Sergeant in Captain Moses Harvey's Company, Colonel David Wells' Regiment Massachusetts Militia.

203

1891. NICHOLS, GEORGE LIVINGSTON, JR., 497

Great-grandson of Lieutenant Isaac Nichols (1748-1835), Captain Abraham Livingston's Company, Colonel James Livingston's Regiment, "Additional Continental," New York, December 18, 1776.

1887. NICHOLSON, CHRISTIE FEW, 256

Great-great-grandson of Commodore James Nicholson (1737-1804), in command of Maryland ship-of-war "Defence," 1775; in command of Continental ship-of-war "Virginia," 1776; Commander-in-Chief Continental Navy, 1777; in command of Continental frigate "Trumbull," 1780.

1888. NICOLL, HENRY DENTON, M. D., 413

Great-grandson of Captain John Nicoll, 2d Regiment Ulster County Militia, New York, Colonel James Clinton.

1890. NORTON, JOHN TREADWELL, 485

Great-great-grandson of Major Ichabod Norton (1736-1825), Captain in 3d Company, Colonel Samuel Mott's Battalion Connecticut State Troops, June, 1776; served in Northern Department, under General Gates, 1776-7; Major 15th Regiment Connecticut Militia, Colonel Isaac Lee, May, 1779.

Also, Great-great-grandson of John Treadwell (1741-1828), Member of Connecticut Assembly, 1776 to 1785.

1891. NORVELL, DUNCAN ROBERTSON, 622

Grandson of Lieutenant Lipscomb Norvell (1756-1843), Ensign and Paymaster 5th Regiment Virginia Continental Infantry, Colonel Josiah Parker, January 15, 1778; Ensign in Captain Valentine Peyton's Company, 3d Regiment Virginia Continental Infantry, Colonel William Heth, May, 1778; 2d Lieutenant same, September, 1778; 1st Lieutenant same, February, 1780.

204

Elected.   No. of
Insignia.

1891. NORWOOD, LEWIS MORRIS,   679

Great-grandson of Captain William Willcocks (1734-
1826), 1st Battalion New York City Militia (New
York "Independents"), Colonel John Lasher, 1776;
served in Battle of Long Island, August 27, 1776;
previously (January 31, 1776), Lieutenant in same.

1890. NOYES, CHARLES HARDING,   483

Great-grandson of Captain Seth Harding (1740-1781),
Connecticut brig-of-war "Defence," 1776; Connecticut State man-of-war "Oliver Cromwell," 1777, and
Continental frigate "Confederacy," 1778; captured
in March, 1781; taken to England, and died there
while a prisoner.

Also, Great-grandson of Major-General Samuel Holden
Parsons (―― 1787), Colonel 10th Regiment Connecti-
cut Continental Infantry, 1776; Brigadier-General
Connecticut Army, 1776; Major-General Connecticut
Army, 1780; retired on account of ill health, 1782;
in continuous active service from 1776 to 1782.

Also, Great-grandson of Titus Hosmer (1736-1780),
Speaker of Connecticut Assembly, 1773-80; Member of Continental Congress, 1776-7; appointed Judge
of United States Maritime Court of Appeals, 1780,
but died before entering upon his duties.

1891. NOYES, CHARLES PHELPS,   680

Grandson of Lieutenant Thomas Noyes (1751-1819),
Lieutenant 11th Company, 2d Regiment Rhode Island
Militia, Colonel Babcock, August 26, 1776; 1st Lieu-
tenant of Rhode Island State Artillery, May 29, 1777.

Also, Great-grandson of Colonel Joseph Noyes (1727-
1802), Colonel 1st Regiment Kings County (Rhode
Island) Militia, May 1, 1775; Member of Rhode Island
General Assembly, 1776, 1780 and 1783.

1889. NOYES, JAMES ATKINS,   45

Great-grandson of Lieutenant Roger Adams, Private in
Captain Amariah Fuller's Company, Newton (Massachusetts) Militia, Lexington Alarm, April 19, 1775;
Private in same, September 2, 1778; later Lieutenant
in same.

205

1891. O'CONNOR, WILLIAM SCOTT,   737

Great-great-grandson of Captain David Phillips
(1742–1829), Captain of 2d Company, 7th Battalion
Chester County Pennsylvania Militia, Colonel William Gibbons, May 17, 1777.

1889. OLCOTT, J. VAN VECHTEN,

Great-great-grandson of Rev. John Mason, Chaplain
3d New York Line.

1889. OLNEY, GEORGE WASHINGTON,   248

Grandson of Captain Stephen Olney, Ensign in Captain
John Angell's Company, 2d Regiment Rhode Island
Militia, Colonel Hitchcock, May 1775, at Bunker Hill;
1st Lieutenant in Captain Coggeshall's Company,
11th Regiment Continental Infantry, Colonel Hitchcock, January, 1776; Commissioned Captain in 2d
Regiment Rhode Island Continental Infantry, January 1, 1777; served at seige of Yorktown, and severely
wounded in that engagement.

1890. OLYPHANT, FRANK MURRAY,

Great-grandson of Surgeon David Olyphant, Deputy
Director-General of Continental Hospital Department, Southern Army; also Member of South Carolina
Legislative Council, 1776; Member of South Carolina
Provincial Congress, 1775-6; Member of South Carolina Committee of Safety, 1775-6.

1888. OLYPHANT, JOHN KENSETT,   24

Great-grandson of Surgeon David Olyphant, Deputy
Director-General of Continental Hospital Department, Southern Army; also Member of South Carolina Legislative Council, 1776; Member of South
Carolina Provincial Congress, 1775-6; Member of
South Carolina Committee of Safety, 1775-6.
Also, Great-great-grandson of William Vernon (1719–
1806), President of the Continental Navy Board,
Rhode Island.

206

1889. OLYPHANT, ROBERT,   **22**

Great-grandson of Surgeon David Olyphant, Deputy Director-General of Continental Hospital Department, Southern Army; also Member of South Carolina Legislative Council, 1776; Member of South Carolina Provincial Congress, 1775-6; Member of South Carolina Committee of Safety, 1775-6.

Also. Great-great-grandson of William Vernon (1719-1806), President of the Continental Navy Board, Rhode Island.

1890. OLYPHANT, ROBERT MORRISON,

Grandson of Surgeon David Olyphant, Deputy Director-General of Continental Hospital Department, Southern Army; also Member of South Carolina Legislative Council, 1776; Member of South Carolina Provincial Congress, 1775-6; Member of South Carolina Committee of Safety, 1775-6.

1889. OLYPHANT, TALBOT,   **161**

Great-grandson of Surgeon David Olyphant, Deputy Director-General of Continental Hospital Department, Southern Army; also Member of South Carolina Legislative Council, 1776; Member of South Carolina Provincial Congress, 1775-6; Member of South Carolina Committee of Safety, 1775-6.

1890. OLYPHANT, REVEREND VERNON MURRAY,

Great-grandson of Surgeon David Olyphant, Deputy Director-General of Continental Hospital Department, Southern Army; also Member South Carolina Legislative Council, 1776; Member South Carolina Provincial Congress, 1775-6; Member of South Carolina Committee of Safety, 1775-6.

Also, Great-great-grandson of William Vernon (1719–1806), President of the Continental Navy Board, Rhode Island.

1885. OWENS, JAMES,

Nephew and Representative of Lieutenant Jonathan Owens, Colonel Luddington's Regiment Dutchess County Militia, New York. 1778.

1890. PAGE, RICHARD CHANNING MOORE, *M. D.*,   310

Grandson of Major Carter Page, Virginia Line.

Also, Great-grandson of Colonel Archibald Cary, Lieutenant Spottsylvania Minute Men, September 12, 1775; later Colonel Virginia Militia; Member of Virginia Convention, 1775–6; Speaker of the Upper House Virginia Senate, 1776.

Also, Great-grandson of Lieutenant-Colonel Hugh Nelson, Virginia Minute Men, Colonel Champion Travis, October 12, 1775; Member of Virginia Convention, 1775–6.

1891. PAGE, WALTER GILMAN,

Great-grandson of Fifer Lemuel Page (1757–1822), Fifer in Captain Philip Thomas' Company, Colonel James Reed's Regiment New Hampshire Militia, April 20, 1775; Private in Captain Abijah Smith's Company, Colonel Enoch Hale's Regiment New Hampshire Militia, September 21, 1776; Fifer in Captain Solomon Stone's Company, same Regiment, July 12, 1777; Fifer in Captain Samuel Cunningham's Company, Colonel Enoch Hale's Regiment New Hampshire Militia, on service with the Continental Army in Rhode Island, August 10, 1778.

1891. PARKE, HUDSON HOVEY,

Great-grandson of Private Elisha Parke (1746–1812), Captain James Morgan's Company, 8th Regiment Connecticut Militia, Lieutenant-Colonel Oliver Smith, September 8 to November 17, 1776; served around New York.

208

1891. PARKER. DANGERFIELD, Lieutenant-Colonel. U. S. A.,   633

Grandson of Lieutenant William Harwar Parker, of
Virginia. Continental Navy; honorably discharged
at close of war.

1887. PARKIN, HENRY GRENVILLE,

Great-great-grandson of Colonel Ethan Allen. Vermont.

.1888. PARSONS. ALBERT ROSS,   74

Great-grandson of Sergeant Aaron Parsons, Jr. (1736
1799), Sergeant in Captain Gideon Burt's Company.
Colonel Timothy Danielson's Regiment Massachusetts Militia, April 28, 1775; served at siege of Boston;
later in Continental service at West Point.

Also, Great-great-grandson of Sergeant Aaron Parsons
3d (1761-1815), Sergeant in Captain William Hitchcock's Company 6th Regiment Massachusetts Continental Infantry, July 3, 1780; served with the 3d
Division of 6 months' men under Lieutenant Daniel
Frye of the "Artificers," 1780.

Also, Great-grandson of Private Samuel Averill,
of Colonel Seth Warner's Regiment "Additional
Continental" Infantry.

.1891. PARSONS. JACOB COX,   610

Great-grandson of Private Jacob Hiltzheimer (1729-
1798), 1st Battalion Pennsylvania State Militia, December 17, 1776: detached to Quartermaster-General's Department under General Mifflin.

Also, Great-grandson of Captain Hezekiah Parsons,
Captain of Enfield (Connecticut) Militia, "Lexington
Alarm," April 19, 1775; marched to relief of Boston;
at Ticonderoga, 1775; Captain 2d Company, 3d Bat-
tallion Connecticut Militia, Colonel Comfort Sage.
Wadsworth's Brigade; served around New York.
1776.

Also, Grandson of Private Jacob Cox (1761-1812). Private in Captain William Price's Company Chester
County (Pennsylvania) Militia. Colonel John Han-
num, July 16. 1777.

209

1890. PARSONS, JOHN D., JR.,   445
    Great-grandson of Corporal Henry Bowne (1752-1825),
    New Jersey Line.

1891. PATTERSON, EDWARD LIDDON,
    Great-great-grandson of Lieutenant-Colonel Christo-
    pher Stuart (—— 1799), Captain 5th Pennsylvania
    Battalion, January 5, 1776; Captain 6th Regiment,
    Major 5th Regiment, September 20, 1776; Lieutenant-
    Colonel 3d Regiment, April 17, 1780, Pennsylvania
    Line.

1887. PATTERSON, JACOB M.,   197
    Great-grandson of Lieutenant Samuel Patterson (1742-
    1822), Captain Olmsted's Company, Colonel Bezaleel
    Beebe's Regiment Connecticut Militia.

1890. PATTERSON, JOHN H., Major U. S. A.,   334
    Great-grandson of Lieutenant-Colonel Christopher
    Stuart (—— 1799), Captain 5th Pennsylvania Battal-
    ion, January 5, 1776; Major 5th Regiment, Septem-
    ber 20, 1776; Lieutenant-Colonel 3d Regiment, April
    17, 1780, Pennsylvania Line.

1888. PEABODY, CHARLES AUGUSTUS, JR.,
    Great-grandson of Captain Richard Peabody (1731-
    1820), Colonel Wigglesworth's Regiment Massachu-
    setts Militia, at Ticonderoga, 1777.

1888. PEET, JOHN NORTHROP,
    Great-grandson of Captain John Webb, Lieutenant
    in "Sheldon's Dragoons," January 10, 1777; Cap-
    tain in same, January 1, 1778; Aide-de-Camp to
    Major-General Robert Howe, 1781; served to close
    of war.

1891. PELL, ARTHUR,
    Great-great-grandson of Major-General Philip Schuyler
    (1733-1804), Major-General Continental Army, 1775;
    resigned 1779; Delegate to Continental Congress,
    1775-7; Member New York Provincial Congress,
    1778-9; Member of New York Senate, 1781-4.

1891. PELL, WILLIAM CRUGER,   626

Great-great-grandson of Major-General Philip Schuyler (1733-1804), Major-General Continental Army,
1775; resigned 1779: Delegate to Continental Congress, 1775-7; Member New York Provincial Congress, 1778-9: Member New York State Senate,
1781-4.

1890. PELTZ, JOHN DEWITT,

Great-great-grandson of Captain John L. DeWitt
(1731-1803), Captain 2d Rhinebeck Company 1st Regiment Ulster County (New York) Minute Men, Colonel Jonathan Van Ness, October 17, 1775; Captain
in Colonel Abraham Hasbrouck's Regiment Ulster
County Militia, October 25, 1775.

1888. PERKINS, CHARLES ELWELL,   191

Great-grandson of Lieutenant-Colonel David Cobb
(1748-1830), Lieutenant-Colonel in 16th Regiment
Massachusetts Continental Infantry, Colonel Henry
Jackson, 1776-9; Aide-de-Camp to the Commander-
in-Chief, 1781; Member Massachusetts Provincial
Congress, 1775; Brevet Lieutenant-Colonel, 1783.
Also, Great-grandson of Captain Noah Hall, Colonel
Abiel Mitchell's Regiment Massachusetts Infantry.
Also, Great-grandson of Private Joseph Perkins,
Private in Lieutenant Daniel Wheelwright's Com-
pany Massachusetts Militia, August, 1776; Private in
Captain Nathaniel Cousens' Company, Major Little-
field's Battalion York Militia, in Penobscot Expedi-
tion, 1779.

1887. PERKINS, EDWARD C.,

Great-grandson of Commissary James Davenport, Continental Army, Connecticut.

211

Elected.

No. of
Insignia.

1890. PERRY, ALEXANDER JAMES, Brevet Brigadier-General,
U. S. A.,   481

Grandson of Christopher Raymond Perry (1761–1818),
served on the "Miflln," Commander Babcock ; captured, confined in prison ship "Jersey ;" escaped
after three months' confinement; subsequently served
as Midshipman on Continental frigate "Trumbull,"
Captain James Nicholson.

1890. PERRY, WILLIAM STEVENS, Right Rev., D. D., LL.D.,
D. C. L., Bishop of Iowa.   314

Grandson of Lieutenant Abel Perry, Continental Line,
Massachusetts, 32d Regiment Continental Foot.
Also, Great-grandson of Captain William Stevens, 2d
Regiment Continental Corps of Artillery.

1888. PERRY, WILLIAM SUMNER,

Great-grandson of Christopher Raymond Perry (1761–
1818), served on the "Miflln," Commander Babcock ;
captured, confined in prison ship "Jersey;" escaped
after three months' confinement; subsequently served
as Midshipman on Continental frigate "Trumbull,"
Captain James Nicholson.

1889. PHILLIPS, WENDELL C., *M. D.*,   221

Great-great-great-grandson of Colonel Ethan Allen,
Vermont.

1890. PHISTERER, KARL JOSEPH,   477

Great-great-grandson of Private Caleb Tuttle (1758–
1836), Captain David Bates' Company, Colonel
Ephraim Martin's Regiment, "Heard's Brigade,"
New Jersey Militia, and Private in Captain Giles
Mead's Company, 1st Regiment New Jersey Line,
Colonel Mathias Ogden.

212

1891.   PIERREPONT, HENRY EVELYN,

Great-grandson of John Jay (1745-1829). Member of
Continental Congress; President of same three years;
prepared draft Constitution of New York, 1777, and
appointed first Chief-Justice under it; Chairman of
New York Council of Safety; Member of New York
Provincial Congress; appointed Colonel of 2d Regiment New York City Militia, October 27, 1775.

Also, Great-grandson of Major and Brevet Lieutenant-
Colonel Matthew Clarkson (1758-1825). Private in
Colonel Ritzema's Corps of American Fusiliers, 1775;
served with Northern Army, 1777-9; acting Aide-de-
Camp to Arnold at Saratoga; appointed Aide-de-Camp
to Major-General Lincoln in Southern Army, 1779, at
Savannah; served as Major of Light Infantry, 1780;
taken prisoner at Charleston; exchanged 1781; served
as Aide-de-Camp to Major-General Lincoln to close of
war; Lieutenant-Colonel by brevet, 1783.

Also, Great-great-grandson of William Livingston
(1723-1790), Brigadier-General New Jersey Militia,
October 28, 1775; Governor of New Jersey, 1776-90;
also Member of Continental Congress.

1885.   PIERREPONT, JOHN JAY,   274

Great-grandson of John Jay (1745-1829), Member of
Continental Congress; President of same three years;
prepared draft Constitution of New York, 1777, and
appointed first Chief Justice under it; Chairman of
New York Council of Safety; Member of New York
Provincial Congress; appointed Colonel of 2d Regiment New York City Militia, October 27, 1775.

Also, Great-grandson of Major and Brevet Lieutenant-
Colonel Matthew Clarkson (1758-1825): Private in
Colonel Ritzema's Corps of American Fusiliers, 1775;
served with Northern Army, 1777-9; acting Aide-de-
Camp to Arnold at Saratoga; appointed Aide-de-Camp
to Major-General Lincoln in Southern Army, 1779, at
Savannah; served as Major of Light Infantry, 1780;
taken prisoner at Charleston; exchanged 1781; served
as Aide-de-Camp to Major-General Lincoln to close of
war; Lieutenant-Colonel by brevet, 1783.

Also, Great-great-grandson of William Livingston
(1723-1790), Brigadier-General New Jersey Militia,
October 28, 1775; Governor of New Jersey, 1776-90;
also Member of Continental Congress.

1890. PIERREPONT, WILLIAM AUGUSTUS, *M. D.,*   402

Great-grandson of John Jay (1745-1829), Member of
Continental Congress; President of same three years;
prepared draft Constitution of New York, 1777, and
appointed first Chief Justice under it; Chairman of
New York Council of Safety; Member of New York
Provincial Congress; appointed Colonel of 2d Regiment New York City Militia, October 27, 1775.

Also, Great-grandson of Major and Brevet Lieutenant-
Colonel Matthew Clarkson (1758-1825); Private in
Colonel Ritzema's Corps of American Fusiliers, 1775;
served with Northern Army, 1777-9; acting Aide-de-
Camp to Arnold at Saratoga; appointed Aide-de-Camp
to Major-General Lincoln in Southern Army, 1779, at
Savannah; served as Major of Light Infantry, 1780;
taken prisoner at Charleston; exchanged 1781; served
as Aide-de-Camp to Major-General Lincoln to close of
war; Lieutenant-Colonel by brevet, 1783.

Also, Great-great-grandson of William Livingston
(1723-1790), Brigadier-General New Jersey Militia,
October 28, 1775; Governor of New Jersey, 1776-90;
also Member of Continental Congress.

1891. PIERSON, JOHN SHAW,

Grandson of Lieutenant Daniel Pierson (1750-1831),
4th Company, Captain William E. Finlay, 3d Battalion, 1st Establishment New Jersey Line, Colonel
Elias Dayton, April 23, 1776; served with Northern
Army.

1891. PILLSBURY, BURKE, *M. D.,*   557

Great-grandson of Private Joshua Pillsbury (1738-1798),
Captain Moses Little's Company Massachusetts Militia, "Lexington Alarm," April 19, 1775.

214

No. of
Insignia.

1888. PINTO. FRANCIS E.,   107

Son of Private William Pinto, Connecticut Militia,
"New Haven Alarm," 1781.

1889. PINTO, WILLIAM A.,   41

Grandson of Private William Pinto. Connecticut Militia,
"New Haven Alarm," 1781.

1891. POLK, WILLIAM M.. *M. D.*,

Great-grandson of Colonel Thomas Polk, Colonel 2d
Battalion North Carolina Militia, December 21, 1775;
Colonel 4th Regiment North Carolina Militia, April
22. 1776; Colonel 4th Regiment North Carolina Con-
tinental Infantry, May 7, 1776; Member of North
Carolina Assembly, and Signer of the Mecklenburg
Declaration of Independence, May 20, 1775; Com-
missary-General of North Carolina.

1889. POMEROY, GEORGE ELTWEED,   166

Great-great-grandson of Brigadier-General Seth Pomeroy (—— 1777); appointed Brigadier-General Continental Army, June, 1775, declined; served as volunteer
at "Bunker Hill;" Colonel 2d Regiment Hampshire
County Militia, February 6, 1776; Member of Massachusetts Provincial Congress, 1774-5.

1888. POND, CHARLES H..   96

Great-great-grandson of Captain Charles Pond, En-
sign in 9th Company, Captain Peter Perritt, 7th
Regiment Connecticut Line, Colonel Charles Webb.
July 6, 1776; 1st Lieutenant 19th Regiment Connecti-
cut Line, Colonel Charles Webb, 1776; Captain 6th
Regiment Connecticut Line, Colonel William Doug-
lass. January 1, 1777; resigned April 20, 1779.
Also, Great-grandson of Colonel Hercules Mooney,
Lieutenant-Colonel in Colonel Pierre Long's Regi-
ment New Hampshire Continental Infantry, August
7, 1776; Colonel of 300 men raised for defense of
Rhode Island, June 23, 1779, to January 16, 1780;
Member New Hampshire Provincial Congress, 1776.

215

1890. POND, WINTHROP,   **315**

Great-great-grandson of Captain Charles Pond, Ensign in 9th Company, Captain Peter Perritt, 7th Regiment Connecticut Line, Colonel Charles Webb, July 6, 1776; 1st Lieutenant 19th Regiment Connecticut Line, Colonel Charles Webb, 1776; Captain 6th Regiment Connecticut Line, Colonel William Douglass, January 1, 1777; resigned April 20, 1779.

1888. POOLE, MURRAY EDWARD,

Great-great-grandson of Lieutenant Samuel Poole, Captain Abiel Pierce's Company, Colonel Nicholas Dike's Regiment Massachusetts Infantry.

Also, Great-great-great-grandson of Samuel Poole, Member of Massachusetts Provincial Assembly, 1778–80, and Member of Committees of Safety and Correspondence.

Also, Great-great-grandson of Private Jesse Mullick, Captain Bailey's Company, Colonel John Hathorn's Regiment Orange County Militia, New York.

Also, Great-grandson of Private Absalom Carey, Captain William Cummings's Company, Colonel Mitchell's Regiment of Militia, stationed at Newburgh.

Also, Great-great-great-grandson of Nathaniel Cooley, Associator, Orange County, New York.

1891. POOR, JAMES HARPER,

Great-grandson of Lieutenant Joseph Poor (1737–1795), Private in Captain Stephen Kent's Company of Volunteers from Essex County, Massachusetts, July 14, 1775; Private same Company, raised for seacoast service, November 1, 1775; Private in Captain Moses Newell's Company Massachusetts Volunteer Infantry, July 9, 1776; 2d Lieutenant in Captain Gideon Foster's Company of Militia, May 4, 1779.

1891. POPE, JAMES WARDEN, Captain U. S. A.,   **711**

Great-great-grandson of Colonel Charles Mynn Thruston (1738–1812), Colonel of "additional Continental" Infantry, Virginia.

216

1885. POPHAM, GEORGE MORRIS, 192

Great-grandson of Major William Popham (1752–1847),
entered the service as Lieutenant of Minute Men
before the formal organization of the regiments for
the war; served in the Battle of Long Island; appointed Aide-de-Camp to General James Clinton,
1777; served with the Sullivan Expedition, 1779;
subsequently transferred to the staff of Baron Steu-
ben with rank of Major.

1890. POPHAM, WILLIAM SHERBROOKE,

Great-grandson of Major William Popham (1752–1847),
entered the service as Lieutenant of Minute Men
before the formal organization of the regiments for
the war; served in the Battle of Long Island; appointed Aide-de-Camp to General James Clinton,
1777; served with the Sullivan Expedition, 1779;
subsequently transferred to the staff of Baron Steu-
ben, with rank of Major.

1888. POTTER, ORLANDO B., 199

Grandson of Corporal Samuel Rice, Corporal 7th Company, Captain Isaac Farwell, 1st Regiment New
Hampshire Continental Infantry, Colonel Cilley,
1780.

1888. *POTTS, FREDERICK A. (died November 9, 1888),

Great-grandson of Thomas Potts, Member New Jersey
Provincial Congress, 1774–6.
Also, Great-grandson of Captain and Brigade Quartermaster John Hughes, Sergeant 6th Battalion Pennsylvania Line, 1776; Ensign same, 1776; Quartermaster 7th Regiment Pennsylvania Line, 1778;
Brigade-Quartermaster 1st Brigade, 1778; Lieutenant
4th Regiment Pennsylvania Line, 1779; Captain 4th
Regiment Pennsylvania Line, 1779; retired from
service, 1781.

217

1883. *POTTS, GEORGE H. (died April 28, 1888).

Grandson of Thomas Potts, Member New Jersey Provincial Congress, 1774-6.

Also, Grandson of Captain and Brigade Quartermaster John Hughes, Sergeant 6th Battalion Pennsylvania Line, 1776; Ensign same, 1776; Quartermaster 7th Regiment Pennsylvania Line, 1778; Brigade-Quartermaster 1st Brigade, 1778; Lieutenant 4th Regiment Pennsylvania Line, 1779; Captain 4th Regiment Pennsylvania Line, 1779; retired from service, 1781.

1889. POWERS, CHARLES ANDREW. *M. D.*,   268

Great-great-grandson of Private Eliot Powers (1732–1783). Private in Temple New Hampshire Militia, "Lexington Alarm," April 19, 1775; Private in Captain Gershom Drury's Company Temple Militia; marched from Temple to reinforce the Continental Army at Ticonderoga, June 29, 1777.

Also, Great-grandson of Private John Stone (1764–1845). Private in Captain Samuel Twitchell's Company New Hampshire Volunteers. Colonel Enoch Hale, August 10, 1778; served in Rhode Island.

Also, Great-great-grandson of Private Benjamin Cutler, Private in Captain Abijah Smith's Company, Colonel Nahum Baldwin's Regiment New Hampshire Militia, September 22, 1776; Private in Captain Samuel Twitchell's Company, New Hampshire Volunteers, Colonel Enoch Hale, August 10, 1778; served in Rhode Island.

Also, Great-great-grandson of Private Benjamin Pierce (1725 ——), Private in Captain Samuel Lamson's Company Leicester Massachusetts Militia, "Lexington Alarm," April 19, 1775; Private in Captain Nathan Fuller's Company 37th Regiment Massachusetts Continental Infantry, Colonel William Bond, 1775; Private in Captain Hudson Ballard's Company, Colonel Whitcomb's Regiment Massachusetts Militia, November 27, 1776, at Ticonderoga; Private in Captain Smith's Company, 15th Regiment Continental Infantry (Massachusetts), Colonel Bigelow, April 1, 1777.

1889. PRALL, JOHN HOWARD,   71

Great-grandson of Lieutenant John Prall, New Jersey Militia.

1889. *PRALL, JOHN PARKER (died March 5, 1891),

Grandson of Lieutenant John Prall, New Jersey Militia.

1889. PRATT, HENRY,   34

Grandson of Lieutenant Samuel Pratt, of Colonel Proctor's Regiment Massachusetts Militia, in charge of Coast Defences about Chelsea, Massachusetts.

1888. PRENTICE, ROBERT KELLY,   802

Great-great-grandson of Major Nathaniel Sartell Prentice, Captain 3d Company 16th Regiment New Hampshire Militia, Colonel Bellows, March 5, 1776; elected Major in Colonel Nahum Baldwin's New Hampshire Regiment, September 17, 1776, but did not serve; Member New Hampshire Provincial Congress, 1776.

1889. PRENTICE, WILLIAM SATTERLEE PACKER,   80

Great-grandson of Major Nathaniel Sartell Prentice, Captain 3d Company 16th Regiment New Hampshire Militia, Colonel Bellows, March 5, 1776; elected Major in Colonel Nahum Baldwin's New Hampshire Regiment, September 17, 1776, but did not serve; Member New Hampshire Provincial Congress, 1776.

1891. PRICE, ALFRED BRYANT,   524

Grandson of Private Joseph Green (1757-1842), Continental Line, New Jersey.

1889. PRIME, EDWARD,   277

Great-grandson of Paymaster Comfort Sands (1748-1834), Paymaster of Westchester, Dutchess, Orange and Ulster Counties Militia, April 4, 1777; Member of New York Committee of One Hundred, May, 1775; Member of New York Provincial Congress, 1775-6; Member of New York Committee of Safety, January 10, 1776; Auditor-General of the Colony of New York, 1776.

Elected.

1890. PROVOST, DAVID,   307

Grandson of Private John Provost (1760-1832), Middlesex County Militia, New Jersey.

1890. PRUYN, AUGUSTUS,

Great-grandson of Lieutenant Casparus Pruyn (1734–1817), 1st Regiment Albany County Militia, New York, Colonel Jacob Lansing, Jr.

1888. PRUYN, JOHN VAN SCHAICK LANSING (Life Member),   216

Great-grandson of Lieutenant Casparus Pruyn (1734–1817), 1st Regiment Albany County Militia, New York, Colonel Jacob Lansing, Jr.
Also, Great-grandson of Quartermaster Christopher Lansing, 3d Albany County Militia, New York.

1890. PUMPELLY, JOHN HOLLENBACK,   421

Great-grandson of Colonel Elizur Talcott (1709-1797), 6th Regiment Connecticut Militia, 1776.

1890. PUMPELLY, RAPHAEL,   798

Great-grandson of Colonel Elizur Talcott (1709–1797), 6th Regiment Connecticut Militia, 1776.

1889. PUTNAM, ALBERT EDWARD,   16

Great-grandson of Captain Jeremiah Putnam, Essex County Militia, Massachusetts.

1891. PUTNAM, HARVEY WORTHINGTON,

Great-great-grandson of Colonel Benjamin Simonds (1726-1807), Colonel 2d Regiment Berkshire County (Massachusetts) Militia, 1775; Colonel 7th Regiment Berkshire County Militia, 1776; Colonel 3d Regiment Berkshire County Militia, April 4, 1777.

220

1891. RAMSEY, FRANK DEWITT, Lieutenant, U. S. A.,   501

Great - great - grandson of Corporal Abner Smith,
"Delevan's" Westchester County Light Horse,
January, 1780; previously Private in 1st Company,
Captain James Rosekrans, 5th Regiment New York
Line, Colonel Dubois, March 20, 1778.

1890. RANKIN, EGBERT GUERNSEY, M. D.,

Great-grandson of Major Henry Schenck (1743–1799),
2d Regiment Dutchess County Minute Men, Colonel
Jacobus Swartwout; Member of 2d and 3d New York
Provincial Congress.

Also, Great-great-grandson of Colonel Jacob Blackwell
1717 ——), Queens County Militia, and Member New
York Provincial Congress.

1888. RAY, JAMES,

Grandson of Lieutenant-Colonel Marinus Willett (1740–
1830), Captain in Colonel McDougall's Regiment,
raised for Continental service, June 28, 1775; served
with Montgomery in Canada; Lieutenant-Colonel 1st
New York Line, Colonel Van Schaick, March 21,
1776; at Fort Stanwix, 1777; at Monmouth, 1778;
with Sullivan's Expedition, 1779; Lieutenant-Colonel
commanding 5th New York Line, January 1, 1780;
Lieutenant-Colonel commanding New York Levies,
April 27, 1781–3; Colonel commanding Tryon County
Militia, April 10, 1782.

1889. RAYMOND, MARCIUS DENISON.

Grandson of Private Newcomb Raymond (1763–1852),
Private in Captain Olmstead's Company, Colonel
Roger Eno's Regiment Connecticut Militia, served
on the Hudson, 1778; Private in 4th Regiment Connecticut Line, Colonel Heman Swift, January 29,
1780; Private in Captain Converse's Company, 2d
Regiment Connecticut Line, Colonel Swift, January
1, 1781.

Also, Great-grandson of Private John Gray, 3d New
York Line, Colonel Gansevoort, December 11, 1776.

1889.   READ, HARMON PUMPELLY.   270

   Great-great-grandson of George Read (1733-1798), Mem-
      ber of Continental Congress; Signer of the Declara-
      tion of Independence; President of the Delaware
      Constitutional Convention; Judge of the Admiralty,
      1782.

1884.   REDDING, CHARLES HAROLD EDGAR.   147

   Great-great-grandson of Captain Kent Wright, detached
      Company Connecticut Militia, died of wounds re-
      ceived in action at White Plains, New York.
   Also, Great-great-grandson of Lieutenant John Hubbell
      (1746-1830), Sergeant in Captain Abijah Sterling's
      Company, Connecticut Militia, 1777; Lieutenant in
      Captain Dimon's Company, Connecticut Militia, 1775.

1890.   REDINGTON, LYMAN WILLIAMS.   525

   Grandson of Private Jacob Redington (1759-1843),
      Private in Captain King's Company, Colonel Whit-
      ing's 17th Regiment Albany County Militia, 1775-6;
      Private in 7th Regiment Massachusetts Continental
      Infantry, Colonel John Brooks, July 13, 1780; Pri-
      vate in Captain Pike's Company, 6th Regiment Mas-
      sachusetts Continental Infantry; transferred to 10th
      Massachusetts; transferred to Captain Kirby Smith's
      Company, 2d Regiment Massachusetts Continental
      Infantry, 1781; served to close of war.
   Also, Great-great-grandson of Captain Amasa Sheldon
      (—— 1780), Captain 4th Company, 5th New Hamp-
      shire, May 3, 1776; Captain in Colonel Brewer's New
      Hampshire Regiment, September, 1776; Captain in
      Colonel Elisha Porter's Regiment New Hampshire
      Militia, in expedition northward, July 10, 1777; also
      served in Colonel David Well's Regiment in North
      ern Department, September 23, 1777, to October 18,
      1777.

222

No. of
Insignia.

1885. REED, THEO. FRELINGHUYSEN, 133

Great-grandson of Private Elnathan Reed, Middlesex
County Militia, Massachusetts.
Also, Grandson of Private Joshua Reed, Middlesex
County Militia, Massachusetts.
Also, Grandson of Sergeant David Haynes Foster,
Suffolk County Militia, New York.

1891. REMINGTON, CYRUS KINGSBURY, 704

Great-grandson of Captain Abner Granger (1735-1816),
2d Lieutenant in Captain Phineas Lovejoy's Company, 3d Battalion Connecticut State Troops, Colonel
Roger Enos, November, 1776, to March 1, 1777; 2d
Lieutenant in Colonel Roger Enos' Battalion Connecticut State Troops, June, 1777; Captain in Colonel Samuel Canfield's Regiment Connecticut Militia,
at Horse Neck, 1782.

1887. REVERE, AUG. LE FEVBRE,

Great-grandson of Lieutenant-Colonel Paul Revere,
Massachusetts Artillery, Continental Army.
Also,Great-grandson of Lieutenant Thomas Lamb, Col-
onel Henry Jackson's Regiment, Massachusetts Line.

1890. RHINELANDER, PHILIP, 374

Great-grandson of Lieutenant Jesse Oakley, 5th Regiment New York Militia, Beekman's Precinct, Colonel William Humphrey: Secretary of Dutchess
County Committee of Safety, June 25, 1776.

1890. RHINELANDER, T. J. OAKLEY, 487

Great-grandson of Lieutenant Jesse Oakley, 5th Regi-
ment New York State Militia, Beekman's Precinct,
Colonel William Humphrey: Secretary of Dutchess
County Committee of Safety, June 25, 1776.

223

         No. of Insignia.

1890. RIKER, EDWARD WOOD, 370

> Great-great great-grandson of Private James Wallace,
> 5th Company, Captain Aarson, 3d Regiment New
> York Line, Colonel Gansevoort, January 13, 1777.
> *Also,* Great-grandson of Private Ananias Weed (1752–
> 1820), Private in Captain Joseph Hull's Company,
> Stamford, Connecticut Militia, "Lexington Alarm,"
> April, 1775; Private in 1st Company, 5th Regiment,
> Connecticut State Troops, Colonel David Waterbury,
> May 6, 1775; 2d Sergeant in 7th Company, Captain
> Nathaniel Webb, same regiment, February 25, 1776;
> Sergeant in Colonel Charles Webb's Regiment, 1776,
> at White Plains and Trenton; Private in Captain
> Bell's Company of Militia, "Danbury Raid," 1777;
> Private in Captain Wales' Company Connecticut
> Militia, August 25, 1777.

1889. RIKER, HENRY LAURENS,

> Great-grandson of Lieutenant Samuel Riker (1743–1823),
> of Captain Daniel Lawrence's Troop of Light Horse,
> Queens County Militia, New York, and Member of
> Queens County Committee of Safety, 1776.

1887. RIKER, JOHN JACKSON, 14

> Great-grandson of Lieutenant Samuel Riker (1743–1823),
> of Captain Daniel Lawrence's Troop of Light Horse,
> Queens County Militia, New York, and Member of
> Queens County Committee of Safety, 1776.

1890. RIKER, JOHN LAWRENCE,

> Grandson of Lieutenant Samuel Riker (1743–1823), of
> Captain Daniel Lawrence's Troop of Light Horse,
> Queens County Militia, New York, and Member of
> Queens County Committee of Safety, 1776.

1889. RIKER, RICHARD, 304

> Great-grandson of Lieutenant Samuel Riker (1743–1823),
> of Captain Daniel Lawrence's Troop of Light Horse,
> Queens County Militia, New York, and Member of
> Queens County Committee of Safety, 1776.

Elected.	No. of Insignia.

1890. RIKER, SAMUEL, JR.,

Great-grandson of Lieutenant Samuel Riker (1743-1823), of Captain Daniel Lawrence's Troop of Light Horse, Queens County Militia, New York, and Member of Queens County Committee of Safety. 1776.

1891. ROBBINS, ROWLAND A.,   577

Great-grandson of Sergeant Frederick Robbins (1756-1821), Private in Captain John Chester's Company, 2d Regiment Connecticut Continental Infantry, Colonel Spencer, May 12, 1775; served at Siege of Boston; Sergeant in Captain Chester Wells' Company, 6th Battalion, Wadsworth's Brigade Connecticut Militia, June 6, 1776.

1890. ROBERTS, CHARLES.   430

Great-great-grandson of Private John Roberts (1727-1796), Colonel Seth Warner's Regiment, Continental Army, Vermont. February 19, 1777.

Also, Great-grandson of Sergeant Christopher Roberts (1753-1832), Captain Thomas Barney's Company, Vermont Militia, Colonel Ira Allen, in service from 1775 to 1783.

1890. ROBERTS, EVELYN PIERREPONT,   446

Great-great-grandson of Private John Roberts (1727-1796), Colonel Seth Warner's Regiment, Continental Army, Vermont. February 19, 1777.

Also, Great-grandson of Sergeant Christopher Roberts (1753-1832), Captain Thomas Barney's Company, Vermont Militia, Colonel Ira Allen, in service from 1775 to 1783.

1891. ROBERTS, THOMAS BENJAMIN GRIGGS,

Great-grandson of Lieutenant John Whitlock (—— 1777), 1st Regiment Monmouth County Militia, New Jersey, killed in action at Middletown, New Jersey, February 13, 1777.

1889. ROBERTSON, HENRY MONTAGUE,

Great-grandson of Private John Moody, Cavalry Virginia.

225

1891. ROBESON, HENRY BELLOWS, Captain, U. S. N.,   609

Great-grandson of Lieutenant-Colonel Joseph Bellows
(1744–1817), Major 8th Regiment, Worcester County,
Massachusetts Militia, 1776; Captain Massachusetts
Continental Infantry, October, 1777, at "Saratoga."
Also, Great-great-grandson of Reverend Nathanael
Taylor (1722–1800), of New Milford, Connecticut,
contributed one year's salary to the cause, as shown
by the Parish records, April, 1779.

1849. ROBINSON, ALFRED BROOKES.

Great-great-grandson of Major John Chipman, of Vermont (1744–1829), 2d Lieutenant in Captain John
Grant's Company, Colonel Seth Warner's Regiment
"Green Mountain Boys," July 27, 1775; 1st Lieuten-
ant in Captain Smith's Company same Regiment,
1776; at Ticonderoga, March, 1777; "Bennington,"
"Saratoga" and "Fort George"; promoted Captain;
taken prisoner at "Fort George"; Major 2d Regi-
ment New York Levies, Lieutenant-Colonel John
Harper, June 16, 1780.
Also, Great-great-grandson of Captain Abial Peirce
(1733–1811), Middleboro' Minute Men, at Lexington,
April 19, 1775; later, Captain in Colonel Nicholas
Dike's Regiment Massachusetts Continental Infantry.

1890. ROBINSON, CHARLES P.,

Great-grandson of Captain Abner Robinson (1738–
1815), Sergeant in Lieutenant Jonathan Palmer's
Company of Windham, Connecticut Militia, "Lex-
ington Alarm," April 19, 1775; Ensign in Captain
Obadiah Johnson's Company, 3d Regiment, Con-
necticut Continental Infantry, Colonel Israel Put-
nam, May 1, 1775; 2d Lieutenant in Captain Vine
Elderken's Company, Colonel Samuel Mott's State
Battalion, June, 1776; Captain in Colonel Samuel
McClellan's Regiment Connecticut Militia, Tyler's
Brigade, in Rhode Island, March 1, 1778; Captain
Connecticut Militia, 1781.

1890. ROBISON, WILLIAM,   **447**

Great-great-grandson of Lieutenant Isaac Bogert
(1741-1818), Captain Thomas DeWitt's Company, 3d
New York Line, Colonel Gansevoort, November 21,
1776, and Captain New York Levies under Lieutenant-Colonel H. K. Van Rensselaer, October 20, 1779.

1891. ROCHESTER, DE LANCEY, M. D.,

Great-grandson of Colonel Nathaniel Rochester (1752-
1831), Paymaster, with rank of Major, North Carolina Line, August, 1775; Paymaster 7th Regiment
North Carolina Militia, 1776; Lieutenant-Colonel
Orange County (North Carolina) Militia, April 22,
1776; promoted Colonel of same, 1777; Deputy Commissary-General of military and other stores in North
Carolina, May 10, 1776; Member of Orange County
(North Carolina) Committee of Safety, 1775; Member
of North Carolina Provincial Congress, 1776.

1891. ROCHESTER, NATHANIEL,   **558**

Great-grandson of Colonel Nathaniel Rochester (1752-
1831), Paymaster, with rank of Major, North Carolina Line, August, 1775; Paymaster 7th Regiment
North Carolina Militia, 1776; Lieutenant-Colonel
Orange County (North Carolina) Militia, April 22,
1776; promoted Colonel of same, 1777; Deputy Commissary-General of military and other stores in North
Carolina, May 10, 1776; Member of Orange County
(North Carolina) Committee of Safety, 1775; Member
of North Carolina Provincial Congress, 1776.

1889. ROCKWOOD, GEORGE GARDNER,   **262**

Great-grandson of Elijah Gardner, Associator, Dutchess
County, New York.

1891. RODGERS, ROBERTSON,

Great-grandson of Rev. John Rodgers, D. D. (1727-
1811), Chaplain in Heath's Brigade, Continental Army,
New York, 1776; Chaplain of New York State Convention, 1777.

1892.   ROE, CHARLES FRANCIS,   792

Great-grandson of Private Stephen Roe (1758-1838),
Private in Captain Job Wright's Company, 1st Reg-
iment New York Continental Infantry, Colonel
Goose Van Schaick, March 1, 1776.

1886.   ROE, WILLIAM JAMES,

Great-grandson of 1st Lieutenant James Roe, 2d Quar-
termaster 1st Regiment Ulster County Militia, Colonel
Abraham Hasbrouck, 1775; 1st Lieutenant, Captain
Simon Lefevre's Company same Regiment, 1778.
Also, Great-grandson of Lieutenant Norman Clark, Pri-
vate Captain Boaz Moore's Company, Colonel Doo-
little's Regiment Massachusetts Militia, "Lexington
Alarm," April 19, 1775; 2d Lieutenant Captain Flint's
Company, Colonel Jonathan Holman's Regiment Mas-
sachusetts Militia, 1776; wounded at Battle of Harlem
Plains, September, 1776, and served under General
Stark, 1777.
Also, Great-grandson of John Franklin, appointed by
General Washington, Agent for Prisoners at New
York, 1780.

1885.   ROOSA, DANIEL B. ST. JOHN, *M. D.*,

Great-grandson of First Lieutenant Isaac Roosa, 2d
Company, Captain John Davis, 4th New York Line,
Colonel Henry B. Livingston; later Lieutenant
Hanover Precinct Company Associated Exempts.

1891.   ROOSEVELT, FRANK,   656

Great-great-grandson of Thomas Potts (1735-1785),
Member New Jersey Provincial Congress, 1774-6.

1887.   RUNK, REV. EDWARD J.,

Great-grandson of Lieutenant Jacob Runk, 3d Regi-
ment Hunterdon County Militia, New Jersey.
Also, Great-grandson of Private William Todd, 2d
Battalion Continental Army, New Jersey.
Also, Great-great-grandson of Lieutenant John Stagg,
Malcolm's 2d Regiment New York City Militia, 1776.

228

Elected.   No. of
Insignia.

1890. RUTHERFURD, JOHN ALEXANDER.   **365**

Great-grandson of Lieutenant William Walton Morris, 2d Continental Corps of Artillery, Colonel Lamb, New York, August 21. 1781.

Also, Great-great-grandson of Brigadier-General Lewis Morris (1726-1798), Brigadier-General Westchester County Militia, 1776; Delegate to Continental Congress, 1774-7; Signer of the Declaration of Independence.

Also, Grandson of David Brooks, of Pennsylvania, Assistant Clothier-General, Continental Army.

1890. RUTHERFURD, WALTER.   **366**

Great-grandson of Lieutenant William Walton Morris, 2d Continental Corps of Artillery, Colonel Lamb, New York, August 21. 1781.

Also, Great-great-grandson of Brigadier-General Lewis Morris (1726-1798), Brigadier-General Westchester County Militia, 1776; Delegate to Continental Congress, 1774-7; Signer of the Declaration of Independence.

Also, Grandson of David Brooks, of Pennsylvania, Assistant Clothier-General, Continental Army.

1891. RUXTON, PHILIP,   **703**

Great-great-grandson of Colonel William Barton (1748-1831), Colonel Rhode Island Continental Infantry, December 24, 1777; presented with a sword by the Continental Congress in recognition of his services in capturing the British General Prescott, July 9, 1777.

1891. SAGE, DEAN.

Great-grandson of Reverend William Linn, D. D. (—— 1808). Chaplain 5th and 6th Battalion Pennsylvania Continental Infantry, February 15, 1776.

1889. SALISBURY, RICHARD LOOMIS.   **209**

Great-grandson of Lieutenant Abner Everett, Sussex County Militia. New Jersey.

1890.   SALTER, WILLIAM TIBBITS,   594

Grandson of Mariner Richard Salter Tibbits (1762–
1821). Captain Samuel Gerrish's letter-of-marque,
New Hampshire.

1887.   SANDFORD, ELLIOTT,

Great-grandson of Captain Thomas White, Massachusetts Militia.
Also, Grandson of Private Joseph Sandford, Massachusetts Militia.

1887.   SANDFORD, JARED,   224

Great-grandson of Silas Halsey, Associator, Suffolk
County, New York.

1889.   SANDS, JOHN AUGUSTINE,   247

Great-great-grandson of Paymaster Comfort Sands
(1748–1834), Paymaster of Westchester, Dutchess,
Orange and Ulster Counties Militia, April 4, 1777;
Member of New York Committee of One Hundred,
May, 1775; Member of New York Provincial Con-
gress, 1775-6; Member of New York Committee of
Safety, January 10, 1776; Auditor-General of the
Colony of New York, 1776.

1889.   SANDS, LOUIS JOSEPH,   337

Great-grandson of Paymaster Comfort Sands (1748–
1834), Paymaster of Westchester, Dutchess, Orange
and Ulster Counties Militia, April 4, 1777; Member
of New York Committee of One Hundred, May,
1775; Member of New York Provincial Congress,
1775-6; Member of New York Committee of Safety,
January 10, 1776; Auditor-General of Colony of
New York, 1776.

1891.   SANFORD, FREDERICK CROSWELL,   726

Great-great-grandson of Sergeant Elihu Sanford (1759–
1839). Corporal 8th Regiment Connecticut Line, Colonel John Chandler, February 16, 1777; Sergeant in
same, May 27, 1778; Sergeant in Captain David Dor-
rance's Company, 5th Regiment Connecticut Line,
Lieutenant-Colonel Isaac Sherman, January 1, 1781.

Also, Great-grandson of Ensign Elihu Lyman (1760
——). Ensign in 17th Regiment Connecticut Line,
Colonel Huntington, 1776; wounded, taken prisoner
in Battle of Long Island, August 27, 1776; exchanged
May, 1778.

1891. SANFORD, GEORGE BLISS, Lieutenant-Colonel U. S. A.,   624

Great-great-grandson of Sergeant Elihu Sanford (1759–
1839), Corporal 8th Regiment Connecticut Line, Colonel John Chandler, February 16, 1777; Sergeant in
same, May 27, 1778; Sergeant in Captain David Dor-
rance's Company, 5th Regiment Connecticut Line,
Lieutenant-Colonel Isaac Sherman, January 1, 1781.
Also, Great-grandson of Ensign Elihu Lyman (1760
——), Ensign in 17th Regiment Connecticut Line,
Colonel Huntington, 1776; wounded, taken prisoner
in Battle of Long Island, August 27, 1776; exchanged
May, 1778.

1891. SANFORD, WILLIAM HENRY,

Great-grandson of Private Jonah Sanford (1735–1817),
Private in Captain Jesse Curtis' Company, Colonel
Noadiah Hooker's Regiment Connecticut Militia, in
United States Service on the Hudson, 1777.

1888. SATTERLEE, DOUGLAS RATHBONE,

Grandson of Sergeant Uriah Gregory, 12th Regiment
Albany (Half-Moon) Militia, New York (Colonel Van
Shoovoens).
Also, Great-grandson of Private Benedict Satterlee
(of Connecticut), Wyoming Militia, Pennsylvania.

1886. SATTERLEE, EDWARD RATHBONE,

Great-grandson of Lieutenant-Colonel Christopher
Yates, 2d Regiment Albany County Militia, Colonel
Abraham Wemple, and Deputy to 3d New York
Provincial Congress, 1776, and Member of Committee
of Safety.

Also, Great-great-grandson of Colonel Jacob Lansing,
Jr., 1st Regiment New York State Militia.
Also, Great-grandson of Lieutenant Jacob G. Lansing,
1st Regiment New York State Militia, Colonel Jacob
Lansing, Jr.
Also, Great-great-grandson of Private Benedict Satter-
lee (of Connecticut), Wyoming Militia, Pennsylvania.

1886. SATTERLEE, F. LEROY, *M. D.*,   163

Great-grandson of Robert Livingston, who gave the use
of his foundry to the Continental Army.
Also, Great-grandson of Private Benedict Satterlee
(of Connecticut), Wyoming Militia, Pennsylvania.

1888. SATTERLEE, GEORGE B.,

Great-grandson of Robert Livingston, who gave the use
of his foundry to the Continental Army.
Also, Great-grandson of Private Benedict Satterlee (of
Connecticut), Wyoming Militia, Pennsylvania.

1886. SATTERLEE, SAMUEL K.,   17

Great-grandson of Private Benedict Satterlee (of Connecticut), Wyoming Militia, Pennsylvania.

1886. SATTERLEE, WALTER,

Great-great-grandson of Robert Livingston, who gave
the use of his foundry to the Continental Army.
Also, Great-grandson of Private Benedict Satterlee (of
Connecticut), Wyoming Militia, Pennsylvania.

1889. SCHENCK, GEORGE ELLIOTT PENDLETON,

Great-grandson of Captain John Schenck, (1750–1783),
Ensign in Captain Cathcart's Company, 1st Regi-
ment Monmouth County (New Jersey) Militia;
Lieutenant in Captain Hunn's Company, same;
Captain in same, October 12, 1777.

232

No. of
Insignia.

1891. SCHERMERHORN, CHARLES AUGUSTUS,   663

Great-grandson of Brevet-Colonel Ebenezer Stevens
(1751–1823), one of "Boston Tea Party," 1773; 1st
Lieutenant in Train Artillery in the Army of Observation, 1775, posted on Boston Neck during the
action at Bunker's Hill, 1775, Captain Massachusetts
Artillery, 1775; Captain Knox's Artillery, 1775; detached to succour Arnold's Expedition against Quebec, 1776; Major in Artillery, 1776; in command of
Artillery at Ticonderoga, 1777; in command of Artillery at Stillwater and Saratoga; brevetted Lieutenant-Colonel of Foot by Congress, 1778; Lieutenant-
Colonel Artillery, 1778 (Lamb's); in command of
Artillery Southern Expedition, 1781; one of the
three alternate commanders of Artillery in the
trenches before Yorktown, 1781; brevetted Colonel
at close of war.

1889. SCHOONMAKER, LUCAS ELMENDORF,

Grandson of Captain Frederick Schoonmaker, Cap-
tain of Mounted Volunteers, Ulster County (New
York) Militia, October 25, 1775; Captain in 3d
Regiment Ulster County Militia, Colonel Pawling,
February 25, 1778.

1890. SCHUYLER, PHILIP,   405

Great-great-grandson of Major-General Philip Schuyler
(1733–1804), Major-General Continental Army, 1775:
resigned 1779; Delegate to Continental Congress,
1775-7; Member New York Provincial Congress,
1778-9; Member New York State Senate, 1781-4.
Also, Great-grandson of Brevet-Colonel Alexander
Hamilton (1757–1804), Captain of New York Provincial Artillery, 1776; Lieutenant-Colonel and
Aide-de-Camp to the Commander-in-Chief, 1777;
Colonel by brevet at close of war.

1886. SCHUYLER, SPENCER D.,

Great-grandson of Colonel Philip P. Schuyler, 3d Regiment Rensselaer Battalion New York Militia.

233

1890. SEAMAN, ALFRED P. W.,

Great-grandson of 2d Lieutenant Daniel Searing
(1759-1833), Captain Sneden's Company, Westchester
County Militia, New York, March 9, 1776.

1886. SEELY, HENRY W.,

Great-great-grandson of Colonel Sylvanus Seeley, Cap-
tain Colonel Martin's Battalion "Heard's" Brigade
New Jersey Militia, 1776; Captain Eastern Battalion
Morris County Militia, 1777; Major of same, 1777;
Colonel of same, 1777, and Colonel of Battalion of
State Troops.

1890. SHELDON, GEORGE RUMSEY,   358

Great-grandson of Sergeant Job Sheldon, Colonel Olney's
Regiment, Rhode Island Line.

1886. SHELDON, WILLIAM CRAWFORD, JR.,   30

Great-grandson of Sergeant Job Sheldon, Colonel Olney's
Regiment, Rhode Island Line.

1890. SHELTON, GEORGE GREGORY, M. D.,   489

Great-great-grandson of Private Elijah Gregory,
served with Wooster's Brigade in Westchester
County (New York) Militia, 1776; Private in Captain Jabez Gregory's Company, 9th Regiment Connecticut Militia, killed in acton near West Point,
1777.

1890. SHELTON, WILLIAM ATWOOD,

Great-great-grandson of Private Elijah Gregory,
served with Wooster's Brigade in Westchester
County (New York) Militia, 1776; Private in Captain Jabez Gregory's Company, 9th Regiment Connecticut Militia, killed in action near West Point,
1777.

1891. SHERMAN, BENJAMIN PRESCOTT,   661

Grandson of Roger Sherman (1721-1793), Member of
Continental Congress from Connecticut, 1775-89;
Signer of the Declaration of Independence.

234

1889. SHERRILL, CHARLES HITCHCOCK, JR..

Great-grandson of Dirck Wynkoop, Associator, Ulster County, New York, 1775; Member of New York Provincial Congress, 1775-6; Judge of Court of Common Pleas, 1777; Member of New York Assembly, 1780-1.

1887. SHORT, EDWARD LYMAN, 775

Great-grandson of Lieutenant Elihu Lyman, Private in Captain Eldad Wright's Company of Minute Men that marched from Northfield and Warwick, Massachusetts, to Cambridge, April 20, 1775; 1st Lieutenant Captain Ephraim Burr's Company, 21st Regiment Continental Infantry, Colonel John Ward.

1884. SHRADY, JACOB.

Grandson of Private John J. Schreder, Private in Captain De Witt's Company, 3d Regiment New York Line, Colonel Gansevoort, 1778; transferred to 1st Regiment New York Line, Colonel Van Schaick; served to close of war.

1884. SHRADY, JOHN, M. D., 257

Grandson of Private John J. Schreder, Private in Captain De Witt's Company, 3d Regiment New York Line, Colonel Gansevoort, 1778; transferred to 1st Regiment New York Line, Colonel Van Schaick; served to close of war.

1884. SHRADY, WILLIAM.

Grandson of Private John J. Schreder, Private in Captain De Witt's Company, 3d Regiment New York Line, Colonel Gansevoort, 1778; transferred to 1st Regiment New York Line, Colonel Van Schaick; served to close of war.

1890. SHURTLEFF, ROSWELL MORSE.

Grandson of Private Asahel Shurtleff (1757-1830), Captain Jonathan Parker's Company, 3d Battalion Connecticut State Troops, Colonel Sage (Wadsworth's Brigade), June, 1776.

235

1886. SILLCOCK, JOHN J.,   198

Great-grandson of Private Joseph Sillcocks, Middlesex
County Militia, New Jersey.

1889. SILLCOCKS, THEODORE WYCKOFF,   741

Great-grandson of Private Gabriel Sillcocks (1752-1825),
Captain Luce's Company, 2d Battalion, 2d Establishment, Continental Army, New Jersey.

1889. SILLCOCKS, WARREN SCOTT,   742

Grandson of Private Gabriel Sillcocks (1752-1825), Captain Luce's Company, 2d Batallion, 2d Establishment,
Continental Army, New Jersey.

1889. SILLCOCKS, WARREN SCOTT, JR.,

Great-grandson of Private Gabriel Sillcocks (1752-1825),
Captain Luce's Company, 2d Battalion, 2d Establishment, Continental Army, New Jersey.

1891. SILLIMAN, BENJAMIN DOUGLAS,   502

Grandson of Brigadier-General Gold Selleck Silliman
(1732-1790), Colonel 4th Regiment Connecticut Militia,
1775; Colonel 1st Regiment Connecticut Militia,
Wadsworth's Brigade, 1776; Colonel Connecticut
Light Horse Militia, 1776; Brigadier-General 4th
Brigade Connecticut Militia, 1776; resigned January
1781, but served continuously on alarms to close of
war; captured, 1779; held prisoner on Long Island
until exchanged for the Loyalist Judge Jones, January, 1782.

1889. SINCLAIR, GEORGE TERRY,

Great-great-grandson of Private Robert Kennon, 5th
Regiment Line, Virginia.

1890. SKILLMAN, FRANCIS,   312

Great-grandson of Lieutenant Thomas Skillman (1736-
1814), Captain Titus's Company, Kings County Militia,
New York.

236

Also, Great-grandson of Ensign Martin Schenck (1743–
1792), Captain Johnson's Company, Kings County
Militia, New York.
Also, Great-grandson of Adrian Onderdonck (1726–1791),
Queens County Committee of Safety, New York.

1889. SLADE, HENRY LEWIS,

Great-grandson of Private James Thomas (1737–1794),
Captain Benedict Arnold's Company, 1st Regiment
Connecticut Militia, Colonel Wooster, May 25, 1775;
marched to seige of Boston.

1892. SLADE, WILLIAM GERRY, 776

Great-grandson of Private Joseph Dale (1731–1801),
Captain Samuel Reed's Company, Colonel William
Prescott's Regiment Massachusetts Minute Men,
"Lexington Alarm," April 19, 1775.

1891. SLAUSON, ALFRED T., 614

Great-grandson of Major Ebenezer Slauson, Colonel
Joseph Drake's Regiment Westchester County
Minute Men, February 22, 1776; Captain and Major
in Colonel Joseph Benedict's Regiment Westchester
County Associated Exempts, October 19, 1779.

1891. SLOCUM, HERBERT JERMAIN, Lieutenant U. S. A.,

Great-great-grandson of Captain Samuel L'Hommedieu
(1744–1834), 8th Company, 2d Regiment Suffolk
County (New York) Militia, August 27, 1776; served
in Battle of Long Island.

1891. SLOCUM, STEPHEN L'HOMMEDIEU, Lieutenant U. S. A., 613

Great-great-grandson of Captain Samuel L'Hommedieu
(1744–1834), 8th Company, 2d Regiment Suffolk
County (New York) Militia, August 27, 1776; served
in Battle of Long Island.

247

237

Elected.

No. of Insignia.

1888. SMEDBERG, EDMUND MORTON, 309

Great-great-grandson of Colonel Charles Rumsey (1736–1780), County Lieutenant Cecil County Militia, Maryland, 1777; Colonel of "Elk" Battalion Cecil County Militia, 1776; Member Maryland Convention, 1775; Member Maryland Council of Safety, 1776.

1890. SMITH, ANDREW HEERMANCE, M. D., 529

Great-grandson of Captain Jacob Hermance (1717–1784), 3d Regiment New York Levies, Colonel Morris Graham, 1780; previously (July 1, 1780), Lieutenant in Colonel Lewis Dubois' Regiment New York Levies.

1889. SMITH, ANDREW KINGSBURY (Colonel U. S. A.), 271

Grandson of Private Andrew Kingsbury, Private in Captain Brigham's Company 8th Regiment Connecticut Line, Colonel Chandler, April 28, 1777; transferred to the General Hospital Department where he served as Clerk; appointed Storekeeper in Continental Surgeons' Department, December 15, 1778; appointed 1st Clerk in the office of Deputy-Quartermaster-General Ralph Pomeroy, May, 1781, where he served to close of war.

1891. SMITH, AUGUSTUS COLEMAN,

Great-great-grandson of Lieutenant-Colonel Elihu Hall (1723–1790), 2d Major of Susquehanna Battalion Maryland Militia, January 6, 1776; later Lieutenant-Colonel Maryland Militia.

1890. SMITH, GEORGE PUTNAM, 517

Great-great-grandson of Brigadier-General Joseph Palmer (1718–1788), Member of Massachusetts Provincial Congress, 1774–5; Member of Massachusetts Committee of Safety, 1775; Quartermaster-General Massachusetts Militia, 1775; Colonel 5th Regiment Suffolk County Militia, February 6, 1776; Brigadier-General Massachusetts Militia, May 9, 1776.

238

1890. SMITH, GOUVERNEUR MATHER, *M. D.*, 456

Great-grandson of Dr. Samuel Mather (1739 1814), of
Connecticut, in medical service Connecticut Militia in
New Jersey, 1776; also Captain Connecticut Militia.
1776.

Also, Great-great-grandson of Dr. Eleazar Mather, appointed by the General Assembly of Connecticut on
a Committee to examine candidates to serve as Surgeons or Surgeon's Mates in the Continental Army
or Navy, October, 1776.

1890. SMITH, HENRY COLE, 434

Great-great-grandson of Corporal Noah Smith (1704-
1793), Corporal in Captain Seymour's Company 9th
Regiment Connecticut Militia, Colonel John Mead,
January 24, 1776; Private in Captain Eliphalet's
Company, Connecticut Coast Guards, March 16,
1780; Private in 7th Regiment Connecticut Line,
Colonel Heman Swift, July 24, 1780.

Also, Great-great-grandson of Lieutenant Stephen
Dodge (1732 1812), Ensign in Captain Amos Chap-
pell's Company 1st Battalion Connecticut State
Troops, Colonel Samuel Whiting, November 1776; 2d
Lieutenant in Colonel Roger Enos' Regiment Con-
necticut State Troops, June, 1777; Lieutenant in
Connecticut Provisional State Troops, 1781.

1887. SMITH, REVEREND J. TUTTLE, *D. D.*, 219

Grandson of Private Benjamin Smith, 4th Company,
4th Regiment, New York Line, Colonel Henry B.
Livingston.

1890. SMITH, LEWIS BAYARD, 459

Great-grandson of Dr. Samuel Mather (1739-1814), of
Connecticut, in medical service Connecticut Militia in
New Jersey, 1776; also Captain Connecticut Militia,
1776.

Also, Great-great-grandson of Dr. Eleazar Mather, appointed by the General Assembly of Connecticut on
a Committee to examine candidates to serve as Surgeons or Surgeon's Mates in the Continental Army
or Navy, October, 1776.

1890. SMITH, THOMAS CHARLES,   699

Great-grandson of Private Amos Morris (1726 1801),
Captain William Van Duersen's Company Connecti-
cut State Guards, on duty at New Haven during the
"Alarm," 1781.

1891. SMITH, THOMAS EDWARD VERMILYE,

Great-grandson of Ebenezer Hazard (1745 1817),
Postmaster of the District of New York, October 5.
1775; Surveyor of the General Post Offices of the
United States, 1777–82; Postmaster-General of the
United States, January 28, 1782, to September 29,
1789.

1884. SMITH, THOMAS WEST,   151

Great-grandson of Sergeant Michael Smith, Private in
Captain Beekman's Company New York Militia, Colonel John Lasher, 1775; Sergeant in same Regiment,
1776; served throughout the war.

1890. SMITH, WILLIAM ALEXANDER,   369

Grandson of Captain Robert Smith (1752 1838), Malcolm's 1st Regiment New York City Militia, Colonel
Malcolm.

1891. SNIFFEN, ELISHA.

Great-great-grandson of Lieutenant-Colonel Thomas
Tillinghast (1742–1821), Major Kent County (Rhode
Island) Militia, 1776; Recruiting Officer Rhode Island
Militia, August, 1777; Lieutenant-Colonel 1st Regi-
ment Kent County Militia, May, 1778, to May, 1781;
Member of Rhode Island Assembly, 1772–9; Member
of Rhode Island Council of War, 1779.

1891. SPINING, REV. GEORGE LAWRENCE, D. D.,   630

Grandson of Private Isaac Spining, (1759–1825), Captain Harriman's Company, 1st Regiment Essex
County (New Jersey) Militia, and Private 1st Battalion 2d Establishment New Jersey Line.

1887. SPRAGUE, CHARLES E.,

Great-grandson of Sergeant Simes Edgerton, Private 4th Regiment Connecticut Line, Colonel John Durkee, 1780; Sergeant Captain Charles Miel's Company, 1st Battalion (Major Edward Shipman) Waterbury's State Brigade, Connecticut Militia, 1781.

Also, Great-grandson of Captain Elisha Avery, Private Norwich Militia, "Lexington Alarm," 1775; Private in Captain Parsons' Company, 6th Regiment Connecticut Militia, 1775; Corporal 1st Regiment Connecticut Line, Colonel Jedediah Huntington, 1777; Captain Connecticut Militia under Colonel Ledyard, killed at Fort Griswold, September 6, 1781.

1886. SQUIER, FRANK,   124

Grandson of Sergeant Ephraim Squier (1747 ——), Private Captain Thomas Knowlton's Company (from Ashford) Connecticut Militia, "Lexington Alarm," 1775; served in the Artillery at "Bunker Hill," 1775; served with Arnold's Expedition to Canada, 1775-6; Sergeant Captain Isaac Stone's Company, Colonel Jonathan Latimer's Regiment Connecticut Militia, Poor's Brigade at "Saratoga," 1777.

1891. STAATS, JOHN HENRY.   640

Great-grandson of Lieutenant Philip Staats (1747-1822), Captain Nicholas Staats' Company, 3d Regiment Albany County Militia, Colonel Killian Van Rensselaer, October 20, 1775.

1889. STAFFORD, MARTIN H.,   43

Great-grandson of Private Ichabod Stafford, Rhode Island Militia.

Also, Great-great-grandson of Private William Stafford (1712-1803), Colonel John Topham's Regiment Rhode Island Militia, May, 1775, to 1778.

Also, Great-grandson of Private Abel Hawley (1750-1836), Captain James Stoddard's Company, Colonel Noadiah Hooker's Regiment Connecticut Militia, May, 1777.

1889. STAFFORD, WILLIAM FREDERICK. 65

Great-grandson of Private Ichabod Stafford, Rhode Island Militia.

Also, Great-great-grandson of Private William Stafford (1712–1803), Colonel John Topham's Regiment Rhode Island Militia. May, 1775, to 1778.

Also, Great-grandson of Private Abel Hawley (1750–1836), Captain James Stoddard's Company, Colonel Noadiah Hooker's Regiment Connecticut Militia. May, 1777.

1886. STANTON, F. McMILLAN. 85

Great-great-grandson of Private Benjamin Westervelt, 2d New York Militia.

Also, Great-grandson of Private Benjamin Westervelt, Jr., 2d New York Militia.

1891. STANTON, HENRY. 559

Great-grandson of Colonel James Livingston (1747–1832), Colonel of " Additional " Continental Infantry, March 20, 1775, to 1781, on active service in Canada and on the Hudson; Member of New York Provincial Congress, 1775–6; Chairman Dutchess County Committee of Safety.

1884. STANTON, JOHN R., 185

Great-great-grandson of Private Benjamin Westervelt, 2d New York Militia.

Also, Great-grandson of Private Benjamin Westervelt, Jr., 2d New York Militia.

1890. 'STANTON, STILES FRANKLIN. 773

Great-grandson of Lieutenant Peter Tappan (1764–1846), 1st Lieutenant in Captain John Schenck's Company of Poughkeepsie Minute Men, October 17, 1775; 2d Lieutenant in 2d Regiment Continental Corps of Artillery, Colonel Lamb, August 21, 1781.

Also, Great-great-grandson of Major Christopher Tappan " Northern " Regiment of Minute Men, Ulster County, Colonel DeWitt, and Member of New York Provincial Congress, 1775.

242

Elected.

No. of Insignia.

1891. STEELE, JOSEPH SELDEN,

Great-great-great-grandson of Private Ebenezer Steele
(1727–1821), in Captain Abraham Sedgwick's Company
Connecticut Militia; served around New York, 1776.
Also, Great-great-grandson of Private Josiah Steele
(1758–1825), in Captain William Judd's Company, 3d
Regiment Connecticut Line, Colonel Wyllys, April
20, 1777.
Also, Great-great-grandson of Colonel Samuel Selden,
Sr. (1723–1776), Colonel of 4th Battalion, Wadsworth's Brigade Connecticut Militia, June 20, 1776;
taken prisoner in retreat from New York, September
15, 1776; died while prisoner in New York, October
11, 1776.
Also, Great-grandson of Lieutenant Samuel Selden, Jr.
(1748–1819), Lieutenant in Connecticut Militia Re-
serve; called into active service on the Hudson
under Colonel Samuel Canfield, September and October, 1781.

1888. STEVENS, ALEXANDER HENRY,

Grandson of Brevet Colonel Ebenezer Stevens (1751–
1823), one of "Boston Tea Party," 1773; 1st Lieutenant in Train Artillery in the Army of Observation,
1775, posted on Boston Neck during the action at
Bunker's Hill, 1775; Captain in Massachusetts Artillery, 1775; Captain in Knox's Artillery, 1775; detached to succour Arnold's Expedition against Quebec,
1776; Major in Artillery, 1776; in command of Artillery at Ticonderoga, 1777; in command of Artillery
at Stillwater and Saratoga; brevetted Lieutenant-
Colonel of Foot by Congress, 1778; Lieutenant-Colonel
in 2d Regiment Continental Corps of Artillery,
Colonel Lamb, 1778; in command of Artillery in
Southern Expedition, 1781; one of three alternate
commanders of Artillery in the trenches before
Yorktown, 1781; brevetted Colonel at close of war.
Also, Great-grandson of Colonel William Perkins,
Captain in Knox's Regiment Artillery, 1776; Captain
in Colonel Crane's Regiment Artillery, 1777; later
Colonel commanding the Castle in Boston Harbor.

1876. STEVENS, JOHN AUSTIN,

Grandson of Brevet Colonel Ebenezer Stevens (1751-
1823), one of "Boston Tea Party," 1773; 1st Lieutenant in Train Artillery in the Army of Observation,
1775, posted on Boston Neck during the action at
Bunker's Hill, 1775; Captain in Massachusetts Artillery, 1775; Captain in Knox's Artillery, 1775; detached to succour Arnold's Expedition against Quebec,
1776; Major in Artillery, 1776; in command of Artillery at Ticonderoga, 1777; in command of Artillery
at Stillwater and Saratoga; brevetted Lieutenant-
Colonel of Foot by Congress, 1778; Lieutenant-Colonel
in 2d Regiment Continental Corps of Artillery,
Colonel Lamb, 1778; in command of Artillery in
Southern Expedition, 1781; one of three alternate
commanders of Artillery in the trenches before
Yorktown, 1781; brevetted Colonel at close of war.

Also, Great-grandson of Colonel William Perkins,
Captain in Knox's Regiment Artillery, 1776; Captain in Colonel Crane's Regiment Artillery, 1777;
later, Colonel commanding the Castle in Boston
Harbor.

1890. STEVENSON, WILLIAM PAXTON.   478

Great-great-grandson of Captain John Paxton (1740-
1823), Captain Associated Company Pennsylvania
Militia, September 11, 1776; Captain 2d Lancaster
Battalion Pennsylvania Militia, 1777.

Also, Great-grandson of First Lieutenant Joseph
Stevenson, 8th Company, 6th Battalion Cumberland
County (Pennsylvania) Associators, Colonel Samuel
Culbertson, July 31, 1777.

Also, Great-grandson of First Lieutenant Alexander
Russell (1758-1836), 2d Lieutenant 7th Regiment
Pennsylvania Continental Infantry, Colonel William
Irvine, January, 1777; promoted 1st Lieutenant
same, September 1, 1777.

Also, Great-great-grandson of Colonel Robert McPherson (—— 1789), Colonel of 2d Battalion York County
(Pennsylvania) Militia, July 28, 1775, and Member
of Pennsylvania Convention, 1776.

Also, Great-great-grandson of Colonel James Dunlop
(1727–1821), Major 6th Battalion Pennsylvania Line,
Colonel Irvine, January 10, 1776; Lieutenant-Colonel
10th Regiment Pennsylvania Line, Colonel Joseph
Penrose, October 25, 1776; Colonel 1st Battalion
Cumberland County Associators, July 31, 1777;
Lieutenant-Colonel 6th Battalion Cumberland
County Associators, May 10, 1780.

Also, Great-grandson of ·Captain William Miller
(1755–1831), Ensign in Captain Hays' Company 8th
Battalion Pennsylvania Line, January 9, 1776; 1st
Lieutenant 7th Regiment Pennsylvania Line, Colonel
William Irvine, March 20, 1777; Captain Lieutenant
same, February 2, 1778; Captain same, October 17, 1779.

1889. STILLMAN, THOMAS BLISS,   109

Great-grandson of Sergeant Jesse Starr (―― 1798).
Private in 10th Company, Captain Abel Spicer, 6th
Regiment Connecticut Line, Colonel Parsons, May
8, 1776; Corporal in Captain Gallup's Company,
same Regiment, November 6, 1776; Corporal in
Captain Wooster's Company, Colonel S. B. Webb's
Regiment "Additional Continental" Infantry, April
23, 1777; promoted Sergeant October 9, 1778; en-
listed in Naval Service May 30, 1782; taken prisoner
June 7, 1782; released August 20, 1783.

Also, Great-great-grandson of Private Vine Starr
(1716–1799), Private in Captain Joseph Gallup's Company, 8th Regiment Connecticut Militia, Lieutenant-
Colonel Oliver Smith, September 8, 1776; Private in
Captain Eliphaz Kingsley's Company, Colonel
Jedutha Baldwin's Regiment of Artificers, Continental Army.

1891. STOKES, WILLIAM EARL DODGE,

Great-grandson of Lieutenant Thomas Phelps, Sergeant
in 7th Company, Captain Abel Pettibone, 2d Regiment Continental Line, Colonel John Spencer, May 4,
1775; Ensign in 22d Regiment Continental Infantry,
Colonel Wyllys, 1776; Lieutenant in Captain Jarius
Willcox's Company, Colonel Jedutha Baldwin's Regiment of Artificers, Continental Army, July 24, 1777.

1884. STONE, WILLIAM,

Grandson of Sergeant Jonathan Stone, Sergeant in Captain Henry Farwell's Company of Minute Men, Colonel William Prescott's Regiment Massachusetts Militia; marched from Groton to Lexington April 19, 1775; Corporal in Captain Aaron Jewitt's Company, Colonel Samuel Bullard's Regiment Massachusetts Militia, 1777.

Also. Great-grandson of Private Solomon Stone, Captain Bowker's Company, Colonel Webb's Regiment Massachusetts Militia; raised to reinforce the Continental Army, 1781.

1891. STONE, WILLIAM COOLIDGE, M. D.,   612

Great-grandson of Private Jonathan Coolidge (1750–1810), Captain Frothingham's Company, 3d Regiment Continental Corps of Artillery, Massachusetts, May, 1777; Private in Watertown (Massachusetts) Militia; served with Continental Army, July 4, 1780.

1887. *STORM, THOMAS (died May 1, 1890),

Grandson of Adjutant Thomas Storm, Adjutant 2d Regiment Dutchess County Militia, New York, Colonel Direk Brinckeroff, 1775; Captain in same, Colonel Abraham Brinckeroff, 1778; Member of Dutchess County Committee of Safety, 1776-7; Member of New York Assembly, 1784.

1887. STORM, WALTON,

Great-grandson of Adjutant Thomas Storm, Adjutant 2d Regiment Dutchess County Militia, New York, Colonel Direk Brinckerhoff, 1775; Captain in same, Colonel Abraham Brinckerhoff, 1778; Member of Dutchess County Committee of Safety, 1776-7; Member of New York Assembly, 1784.

1891. STOUT, FREDERICK AQUILA,

Grandson of Lieutenant William Walton Morris, 2d Regiment Continental Corps of Artillery, Colonel Lamb, August 21, 1785.

Also, Great-grandson of Lewis Morris (1726-1798), Brigadier-General Westchester County Militia, 1776; Delegate to Continental Congress, 1774-7; Signer of the Declaration of Independence.

1889. STOW, GEORGE GRANNIS,   552

Great-grandson of Lieutenant Thomas Elwood, Private in Captain David Dimon's Company of Minute Men, that marched from Fairfield to the relief of Boston, on Lexington Alarm, April 19, 1775; Private in Captain Dimon's Company, 5th Regiment Connecticut Line, Colonel David Waterbury, May 10, 1775; Lieutenant of Marines on frigate " Alliance," 32 guns, Captain Peter Landais, afterwards Captain Barry, August 24, 1778; retired from service, May 1, 1783.

1889. STOW, WILLIAM LEWIS.   237

Great-grandson of Lieutenant Thomas Elwood, Private in Captain David Dimon's Company of Minute Men, that marched from Fairfield to the relief of Boston on Lexington Alarm, April 19, 1775; Private in Captain Dimon's Company, 5th Regiment Connecticut Line, Colonel David Waterbury, May 10, 1775; Lieutenant of Marines on frigate " Alliance," 32 guns, Captain Peter Landais, afterwards Captain Barry, August 24, 1778; retired from service May 1, 1783.

1891. STRONG, JAMES HENRY WARD,

Great-grandson of Captain Selah Strong, Captain 3d Regiment Suffolk County Minute Men, Colonel Scudder, April 4, 1776; Captain in Colonel Josiah Smith's Regiment Suffolk County Militia, May 20, 1776; Member New York Provincial Congress, 1775-6.
Also, Great-great-grandson of Major Nathan Woodhull (1720-1804), 1st Regiment Suffolk County Militia, New York.

1889. STRONG, J. MONTGOMERY, JR.,   301

Great-grandson of Philip Livingston (1716-1778), Signer of the Declaration of Independence, New York.

1889. STRONG, JAMES REMSEN,   806

Great-grandson of Captain Selah Strong, Captain 3d
Regiment Suffolk County Minute Men, New York,
Colonel Scudder, April 4, 1776; Captain in Colonel
Josiah Smith's Regiment Suffolk County Militia,
May 20, 1776; Member New York Provincial Con-
gress, 1775 6.

Also, Great-great-grandson of Major Nathan Woodhull
(1720-1804), 1st Regiment Suffolk County Militia,
New York.

1889. STRONG, MURRAY HOFFMAN,

Great-grandson of Captain Selah Strong, Captain 3d
Regiment Suffolk County Minute Men, New York,
Colonel Scudder, April 4, 1776; Captain in Colonel
Josiah Smith's Regiment Suffolk County Militia,
May 20, 1776; Member New York Provincial Con-
gress, 1775-6.

Also, Great-great-grandson of Major Nathan Woodhull
(1720-1804), 1st Regiment Suffolk County Militia,
New York.

1886. STRONG, THERON G.,

Great-grandson of Commissary Adonijah Strong, Colonel Burrall's Regiment Connecticut Militia, and Lieutenant, Captain John Bigelow's Company, Connecticut Artillery.

1889. STRONG, WILSON BUDD,   235

Great-great-grandson of Lieutenant David Lyman, Captain Jonathan Wales's Company, Colonel Dickinson's
Regiment, Massachusetts Militia, August 17, 1777;
previously Lieutenant Massachusetts Militia, 1776;
Aide-de-Camp, 1780.

1890. SUTHERLAND, JOHN LANSING,

Grandson of Lieutenant John Lansing, Jr. (1754-1829),
1st Battalion New York Line, Colonel Goose Van
Schaick, November 21, 1776, and Adjutant 3d Regiment, Tryon County Militia, Colonel Fisher, New
York, 1779.

Elected.

1886. SUYDAM, JOHN R.,

Great-great-grandson of Brigadier-General Nathaniel Woodhull (1722-1776), Colonel Long Island Militia, 1775; Brigadier-General same, 1776; Member New York Provincial Congress, 1775; President of same, 1776; died of wounds received in action at Jamaica, Long Island, September 20, 1776.

1888. SWAN, BENJAMIN L., JR.,   212

Great-grandson of Private Samuel Swan, Private in Captain William Adams' Company, Colonel Thatcher's Regiment Massachusetts Militia, March, 1776.

1889. SWAN, FREDERICK GEORGE,   213

Great-grandson of Private Samuel Swan, Private in Captain William Adams' Company, Colonel Thatcher's Regiment Massachusetts Militia, March, 1776.

1891. SWARTWOUT, EGERTON,

Great-great-grandson of Captain Abraham Swartwout, 3d Regiment New York Line, Colonel Gansevoort.
Also, Great-great-great-grandson of Private Benedict Satterlee (of Connecticut), Wyoming Militia, Pennsylvania.

1888. SWARTWOUT, JOHN H.,   19

Great-grandson of Captain Abraham Swartwout, Captain in 4th Regiment Dutchess County Militia, New York, 1776; Captain 3d Battalion New York Line, Colonel Gansevoort, 1776; Captain 4th Battalion New York Line, Colonel Gansevoort, 1778; Captain Dutchess County Associated Exempts, 1778.
Also, Great-great-grandson of Private Benedict Satterlee (of Connecticut), Wyoming Militia, Pennsylvania.

1887. SWARTWOUT, SATTERLEE,　　　　　　　　　31

Great-grandson of Captain Abraham Swartwout, Captain in 4th Regiment Dutchess County Militia, New York, 1776; Captain 3d Battalion New York Line, Colonel Gansevoort, 1776; Captain 4th Battalion New York Line, Colonel Gansevoort, 1778; Captain Dutchess County Associated Exempts, 1778.

Also, Great-great-grandson of Private Benedict Satterlee (of Connecticut), Wyoming Militia, Pennsylvania.

1890. SWIFT, EDWIN E., *M. D.,*

Great-great-grandson of Brigadier-General Heman Swift, Colonel of State Battalion, raised for service at Ticonderoga, July, 1776; Colonel 7th Regiment Connecticut Line, January 1, 1777; Colonel 2d Regiment Connecticut Line, October, 1781, to close of war; Brigadier-General by brevet at close of war; Member of Connecticut Assembly, 1775.

1889. SWIFT, MOSES ROBINSON,

Great-grandson of Colonel Moses Robinson (1774 ——), Colonel Vermont Militia, July, 1777; Member of Council of Safety, 1777-8; Chief-Justice of Supreme Court, 1778-84.

1890. SWORDS, HENRY COTHEAL,

Great-grandson of Private Isaac Cotheal (1743-1812), 4th Battalion, 2d Establishment, New Jersey Line, wounded and taken prisoner at Woodbridge, April 19, 1777; served thirteen months in New York prison; honorably discharged, May 1, 1778, on account of wounds.

1890. TAGGART, WILLIAM RUSH,　　　　　　　　371

Great-grandson of Private William McGahey (—— 1827), Captain Thomas Church's Company, 4th Pennsylvania Battalion, Colonel Anthony Wayne, 1776.

250

1890. TALBOT, CHARLES NICOLL,   359

Great-grandson of Captain Silas Talbot (—— 1813),
Lieutenant in Captain Levi Tower's Company Rhode
Island Army of Observation, 1775; Captain 1st Battalion Rhode Island Militia, Colonel Varnum, 1776:
Captain 11th Regiment Rhode Island Continental Infantry, Colonel Hitchcock, 1776; Major Continental
Army, 1777; Lieutenant-Colonel Continental Army,
1778; Captain Continental Navy, 1779, in command
of sloop "Argos;" was shot twice through the thigh
and wrist in engagement at Fort Mifflin, October,
1777; shot through the knee in engagement with
British privateers "Dragon" and "Hannah," 1779.

1891. TALBOT, ROBERT BANCKER, *M. D.*,

Great-grandson of Captain Silas Talbot (—— 1813),
Lieutenant in Captain Levi Tower's Company Rhode
Island Army of Observation, 1775; Captain 1st Battalion Rhode Island Militia, Colonel Varnum, 1776;
Captain 11th Regiment Rhode Island Continental Infantry, Colonel Hitchcock, 1776; Major Continental
Army, 1777; Lieutenant-Colonel Continental Army,
1778; Captain Continental Navy, 1779, in command
of sloop "Argos;" was shot twice through the thigh
and wrist in engagement at Fort Mifflin, October,
1777; shot through the knee in engagement with
British privateers "Dragon" and "Hannah," 1779.

1887. TALBOT, THEODORE B.,

Great-grandson of Captain Silas Talbot (—— 1813),
Lieutenant in Captain Levi Tower's Company, Rhode
Island Army of Observation, 1775; Captain 1st Bat-
talion Rhode Island Militia, Colonel Varnum, 1776;
Captain 11th Regiment Rhode Island Continental
Infantry, Colonel Hitchcock, 1776; Major Conti-
nental Army, 1777; Lieutenant-Colonel Continental
Army, 1778; Captain Continental Navy, 1779, in
command of sloop "Argos;" was shot twice through
the thigh and wrist in engagement at Fort Mifflin,
October, 1777; shot through the knee in engagement
with British privateers "Dragon" and "Hannah," 1779.

1883. TALLMADGE, FREDERICK SAMUEL,　　　　　　　4 & 473

Grandson of Major and Brevet Lieutenant-Colonel Benjamin Tallmadge (1754–1835), Captain, 1776; Major in Sheldon's Light Dragoons, 1777; conducted "Secret Service" for the Commander-in-Chief; captured Fort George, Long Island, November 21, 1780, and received special notice of Congress; Lieutenant-Colonel by brevet, 1783.

Also, Great-grandson of William Floyd (1734–1821), Signer of Declaration of Independence, and Colonel 1st Regiment Suffolk County Militia, New York, 1775.

1889. TALLMADGE, HENRY OVERING,

Great-great-grandson of Brigadier and Brevet Major-General George Clinton (1739–1812), Brigadier-General Continental Army, 1776; Member of Continental Congress, 1775; Governor of New York. 1777–95; Major-General by brevet.

Also, Great-grandson of Major and Brevet Lieutenant-Colonel Benjamin Tallmadge (1754–1835), Captain, 1776; Major Sheldon's Light Dragoons, 1777; conducted "Secret Service" for the Commander-in-Chief; captured Fort George, Long Island, November 21, 1780, and received special notice of Congress; Lieutenant-Colonel by brevet, 1783.

Also, Great-great-grandson of William Floyd (1734–1821), Signer of Declaration of Independence, and Colonel 1st Regiment Suffolk County Militia, New York, 1775.

1885. *TAPP, EDWARD WILLIAM (died February 3, 1888),

Grandson of Lieutenant William Tapp (1750–1796), Ensign 5th Company 1st Regiment New York Line, Colonel McDougal, 1775; 2d Lieutenant and Quartermaster same Regiment, 1775; 2d Lieutenant in Colonel Nicholson's Regiment, on service in Canada, 1776; 1st Lieutenant Captain Thomas DeWitt's Company 3d Battalion New York Line, Colonel Peter Gansevoort, 1776; resigned March 20, 1780.

252

TAPP, EDWARD WRIGHT,   258

Great-grandson of Lieutenant William Tapp (1750–
1796). Ensign 5th Company 1st Regiment New York
Line, Colonel McDougal, 1775; 2d Lieutenant and
Quartermaster same Regiment, 1775; 2d Lieutenant
in Colonel Nicholson's Regiment, on service in Can-
ada, 1776: 1st Lieutenant Captain Thomas DeWitt's
Company 3d Battalion New York Line, Colonel
Peter Gansevoort, 1776; resigned March 20, 1780.

Also, Great-grandson of Matross Daniel Whitehead
(1751–1824), Captain Daniel Neil's Eastern Company
of Artillery, New Jersey State Troops.

1890. TAYLOR, ARTHUR WILSON, M. D. (Captain and Assistant-
Surgeon, U. S. A.),   765

Great-grandson of Corporal Jonathan Taylor (1739–
1816), Captain Chase Taylor's Company, Colonel
Thomas Stickney's Regiment Vermont Militia,
" Stark's " Brigade, on service at Ticonderoga, July,
1777.

1889. TAYLOR, FRANCIS BERGH,

Great-grandson of Private Joseph Moringault, South
Carolina Artillery, at seige and capitulation of
Charleston, May, 1780.

1887. TAYLOR, SAMUEL R.,

Great-great-grandson of Captain Benjamin Vail, Orange
County (New York) Militia, killed at Minisink, Delaware County, July 22, 1779.

1889. TAYLOR, SUTHERLAND GAZZAM,   204

Great-grandson of Brigadier and Brevet Major-General
George Clinton (1739–1812), Brigadier-General Continental Army, 1776; Member of Continental Congress, 1775; Governor of New York, 1777–95;
Major-General by brevet.

253

1890. TAYLOR, W. IRVING,   764

Great-grandson of Corporal Jonathan Taylor (1739–
1816), Captain Chase Taylor's Company, Colonel
Thomas Stickney's Regiment Vermont Militia,
"Stark's" Brigade, on service at Ticonderoga, July,
1777.

1891. TERRY, WYLLYS,   516

Great-great-grandson of Colonel Nathaniel Terry
(1730–1792), Major of Enfield Company Connecticut
Militia, "Lexington Alarm," April 19, 1775; Lieutenant-Colonel 19th Regiment Connecticut Militia,
December, 1776; Colonel of same, May, 1777; Member of Connecticut Assembly, 1776.
Also, Great-great-grandson of Major Nathaniel Sartell
Prentice, Captain 3d Company 16th Regiment New
Hampshire Militia, Colonel Bellows, March 5, 1776;
elected Major in Colonel Nahum Baldwin's New
Hampshire Regiment, September 17, 1776, but did
not serve; Member New Hampshire Provincial Con-
gress, 1776.

1891. THOMAS, FREDERIC CHICESTER,

Great-grandson of Lieutenant Joseph Winter (1757–
1820), 13th Beat Company, Captain Benjamin Carpenter, New York City Militia, August 29, 1775, and
Secretary New York Committee of Safety, 1776.

1891. THOMAS, THEODORE,   515

Grandson of Captain Anthony Cuthbert (1751–1832), 6th
Company Artillery, Philadelphia City Militia, April
15, 1780.

1883. THOMPSON, ALEXANDER R., JR.,   246

Great-grandson of Lieutenant Alexander Thompson,
2d Regiment Continental Corps of Artillery, New
York, Colonel Lamb.

254

1891. THOMPSON, AUGUSTUS ANNIN,

Great-great-grandson of Lieutenant-Colonel Jabez Thompson (—— 1776), Major of Derby (Connecticut) Militia, "Lexington Alarm," April 19, 1775: Major 1st Regiment Connecticut Militia, Colonel David Wooster, May 1, 1775, Lieutenant-Colonel 2d Regiment Connecticut Militia, 1776; killed in the retreat from New York, September 15, 1776.

1891. THOMPSON, FREDERICK DIODATI (Life Member),   454

Great-great-grandson of Reverend Stephen Johnson, Chaplain 6th Regiment Connecticut Militia. Colonel S. H. Parsons, May 20, 1775.
Also, Great-great-grandson of Matthew Griswold (1714–1799), Deputy - Governor of Connecticut. 1771–84; Chief-Justice of Connecticut, 1769-84.

1885. THOMPSON, VON BEVERHOUT, *M. D.*,

Great-grandson of Surgeon Walter Smith. Maryland Line; Member of Frederick County Committee of Safety and Correspondence.

1890. THOMPSON, WILLIAM A.,   474

Great-grandson of Lieutenant William Thompson (1742-1777), Private in 1st Company, 5th Regiment Connecticut Militia, Colonel David Waterbury, May 8, 1775: Lieutenant Connecticut Militia; killed in action at Ridgefield, Connecticut (Danbury Raid), April, 1777.

1884. THOMPSON, WILLIAM R.,   48

Great-grandson of Lieutenant Alexander Thompson, (—— 1809), 2d Regiment Continental Corps of Artillery, New York, Colonel Lamb.

1887. THORNALL, CLARENCE EUGENE,   99

Great-grandson of Sergeant Garrett Voorhees, Sussex County Militia, New Jersey; also Private Continental Army, New Jersey.

255

1888. THORNALL, EDWARD VOORHEES,   87

Great-grandson of Sergeant Garrett Voorhees, Sussex
County Militia, New Jersey; also Private Continental Army, New Jersey.

1889. THORNE, ROBERT,

Great-great-grandson of Major Richard Thorne, Queens
County Militia, and Member First Provincial Congress, New York.

1891. TIEMANN, PAUL E., M. D.,   591

Great-great-grandson of Lieutenant Abraham Leggett,
(1755-1842), 5th Regiment New York Line, Colonel
Lewis Dubois, October 2. 1777.

1889. TILLINGHAST, CHARLES WHITNEY, 2d,   254

Great-great-grandson of Lieutenant-Colonel Thomas
Tillinghast (1742-1821), Major Kent County Militia,
Rhode Island, 1776; Recruiting Officer, Rhode Island
Militia, August, 1777; Lieutenant-Colonel 1st Regi-
ment Kent County Militia, May, 1778, to May, 1781;
Member of Rhode Island Assembly, 1772-9; Member
of Rhode Island Council of War, 1779.

1890. TILLINGHAST, JOSEPH J.,

Great-grandson of Lieutenant-Colonel Thomas Tilling-
hast (1742 1821), Major Kent County Militia, Rhode
Island, 1776; Recruiting Officer, Rhode Island Militia,
August, 1777; Lieutenant-Colonel, 1st Regiment
Kent County Militia, May, 1778, to May, 1781; Mem-
ber of Rhode Island Assembly, 1772 9; Member of
Rhode Island Council of War, 1779.

1889. TILLINGHAST, WILLIAM H.,   78

Grandson of Lieutenant-Colonel Thomas Tillinghast
(1742 1821), Major Kent County Militia, Rhode
Island, 1776; Recruiting Officer, Rhode Island Militia,
August, 1777; Lieutenant-Colonel 1st Regiment
Kent County Militia, May, 1778, to May, 1781; Mem-
ber of Rhode Island Assembly, 1772 9; Member of
Rhode Island Council of War, 1779.

256

1886. TOMLINSON, JOHN CANFIELD,   36

Great-great-grandson of Colonel Andrew Adams (—— 1797), Major Connecticut Militia, 1777: Lieutenant-Colonel, 1779; Colonel 17th Regiment Connecticut Militia, 1780; Delegate Continental Congress, 1777-80 (Speaker, 1779-80): Member Connecticut Council of Safety.

Also, Great-great-grandson of Brigade-Major John Canfield, Adjutant Sheldon's Dragoons, 1776; Brigade-Major in Brigadier-General Oliver Wolcott's Detachment, "at Saratoga," 1777; Member of Continental Congress.

1886. TOMLINSON, THEODORE E., JR.,   37

Great-great-grandson of Colonel Andrew Adams (—— 1797), Major Connecticut Militia, 1777: Lieutenant-Colonel, 1779; Colonel 17th Regiment Connecticut Militia, 1780; Delegate Continental Congress, 1777-80 (Speaker, 1779-80); Member Connecticut Council of Safety.

Also, Great-great-grandson of Brigade-Major John Canfield, Adjutant Sheldon's Dragoons, 1776; Brigade-Major in Brigadier-General Oliver Wolcott's Detachment, "at Saratoga," 1777; Member Continental Congress.

1891. TOMPKINS, HAMILTON BULLOCK,

Grandson of Private Gideon Tompkins (1761-1837), Rhode Island Continental Infantry.

1891. TOSTEVIN, WILLIAM L.,

Great-great-grandson of Captain Daniel Brainard, Colonel Comfort Sage's Regiment Connecticut Militia, 1779.

257

1890. TOWLE, GEORGE FRANCIS (Captain and Brevet Lieuten-
       ant-Colonel, U. S. A.),   438

> Great-great-grandson of Lieutenant William Greenleaf
> (—— 1800), Fifer in Captain Moses McFarland's
> Company, Colonel Nixon's Massachusetts Militia,
> January, 1776; Private in Captain Fairchild's Com-
> pany in Colonel Edward Wigglesworth's Regiment
> Massachusetts Militia, February, 1777; promoted
> Corporal; then Sergeant in same, September 11,
> 1777; Ensign in same, 1777; Lieutenant in same,
> February 13, 1778.

1891. TOWLE, HARRY F.,

> Great-grandson of Sergeant Simeon Towle (1752-1823),
> Private in Captain Joseph Parsons' Company New
> Hampshire Minute Men, October 12, 1775; Private in
> Captain Henry Elkin's Company New Hampshire
> Militia, November 5, 1775; Private in Captain Jona-
> than Robinson's Company, Colonel William Whip-
> ple's Regiment New Hampshire Militia, raised to re-
> inforce the Continental Army at New York, 1776;
> Sergeant in Captain Joseph Parsons' Company New
> Hampshire Militia, Colonel David Gilman, December
> 5, 1776; Sergeant same Company, Lieutenant-Col-
> onel Joseph Senter's Regiment New Hampshire Mili-
> tia, to reinforce the Continental Army in Rhode Isl-
> and, June 26, 1777; Private in Captain Parsons'
> Company, Colonel Moses Nichols' Regiment New
> Hampshire Volunteers, in Expedition to Rhode Isl-
> and, August 15, 1778; Private in Captain Nute's
> Company, Colonel Wentworth's Regiment New
> Hampshire Militia, raised for defence of Portsmouth,
> September, 27, 1779.

1889. TOWNSEND, EDWARD NICOLL.

> Grandson of Midshipman Solomon Townsend, Conti-
> nental frigate "Providence," 28 guns, Commander
> Whipple, July 16, 1778.
> Also, Great-grandson of Samuel Townsend, Member
> Provincial Congress, New York, 1774-77.

Elected.

1889. TOWNSEND, ROBERT.

Grandson of Midshipman Solomon Townsend, Continental frigate "Providence," 28 guns, Commander Whipple, July 16, 1778.

Also, Great-grandson of Samuel Townsend, Member Provincial Congress, New York, 1774–77.

1892. TOWNSEND, RUFUS M.,

Great-grandson of Private Rufus Marsh (1758–1814), Captain Christopher Bainester's Company, Colonel David Well's Regiment Massachusetts Militia, on Expedition to Fort Ticonderoga, May 8 to July 8, 1777; Private in Captain Ebenezer Webber's Company, Colonel Ezra May's Regiment Massachusetts Militia, on Expedition to Stillwater, September 20 to October 14, 1777.

Also, Great-great-grandson of Eliashib Adams (1727–1801), Member of Connecticut General Convention, 1775.

1886. TREMAIN, HENRY EDWIN,

Great-grandson of Private Nathaniel Tremain (——1800), Massachusetts Militia.

1888. TRENCHARD, EDWARD. 40

Great-great-grandson of Captain George Trenchard (1720–1780), Captain 1st Battalion Salem County (New Jersey) Militia, Colonel Ebenezer Dick, 1776; Captain New Jersey Light Horse Militia, 1778; Chairman of Committee of Safety and Correspondence, Salem County, New Jersey, 1774–5.

Also, Great-grandson of Captain Joshua Sands, (1758–1835), Commissary's Department, Continental Army.

Also, Great-grandson of Ensign John Barclay (1749–1816), Ensign Philadelphia Associators, 1776; Member of Philadelphia Light Horse, 1780.

259

Elected.   No. of
                                                            Insignia.
1891. TROWBRIDGE, SAMUEL BRECK PARKMAN,

Great-grandson of Lieutenant Luther Trowbridge
(1756–1802), Lieutenant in Captain Parker's Company
7th Regiment Massachusetts Continental Infantry,
Colonel John Brooks, July 1, 1777, to 1782; Lieutenant in Captain Jonathan Maynard's Company same
Regiment, January, 1782.

1889. TUCKER, CUMMINGS HATFIELD, JR.,

Great-great-grandson of Captain Isaac Halsey, Eastern
Battalion Morris County (New Jersey) Militia, 1775;
served throughout the war.

1889. TUCKER, EDWIN B.,

Great-great-grandson of Captain Isaac Halsey, Eastern
Battalion Morris County (New Jersey) Militia, 1775;
served throughout the war.

1889. TUCKER, FRANCIS CUMMINGS,   418

Great-great-grandson of Captain Isaac Halsey, Eastern
Battalion Morris County (New Jersey) Militia, 1775;
served throughout the war.

1889. TUCKER, WILLIAM ALONZO,   66

Great-great-grandson of Captain Isaac Halsey, Eastern
Battalion Morris County (New Jersey) Militia, 1775;
served throughout the war.

1891. TUFTS, WALTER BROWNELL,

Great-great-grandson of Lieutenant Thomas Emerson,
Essex County Militia, Massachusetts, "Lexington
Alarm," 1775.
Also, Great-great-grandson of Sergeant Samuel Brad-
street, Essex County Militia, Massachusetts, "Lex-
ington Alarm," 1775.

1890. TURNER, GILBERT HUBBARD,

Great-great-grandson of Ensign John Turner, 6th Battalion Philadelphia County Militia, Pennsylvania.

No. of
Insignia.

1890.   TURNER, JOHN CLOCK,   339

Great-grandson of Private John Clock (1757-1838).
Captain Bell's Company 9th Connecticut Militia,
Lieutenant-Colonel Mead, December 24, 1776.

1889.   TURNER, THOMAS MORGAN,   93

Great-great-grandson of Ensign John Turner, 6th Battalion Philadelphia County Militia, Pennsylvania.

1890.   TURNER, THORNTON FLOYD,

Great-great-grandson of William Floyd (1734-1821),
Signer of Declaration of Independence, and Colonel
1st Regiment Suffolk County Militia, New York,
1775.

1891.   TURRILL, HENRY STUART. Captain and Assistant-Sur-
geon, U. S. A.,   611

Grandson of Private John Turrill (1756-1829). Captain
Ebenezer Couch's Company, Colonel Andrew
Ward's Regiment Connecticut Militia, February,
1776; served around New York, 1776; later in Continental Service in same Regiment.

1889.   TUTTLE, EZRA B.,   211

Great-grandson of Captain James Green, 2d Regiment
Connecticut Militia Light Horse (Major Elijah Hyde),
at "Saratoga."

1889.   TYLER, HENRY WHITNEY,

Great-grandson of Captain James Green, 2d Regiment
Connecticut Militia Light Horse (Major Elijah Hyde),
at "Saratoga."

1885.   TYLER, MASON W.,   143

Great-grandson of Timothy Edwards, Committee of
Safety for Berkshire County Massachusetts; also
Commissary of Supplies for Massachusetts.
Also, Great-grandson of Dr. William Whitney, mem-
ber of Massachusetts Provincial Congress, 1775.

261

Great-grandson of Lieutenant John Odell (1756–1835),
Private in Captain John Oakley's Company, West-
chester County Militia, August 21, 1775; Private in
Captain Stephen Oakley's Company, Westchester
County Militia, New York, May, 1775, Colonel Samuel
Drake; Private in Captain Seybert Acker's Company,
Colonel Morris Graham's Regiment New York Levies,
May, 1778; Private in Captain Daniel Williams'
Company, Lieutenant-Colonel Albert Pawling's Regi-
ment of New York Levies, raised for defence of the
frontier, May 11, 1780; also General Guide to the
army in Westchester County.

Also, Great-grandson of Lieutenant David Hunt (1757–
1819), Private in Captain Ricker's Company, 2d
Regiment New York Line, May 5, 1778, to February
17, 1779; Quartermaster-Lieutenant 5th Regiment
New York Line, Colonel Lewis Dubois, July 1, 1780;
Quartermaster 3d Regiment New York Levies, Colonel Morris Graham, 1780.

Also, Great-grandson of Lieutenant Jonathan Owens,
Ensign in Captain Isaiah Beal's Company, 2d
Regiment Ulster County Militia, Colonel James
Clinton, October 25, 1775; later Lieutenant in same.

Also, Great-grandson of Lieutenant Gilbert Taylor
(1744–1805), 1st Lieutenant in Captain Nicholas Ber-
rian's Company, Westchester County Militia, New
York, October 31, 1775.

1888.   VAIL, CHARLES MONTGOMERY,

110

Great-grandson of Lieutenant Joseph Vail, 2d Lieutenant in Colonel Drake's and Van Cortlandt's Regiment (3d or Manor of Van Cortlandt); in active
service from August 15, 1778, to November 20, 1781.

Also, Great-great-grandson of Private Gilbert T. Vail,
Orange County Militia, killed at Minisink Massacre,
July 22, 1779.

262

Elected.

No, of
Insignia.

1888. VAIL, JAMES WILLIAM,

Great-grandson of Lieutenant Joseph Vail, 2d Lieutenant in Colonel Drake's and Van Cortlandt's Regiment (3d or Manor of Van Cortlandt); in active service from August 15, 1778, to November 20, 1781. *Also,* Great-great-grandson of Private Gilbert T. Vail, Orange County Militia, killed at Minisink Massacre, July 22, 1779.

1886. VALENTINE, ABRAHAM B.,   **35**

Great-grandson of Edward Briggs, Committee of Safety, Westchester County, New York. 1776-77.

1890. VALENTINE, BENJAMIN EYRE,   **64**

Great-grandson of Lieutenant-Colonel Benjamin Eyre (1747-1789), 2d Battalion Militia, Philadelphia Associators, served throughout the war.

1891. VAN ANTWERP, WILLIAM,

Great-grandson of Private Nicholas Van Antwerp (1760-1825), 1st Battalion New York City Militia. Colonel John Lasher, July 30, 1776. *Also,* Great-grandson of Private Leonard Fisher (——1835), 1st Battalion New York City Militia. Colonel John Lasher, 1776.

1885. VANDERPOEL, JOHN A.,   **344**

Great-grandson of Major and Brevet Lieutenant-Colonel Benjamin Tallmadge (1754-1835), Captain, 1776, Major Sheldon's Light Dragoons: 1777, conducted "secret service" for the Commander-in-Chief; captured Fort George, Long Island. November 21, 1780, and received special notice of Congress: Lieutenant-Colonel by brevet, 1783. *Also,* Great-great-grandson of William Floyd (1734-1821). Signer of the Declaration of Independence. and Colonel 1st Regiment Suffolk County Militia. New York, 1775.

1891. VAN DYK, JAMES,   676

Great-grandson of Captain-Lieutenant John Van Dyk
(1754 1810), Captain 1st Battalion New York City
Militia, Colonel John Lasher, September, 1776; 1st
Lieutenant 2d Regiment Continental Corps of Artillery, Colonel Lamb, November, 1776; promoted Captain Lieutenant, and Major by brevet at close of war.

1889. VAN LENNEP, FREDERIC.

Great-great-great-grandson of Governor Jonathan
Trumbull, LL. D. (1710-1785), Connecticut.

1889. VAN RENSSELAER, CORTLANDT SCHUYLER.

Great grandson of Major James Van Rensselaer, (1747–
1827), Aide-de-Camp (with rank of Captain) to Major-
General Richard Montgomery, 1775; served through
the Canada Campaign at Fort Chambly, St. Johns,
Montreal and Quebec; Aide-de-Camp (with rank of
Major) to Major-General Philip Schuyler, 1776;
served with the Northern Army.

1889. VAN RENSSELAER, REVEREND MAUNSELL, D. D., LL.D.,

Great-grandson of Colonel Killian Van Rensselaer
(1717-1781), Quartermaster 8th Regiment Albany
County Militia (1st Claverack Battalion, New York,
Colonel Robert Van Rensselaer, July 25, 1778;
Colonel 4th Regiment Albany County Militia, April
1, 1778; Member of Albany Committee of Correspondence, 1775.

1888. VAN VECHTEN, ABRAHAM VAN WYCK (Life Member),   29

Grandson of Captain Samuel Van Vechten, 1st Regi-
ment Albany County Militia, New York, Colonel
Van Schaick.
Also, Great-grandson of Theodorus Van Wyck, M. D.,
Member of the New York Provincial Congress, and
Commissioner of Sequestration for Dutchess County.
Also, Great-grandson of Captain Samuel Haight, of
Manor of Cortlandt Regiment, New York, Colonel
Pierre Van Cortlandt.

264

Elected.

No. of
Insignia.

1886. VAN WINKLE, EDGAR BEACH,

Great-great-grandson of Fife-Major Abram Goodwin,
5th New York Line. Colonel Lewis Dubois.

1883. VARNUM, JAMES M.,   70

Great-grandson of Major-General Joseph Bradley Varnum, Captain 7th Regiment Massachusetts Militia
Infantry, 1776: Captain 11th Regiment Massachusetts
Militia Infantry, 1781: later Major-General of Massachusetts Militia.

Also, Great-grandnephew and Representative of Major-
General James M. Varnum, Brigadier-General Continental Army, 1777–9; Major-General commanding
Rhode Island State Militia in United States service,
1780; and Member of Continental Congress.

Also, Great-grandson of Major Augustus Pease, (1757–
1791), Sergeant in Captain Oliver Hanchett's Com-
pany 2d Regiment Connecticut Continental Infantry,
Colonel Israel Putnam, 1775, at siege of Boston;
Major and Aide-de-Camp to Major-General Spencer,
April 21, 1777.

Also, Great-great-grandson of Sergeant Joseph Pease,
Private in Captain Elihu Kent's Company Suffield
(Connecticut) Militia, "Lexington Alarm," April 19,
1775; Private in Captain Oliver Hanchett's Company
2d Regiment Connecticut Continental Infantry, Col-
onel Israel Putnam, May 28, 1775, at siege of Bos-
ton: Private in 2d Regiment Connecticut Line,
Colonel Charles Webb, July 1, 1780; Private in Cap-
tain Samuel Granger's Company, 2d Battalion
Connecticut State Troops, Major Elijah Humphrey,
Waterbury's Brigade, June 30, 1781; Quartermaster
July 12, 1781.

Also, Great-great-great-grandson of Private Josiah
King, in Captain Elihu Kent's Company Suffield
(Connecticut) Militia, "Lexington Alarm," April 19,
1775.

Also, Great-great-grandson of Private Jacob Butler,
Private in Captain Amos Gage's Company, Colonel
Daniel Moore's Regiment New Hampshire Volunteer
Infantry, September 29, 1777, at "Saratoga."

265

Elected.

No. of
Insignia.

Also, Great-great-grandson of Private Andrew Graham (1728-1785). Private in Captain John Hinman's Company 13th Regiment Connecticut Militia, Colonel Benjamin Hinman, August 18, 1776, served around New York; later Surgeon in same Regiment.

1890. VERNON, WILLIAM BRYAN,

Great-great-grandson of William Vernon (1719-1806), President of the Continental Navy Board, Rhode Island.

1885. VER PLANCK, WILLIAM GORDON,   153

Great-great-grandson of Lieutenant-Colonel James Gordon, 12th Regiment Albany County Militia, New York, Colonel Van Schoonhoven; captured, taken to Canada, October 17, 1780; exchanged November 19, 1782.

1891. VIELE, SHELDON THOMPSON,

Great-great-grandson of Lieutenant-Colonel Jabez Thompson (——1776), Major of Derby (Connecticut) Militia, "Lexington Alarm," April 19, 1775; Major 1st Regiment Connecticut Militia. Colonel David Wooster, May 1, 1775; Lieutenant-Colonel 2d Regiment Connecticut Militia, 1776; killed in the retreat from New York, September 15, 1776.

Also, Great-great-grandson of Colonel John Knickerbacker (1723-1812), 14th Regiment Albany County Militia, New York.

1887. WAINWRIGHT, JOHN TILLOTSON,

Great-grandson of Surgeon Thomas Tillotson, Maryland Line, and 1st Lieutenant Queen Anne County Militia, Captain Kent, February 3, 1776.

Also, Great-grandson of Lieutenant-Colonel Robert R. Livingston, Jr., 10th Regiment Albany County Militia, New York.

Also, Great-great-grandson of Robert R. Livingston, Member of Continental Congress, 1776; Member New York Provincial Congress, 1776-8; Secretary for Foreign Affairs, 1781-3; Chancellor New York, 1783.

No. of
Insignia.

1889. Wainwright. William Pratt. Jr.,

Great-grandson of Surgeon Thomas Tillotson, Maryland
Line, and 1st Lieutenant Queen Anne County
Militia, Captain Kent, February 3, 1776.

Also, Great-grandson of Lieutenant-Colonel Robert R.
Livingston, Jr., 10th Regiment Albany County
Militia.

Also, Great-great-grandson of Robert R. Livingston,
Member of Continental Congress, 1776; Member
New York Provincial Congress, 1776-8; Secretary
for Foreign Affairs, 1781-3; Chancellor New York,
1783.

1888. Wakeman, Abram. 39

Great-grandson of Private Ebenezer Wakeman, Captain
Dimon's Company Minute Men, that marched from
Fairfield, Connecticut, on Lexington Alarm, 1775.

1889. Walbridge, Robert Ryckman.

Great-great-grandson of Colonel Ebenezer Walbridge,
(1738-1819), Lieutenant in Captain Gideon Brownson's Company, Colonel Seth Warner's Regiment Vermont Militia, March 3, 1776; Acting Adjutant of the
Regiment in the Canadian Expedition; Colonel Vermont Militia, 1780; Member of Assembly, 1778-80.

1890. Walden, Daniel Treadwell,

Grandson of Assistant Purser Jacob Walden, of New
Hampshire, Continental Sloop-of-War "Ranger,"
Captain John Paul Jones.

1892. Walker, William Augustus, 799

Great-grandson of Quartermaster Thomas Williams
(1754-1811), 3d Regiment New York Line, Colonel
Peter Gansevoort, November 21, 1776.

Elected.

Also, Grandson of Private Joseph Walker (1760 1852), served as guard under Sergeant Breck in Hopkinton (Massachusetts) Militia, April, 1776; Private in Captain Samuel Burbank's Company Massachusetts Militia, for service in Rhode Island, January, 1778; Private in Captain Perry's Company, Colonel Cyprian Howe's Regiment Massachusetts Militia, Rhode Island service, August, 1778; Private in Captain Mc-Farland's Company, Colonel Cyprian Howe's Regiment, for Rhode Island service, September, 1780.

1890. WALLACE, WILLIAM ADDISON,   **475**

Great-grandson of Private Abijah Thompson, (1739–1811), Captain Samuel Belknap's Company, Woburn Militia, Massachusetts, on duty at Cambridge, April 19. 1775.

1891. WARD, REGINALD HENSHAWE,

Great-great-grandson of Major-General Artemas Ward (1727–1800), Major-General Continental Army, October 27, 1774; Commander-in-Chief of Massachusetts forces, May 19, 1775; Commander-in-Chief of Continental forces, June 15, 1775; Senior Major-General Continental Army, June 17, 1775; Member of Massachusetts Provincial Congress, 1775; Member of Massachusetts Executive Council, 1777; Member of Continental Congress, 1779.

1887. WARD, SYLVESTER L. H. (Life Member),   **249**

Great-grandson of Stephen Ward (1730 1797), Member of 1st, 2d and 3d Provincial Congresses from Westchester County, New York; Member of New York Assembly, 1779; Member of New York Senate, 1779–87.

1888. WARLEY, FELIX,

Grandson of Captain Felix Warley, 1st Regiment Line, South Carolina.

268

Elected.

No. of
Insignia.

1890. WARNER, JAMES MEECH,

Great-grandson of Lieutenant Joseph Little (——
1791), Captain Ezekiel Giles' Company of Volunteers
from Plaistow, New Hampshire, joined the Northern
Army at Saratoga, October, 1777.

1883. WARREN, ASA COOLIDGE,   7

Grandson of Private Timothy Warren, Captain John
Holley's Company Massachusetts Militia; served
under General Gates, 1777.

1890. WARREN, CHARLES ELLIOTT,   340

Great-grandson of Private William Warren (1751–
1831), Captain Abram Peirce's Company, Colonel
Thomas Gardner's Regiment, Massachusetts.
Also, Great-grandson of Private Azor Phelps, Captain
Benjamin Allton's Company, Colonel John Rand's
Regiment, Massachusetts Militia, July 22, 1780.

1891. WARREN, EDWARD STEVENS,   598

Great-great-grandson of Lieutenant-Colonel Jabez
Thompson (—— 1776), Major of Derby (Connecticut)
Militia, "Lexington Alarm," April 19, 1775; Major
1st Regiment Connecticut Militia, Colonel David
Wooster, May 1, 1775; Lieutenant-Colonel 2d Regiment Connecticut Militia, 1776; killed in the retreat
from New York, September 15, 1776.

1889. WARREN, HENRY T.,

Great-great-grandson of Colonel Andrew Adams
(—— 1797), Major Connecticut Militia, 1777; Lieutenant-Colonel, 1779; Colonel 17th Regiment Connecticut Militia, 1780; Delegate Continental Congress,
1777–80 (Speaker, 1779–80); Member Connecticut
Council of Safety.
Also, Great-great-grandson of Surgeon John Warren
(1753–1815), Surgeon in Essex County (Massachusetts)
Militia, "Lexington Alarm," April 19, 1775; subsequently appointed Hospital Surgeon in Boston, and
continued so during the war.

269

Also, Great-great-grandson of Brigade-Major John Canfield, Adjutant Sheldon's Dragoons, 1776; Brigade-Major in Brigadier-General Oliver Wolcott's Detachment, "at Saratoga," 1777; Member Continental Congress.

1891. WARREN, WILLIAM YOUNG,   548

Great-great-grandson of Lieutenant-Colonel Jabez Thompson (—— 1776), Major of Derby (Connecticut) Militia "Lexington Alarm," April 19, 1775; Major 1st Regiment Connecticut Militia, Colonel David Wooster, May 1, 1775; Lieutenant-Colonel 2d Regiment Connecticut Militia, 1776; killed in the retreat from New York, September 15, 1776.

1891. WAYNE, REVEREND HENRY N.,

Great-great-grandson of Brigade-Major Jonathan Lawrence, Brigade-Major Queens County Militia, 1775; Lieutenant in Colonel William Malcolm's Regiment "additional Continental," 1777; Captain in Lieutenant-Colonel H. K. Van Rensselaer's Regiment New York Levies, 1779; Captain in Colonel John Harper's Regiment New York Levies, in service of United States, 1780; Member New York Provincial Congress, 1776.

1889. WEBB, FRANCIS PARSONS,

Great-grandson of Colonel Samuel Blachley Webb, 3d Connecticut Line, and Aide-de-Camp to General Washington.

1889. WEBB, LELAND JUSTIN,

Great-grandson of Private Moses Webb (1756–1850), Connecticut Militia.

1890. WEED, HENRY F.,

Grandson of Private John Clock (1757–1838), Captain Bell's Company, 9th Regiment Connecticut Militia, Lieutenant-Colonel John Mead, December 24, 1776.

1889. WEEKS, BARTOW S.,   136

    Great-grandson of Surgeon Ebenezer White, 3d West-
chester County Militia, New York, Colonel Van
Cortlandt, 1778–81.

1891. WELLINGTON, ARTHUR MELLON,   596

    Great-grandson of Lieutenant Benjamin Wellington
(1743–1812), Private in Captain John Bridges' Company, Colonel Eliezer Brooks' Regiment Massachusetts Militia, May 6, 1775; Sergeant in Captain Samuel Farrar's Company same Regiment, September 29,
1777; served with General Gates in Northern Army;
3d Lieutenant 3d Company, 3d Regiment Middlesex
County (Massachusetts) Militia, Colonel Faulkner,
June 7, 1780.

    Also, Great-great-grandson of Lieutenant-Colonel Gor-
don Hutchins (1733–1815), Captain in Colonel John
Stark's Regiment New Hampshire Volunteer Militia,
April 23, 1775; Lieutenant-Colonel in Colonel Na-
hum Baldwin's Regiment New Hampshire Volunteer
Militia, September 17, 1776; served around New York.

1891. WEMPLE, CHRISTOPHER YATES,   509

    Great-grandson of Quartermaster Jacob Van Alstyne,
6th Regiment Albany County Militia, New York,
1775, Colonel Stephen J. Schuyler; later Adjutant
same regiment.

    Also, Great-grandson of Captain Daniel Brainard, Col-
onel Comfort Sage's Regiment Connecticut Militia,
1779.

1891. WEMPLE, EDWARD LANSING,   510

    Great-great-grandson of Quartermaster Jacob Van Al-
styne, 6th Regiment Albany County Militia, New
York, 1775, Colonel Stephen J. Schuyler; later Adjutant same regiment.

    Also, Great-great-grandson of Captain Daniel Brainard,
Colonel Comfort Sage's Regiment Connecticut Militia,
1779.

1891.   WEMPLE, HARRY YATES,   511

Great-great-grandson of Quartermaster Jacob Van Alstyne, 6th Regiment Albany County Militia, New
York, 1775, Colonel Stephen J. Schuyler; later Adjutant same regiment.

Also, Great-great-grandson of Captain Daniel Brainard,
Colonel Comfort Sage's Regiment Connecticut Militia,
1779.

1891.   WEMPLE, HENRY YATES,

Great-grandson of Quartermaster Jacob Van Alstyne,
6th Regiment Albany County Militia, New York,
1775, Colonel Stephen J. Schuyler; later Adjutant
same regiment.

1891.   WEMPLE, JOHN RUSS,

Great-grandson of Quartermaster Jacob Van Alstyne,
6th Regiment Albany County Militia, New York,
1775, Colonel Stephen J. Schuyler; later Adjutant
same regiment.

1891.   WESSELS, HENRY WALTON,   575

Great-great-grandson of Private Elijah Holcombe (1731
——), 3d Company, Captain Roger Enos, 2d Regiment Connecticut Militia, Colonel Joseph Spencer,
1775; Private Captain James Judson's Company,
Major John Skinner's Regiment Connecticut Light
Horse Militia, 1776; Private "Sheldon's" Dragoons,
1781–3.

1886.   WESTON, REVEREND DANIEL CONY, D. D.,   141

Grandson of Adjutant Daniel Cony, Massachusetts
Militia.

1891.   WESTBROOK, FREDERICK E.,   629

Grandson of Ensign Frederick Westbrook (1749–1823),
3d Rochester Company Ulster County Militia, Colonel Levi Pawling, May 3, 1776.

Also, Grandson of Captain Isaac Van Wyck, 2d Regiment, Rondout Precinct, Dutchess County Minute
Men, Colonel Dirck Brinckerhoff, October 17, 1775;
previously (February 26, 1775), Ensign in same.

Elected.

No. of
Insignia.

1890. WETMORE, EDWARD WILLARD,

Great-grandson of Surgeon Elias Willard (1756–1827), Private in Massachusetts Militia; served at Boston, April, 1775; Surgeon in Massachusetts Hospitals, 1777; Surgeon in Colonel Frost's Marine Regiment, stationed on the Hudson, 1777; Surgeon in Military Hospitals at Boston, 1780–5.

1891. WHEELER, REVEREND HORACE LESLIE,

Great-great-grandson of Lieutenant-Colonel Abijah Brown (1736–1818), Captain of Watertown (Massachusetts) Militia, 1775; Lieutenant-Colonel in Colonel Ruggles Woodbridge's Regiment, June, 1776, at "Bunker's Hill"; Lieutenant-Colonel in Colonel Ephraim Wheelock's Regiment Suffolk County (Massachusetts) Militia, 1776; Lieutenant-Colonel in Thomas Poor's Regiment Massachusetts Militia, raised for defence of the North River, June 26, 1776.

Also, Great-grandson of Corporal Eli Jones (1756–1811), Private in Captain Abraham Peirce's Company, Colonel Thomas Gardiner's Regiment Massachusetts Minute Men, at Concord and Lexington, April, 1775; Private in Captain Abijah Lamb's Company, Colonel Jonathan Holman's Regiment Massachusetts Militia, 1776; Private in Captain Isaac Martin's Company, Colonel Joseph Whitney's Regiment Massachusetts Militia, served in Rhode Island, May, 1777; Private in Captain Edward Fuller's Company, Colonel William McIntosh's Regiment Massachusetts Militia, March 19, 1778; Private in Captain Peirce's Company, Colonel Stearns' Regiment, detached to serve for nine months in Continental Army, 1779; Corporal among the Six Months' Men raised in Waltham for Continental service, July 11, 1780.

Also, Great-great-grandson of Deputy Brigade Commissary Stephen Nye (1720–1810), 1st Lieutenant in Elizabeth Island Militia, January 1, 1776; Deputy Brigade Commissary same, 1776; Member of Massachusetts Provincial Congress, 1775.

273

1890. WHIPPLE, CHARLES HENRY, Major, U. S. A.,   482

Great-great-grandson of Stephen Ward (1730-1797),
Member of 1st, 2d and 3d Provincial Congresses, from
Westchester County, New York: Member of New
York Assembly, 1779; Member of New York Senate,
1779 87.

1891. WHITE, REVEREND ERSKINE NORMAN,

Great-grandson of Captain Jonathan Hale (1716-1776),
Captain 6th Company, Colonel Erastus Wolcott's
Regiment Connecticut State Troops, 1776; died in
service near Boston, March 7, 1776.
Also, Great-grandson of Private Moses Stanley, Private
in Major Thomas Brown's Company Coventry (Connecticut) Militia, "Lexington Alarm," April 19, 1775.

1891. WHITE, WILLIAM DARLING,   572

Grandson of Private Antipass White (1739-1820), Colonel Canfield's Regiment Connecticut Militia, Septem-
tember, 1781; at West Point, 1781.

1890. WHITEHEAD, IRA CONDICT, M. D.,   455

Grandson of 2d Lieutenant and Brevet-Captain William
I. Pennington of New Jersey (1757-1826), Sergeant
2d Regiment Continental Corps of Artillery, Colonel
Lamb, March 7, 1777; promoted 2d Lieutenant, September 12, 1778; Captain by brevet.

1891. WHITTEMORE, WILLIAM LAWRENCE,

Great-great-grandson of Private Samuel Whittemore
(1696-1793), Private in Charlestown (Massachusetts)
Company of Minute Men; severely wounded in the
action at Lexington, April 19, 1775.

274

No. of
Insignia.

1889. WILCOX, REYNOLD WEBB, *M. D.*, 139

Great-great-grandson of Lieutenant Timothy Field,
Sergeant in Ensign Jehiel Meigs' Company Guilford
(Connecticut) Militia, "Lexington Alarm," April,
1775; Private in 2d Company, Captain Andrew
Ward, Colonel David Wooster's Regiment Connecticut Militia, 1775; Lieutenant in 7th Regiment Connecticut Militia, Colonel Worthington, 1780; Lieutenant in Captain Peter Vaill's Company, Connecticut Coast Guards, 1781.

Also, Great-grandson of Private Reynold Webb, Captain Kirtland's Company 6th Connecticut Line, Colonel William Douglass, June 2, 1777.

Also, Great-grandson of Sergeant Daniel Meigs (1747–
1822), Sergeant in Ensign Jehiel Meigs' Company
Guilford Militia, "Lexington Alarm," April, 1775;
Sergeant in Captain Peter Vaill's Company, Connecticut Coast Guards, 1781.

1890. WILDMAN, HENRY GREEN,

Great-grandson of Captain James Green, 2d Regiment
Connecticut Militia Light Horse (Major Elijah Hyde),
at "Saratoga."

Also, Great-grandson of Private Philo Canfield, Captain
Nathan Chapman's Company, Colonel John Mead's
Regiment Connecticut Militia.

Also, Great-great-grandson of Lieutenant-Colonel Samuel Canfield, 1st Battalion Connecticut State Troops,
Colonel Samuel Whiting.

1891. WILEY, WILLIAM MELIN, 713

Great-great-grandson of Major John James (1732–1791),,
Major in General Marion's Brigade South Carolina
Militia.

1890. WILLARD, DAVID SEYMOUR,

Great-grandson of Surgeon Elias Willard (1756–1827),
Private in Massachusetts Militia; served at Boston,
April, 1775; Surgeon in Massachusetts Hospitals,
1777; Surgeon in Colonel Frost's Marine Regiment,
stationed on the Hudson, 1777; Surgeon in Military
Hospitals at Boston, 1780–5.

1891. WILLIAMS, CHARLES HOWARD,   740

Great-grandson of Ensign Benjamin Williams (1744-
1835), Captain Parker's Company, Colonel Moses
Nichols' Regiment, Stark's Brigade, New Hampshire
Volunteer Infantry, July 19, 1777, at "Stillwater."

1890. WILLIAMS, ROBERT DAY,

Great-grandson of Corporal Isaac Foot, of Connecticut
(1746-1843), Corporal in 2d Regiment Continental
Corps of Artillery, Colonel Lamb, May 1, 1777.

1890. WILLIAMS, WILLIAM TYLEE,   479

Great-grandson of Private William Lippincott (
1801), Captain Walton's Troop Light Dragoons,
Monmouth County, New Jersey.

1891. WILLIAMSON, NICHOLAS, M. D.,

Great-great-grandson of Colonel James Abeel (1738-
1825), of New Jersey, Deputy Quartermaster General
Continental Army.

1885. WILSON, HENRY APPLEGATE,   464

Great-grandson of Lieutenant and Brevet Captain Wessel Ten Broeck Stout, 2d Lieutenant 4th Battalion 2d
Establishment, New Jersey Line, 1777; transferred to
3d Battalion; Ensign 3d Regiment New Jersey Line;
Lieutenant ditto, 1782; Lieutenant 1st Regiment
New Jersey Line; discharged at close of war; Captain by brevet.

1891. WILSON, ROBERT PRESTON,

Grandson of Ensign Robert Wilson (1763-1811), 2d
Company, Captain John Graham, 1st Regiment New
York Line, Colonel Van Schaick, June 29, 1781.

1889. WINNE, CHARLES KNICKERBACKER, Major, Surgeon
U. S. A.,   131

Great-great-grandson of Ensign Douw J. Fonda, 3d
Regiment New York Line, Colonel Gansevoort, May
29, 1779; mustered to the end of the war.

Also, Great-grandson of Adjutant Jacob Winne, Adjutant of 14th Regiment Albany County (New York) Militia, Colonel Yates, October, 1779; Quartermaster of Lieutenant-Colonel Marinus Willet's Regiment Militia, August 7, 1781.

Also, Great-great-grandson of Colonel John Knickerbacker (1723-1802), 14th Albany County Militia, New York.

1830.   WISNER, CHARLES.

Great-great-grandson of Lieutenant-Colonel Henry Wisner, Major Florida and Warwick Regiment Orange County Militia, 1776; Lieutenant-Colonel same Regiment (Colonel John Hathorn), February 19, 1778; Member New York Provincial Congress, 1775; Member of Continental Congress, 1776.

Also, Great-grandson of Ensign Gabriel Wisner, Orange County Militia (Colonel John Hathorn) ; killed in action at Minisink, on the Delaware, July 22, 1779.

1891.   WISNER, LEWIS SMITH.   625

Great-grandson of Lieutenant-Colonel Henry Wisner, Major Florida and Warwick Regiment Orange County Militia, 1776; Lieutenant-Colonel same Regiment (Colonel John Hathorn), February 19, 1778; Member New York Provincial Congress, 1775; Member of Continental Congress, 1776.

1891.   WISNER, PERCY.

Great-grandson of Ensign Gabriel Wisner, Orange County Militia (Colonel John Hathorn); killed in action at Minisink, on the Delaware, July 22, 1779.

Also, Great-great-grandson of Lieutenant-Colonel Henry Wisner, Major Florida and Warwick Regiment Orange County Militia, 1776; Lieutenant-Colonel same Regiment (Colonel John Hathorn), February 19, 1778; Member New York Provincial Congress, 1775; Member of Continental Congress, 1776.

Elected.

1891. WISNER, WILLIAM HENRY,

Grandson of Ensign Gabriel Wisner, Orange County
Militia (Colonel John Hathorn); killed in action at
Minisink, on the Delaware, July 22, 1779.

Also, Great-grandson of Lieutenant-Colonel Henry
Wisner, Major Florida and Warwick Regiment
Orange County Militia, 1776; Lieutenant-Colonel
same Regiment (Colonel John Hathorn), February
19, 1778; Member New York Provincial Congress,
1775; Member of Continental Congress, 1776.

1891. WITHERBEE, FRANK SPENCER,

Great-great-grandson of First Lieutenant Thomas With-
erby (1747-1828), Captain Thomas Knowlton's Shrews-
bury Company, 6th Regiment Massachusetts Militia,
Colonel Job Cushing, 1777.

1890. WODELL, SILAS, 417

Great-great-grandson of Captain Cornelius Van Wyck,
5th Regiment Dutchess County (New York) Militia,
Colonel Abraham Brinckerhoff, killed at White
Plains, October 31, 1776.

Also, Great-great-grandson of Colonel James Vande-
burgh (1729 ——), 5th Regiment Dutchess County
Militia (Beekman's Precinct), March 10, 1778.

Also, Great-grandson of Private Aaron Hall (1760-
1839), Captain Stephen Hall's Company 7th Regiment Connecticut Continental Infantry, Colonel
Heman Swift, May 15, 1780.

Also, Great-great-grandson of Captain Noah Wheeler
(1744-1823), Ensign in Captain Robert Freeman's
Company 6th Regiment (Charlotte Precinct) Dutchess
County (New York) Militia, Colonel David Souther-
land, October 17, 1775; promoted 1st Lieutenant
March 20, 1778; promoted Captain June 25, 1778.

1887. WOOD, SAMUEL SEYMOUR, 635

Grandson of Private Samuel Wood (1740 ——), Private 8th Company 1st Regiment New York Line,
Colonel Van Schaick, 1776; Private 2d Company 4th
Regiment New York Line, Colonel H. B. Livingston,
1777.

Elected.		No. of Insignia.

1891. WOODHULL, JESSE CALVIN, 715
Great-grandson of Colonel Jesse Woodhull (1735–1799),
Orange County (New York) Militia (Woodhull's),
and Member New York Provincial Congress, 1775.

1891. WOODRUFF, CARLE AUGUSTUS, Captain and Brevet Lieu-
tenant-Colonel, U. S. A., 631
Great-grandson of Captain Israel Carle (—— 1822),
Hunterdon Troop of Light Horse New Jersey Militia,
October 6, 1777.
Also, Great-great-grandson of Lieutenant-Colonel
Thomas Lowry, 3d Regiment Hunterdon County
(New Jersey) Militia, June 19, 1777; later Colonel
same Regiment.

1889. WOODRUFF, CHARLES HORNBLOWER, 343
Great-grandson of Private James Woodruff (1749–
1813), Captain Bezaleel Beebe's Company, Colonel
Andrew Ward, Jr.'s, Regiment Connecticut Militia.
Also, Great-great-grandson of Surgeon-General William
Burnet (1730–1791), Surgeon 1st Battalion 1st Es-
tablishment, New Jersey Line, December 8, 1775;
Surgeon 1st Battalion 2d Establishment, November
28, 1776; Surgeon 1st Regiment; resigned, and ap-
pointed Surgeon-General for Eastern District Con-
tinental Army, 1781–3.
Also, Great-grandson of Josiah Hornblower, Speaker
of Lower House (Assembly) Provincial Congress,
New Jersey, 1780; Member of Upper House (Coun-
cil), 1781–4.
Also, Great-grandson of Captain Joseph Alling, Essex
County Militia, New Jersey, 1776.

1890. *WOODRUFF, HENRY DWIGHT (died November 29, 1891), 408
Great-grandson of Captain Ambrose Sloper (1735–1822),
1st Lieutenant 1st Company, Captain Gad Stanley,
2d Battalion, Colonel Fisher Gay, Wadsworth's Brigade Connecticut Militia, June, 1776; Captain of
Farmington Company of Volunteers, January 15,
1777; Captain in 15th Regiment Connecticut Militia,
1778; Captain of Connecticut Militia, "New Haven
Alarm," 1779; Captain in Provisional Regiment
Connecticut Militia, 1781.

Also, Grandson of Private Samuel Woodruff (1744
1840), Private in 4th Company, Captain David
Welch, 1st Regiment Connecticut Militia, Colonel
David Wooster, 1775; Private in Captain Judson's
Company, Major John Skinner's Regiment Connecti
cut Light Horse Militia, January 7, 1776; Private
in Captain Jesse Curtis' Company, Colonel Hooker's
Regiment in Continental Service at Peekskill, April
5, 1776.

Also, Great-grandson of Lieutenant Elisha Root (1737–
1776), 1st Company, Captain Noadiah Hooker,
Colonel Erastus Wolcott's Regiment Connecticut
Militia, stationed at Eastchester, New York, Jan
uary, 1776; died there in service, September, 1776.

Also, Great-grandson of Lieutenant-Colonel John
Strong (1733–1816), Sergeant 1st Company 4th Regi
ment Connecticut Militia, Colonel Hinman, May,
1775; Ensign 8th Regiment Connecticut Line,
Colonel Chandler, January 1, 1777; promoted Lieu
tenant, April 11, 1778; Major 17th Regiment Con
necticut Militia, Colonel Oliver Wolcott, January,
1780; Lieutenant Colonel same, May, 1783.

1890. WOODRUFF, MORRIS,

Great-grandson of Private James Woodruff (1749–
1813), Captain Bezaleel Beebe's Company, Colonel
Andrew Ward, Jr.'s Regiment Connecticut Militia.

Also, Great-great-grandson of Surgeon General Wil
liam Burnet (1730–1791), Surgeon 1st Battalion 1st
Establishment, New Jersey Line, December 8, 1775;
Surgeon 1st Battalion 2d Establishment, November
28, 1776; Surgeon 1st Regiment; resigned, and ap
pointed Surgeon-General for Eastern District Con
tinental Army, 1781–3.

Also, Great-grandson of Josiah Hornblower, Speaker
of Lower House (Assembly) Provincial Congress,
New Jersey, 1780; member of Upper House (Council),
1781–1784.

Also, Great-grandson of Captain Joseph Alling, Essex
County Militia, New Jersey, 1776.

280

1891. WOODRUFF, THOMAS MAYHEW, Captain U. S. A.,   716

Great-grandson of Captain Israel Carle (—— 1822),
Hunterdon Troop of Light Horse New Jersey Militia,
October 6, 1777.

Also, Great-great-grandson of Lieutenant-Colonel
Thomas Lowry, 3d Regiment Hunterdon County
(New Jersey) Militia. June 19, 1777; later Colonel
same Regiment.

1885. WRIGHT, W. F., *M. D.,*

Great-grandson of Private John Putnam, Private in
Captain William Belcher's Company Connecticut
Militia, marched to relief of Boston on "Lexington
Alarm," 1775; Private 1st Regiment Connecticut
Line, Colonel Jedediah Huntington, 1779.

1887. WYETH, GEORGE EDWARD,

Great-great-grandson of Private Daniel Hawthorne,
Massachusetts Militia.

1887. WYETH, LEONARD J., JR.,

Great-great-grandson of Private Daniel Hawthorne,
Massachusetts Militia.

1889. WYLIE, EDMUND WADE,

Great-grandson of Private Samuel Hicks (1758–1834),
Private from New London in Colonel S. H. Parson's
Company, "Lexington Alarm," 1775; Private in
Captain Calkins' Company, Colonel Latimer's Regi-
ment Connecticut Militia, 1777; Private 2d Regiment
Continental Corps of Artillery, Colonel Lamb, 1780;
Private in Captain Jared's Company of Connecticut
Militia, 1781.

Also, Great-great-grandson of Captain-Lieutenant John
Miles, Corporal in Captain Prentice's Company 5th
Battalion Connecticut Militia, Colonel William Douglass, 1776; 1st Lieutenant 2d Regiment Continental
Corps of Artillery, Colonel Lamb, January 6, 1777;
promoted Captain-Lieutenant in same, October 22.
1779; served to close of war.

1889.   WYLIE, GEORGE SANDFORD,   357

Great-grandson of Private Samuel Hicks (1758–1834),
Private from New London in Colonel S. H. Parson's
Company, "Lexington Alarm," 1775; Private in
Captain Calkins' Company, Colonel Latimer's Regi-
ment Connecticut Militia, 1777; Private 2d Regiment
Continental Corps of Artillery, Colonel Lamb, 1780;
Private in Captain Jared's Company of Connecticut
Militia, 1781.

Also, Great-great-grandson of Captain-Lieutenant John
Miles, Corporal in Captain Prentice's Company 5th
Battalion Connecticut Militia, Colonel William Douglass, 1776; 1st Lieutenant 2d Regiment Continental
Corps of Artillery, Colonel Lamb, January 6, 1777;
promoted Captain-Lieutenant in same, October 22,
1779; served to close of war.

1889.   YEATON, ALBERT SULLIVAN,   46

Great-grandson of Captain Ebenezer Sullivan (1753–
1799) of New Hampshire, Captain in 16th Regiment
Continental Infantry, Colonel John Patterson, 1776;
taken prisoner at the "Cedars," 1777; and Aide-de-
Camp to Major-General John Sullivan.

Total Membership, January 12, 1892, -   -   -   902

In Memoriam.

Date of Initiation.	Name.	Died.
1883.	JOHN MERCHANT.	July 7, 1886.
1884.	MOREY HALE BARTOW,	1886.
1886.	THOMAS W. CHRYSTIE.	Jan. 18, 1888.
1885.	EDWARD WILLIAM TAPP.	Feb. 3, 1888.
1887.	JAMES A. FOSTER.	March 10, 1888.
1883.	JOSEPH W. DREXEL.	March 25, 1888.
1883.	GEORGE H. POTTS,	April 28, 1888.
1886.	N. W. T. HATCH.	May 8, 1888.
1888.	Rev. S. J. M. MERWIN.	Sept. 12, 1888.
1888.	FREDERICK A. POTTS.	Nov. 9, 1888.
1889.	PETER CARPENTER BAKER.	May 19, 1889.
1885.	JOHN FITCH.	Sept. 1, 1889.
1889.	RICHARD HOFFMAN BENSON,	Sept. 29, 1889.
1886.	EDWARD NICOLL DICKERSON.	Dec. 12, 1889.
1887.	JAMES RENWICK GIBSON, JR..	March 5, 1890.
1887.	THOMAS STORM.	May 1, 1890.
1886.	ROBERT RAY HAMILTON,	Aug. 23, 1890.
1888.	CHARLES LOUIS FINCKE.	Nov. 11, 1890.
1889.	JOHN PARKER PRALL.	March 5, 1891.
1887.	BOLTON, JAMES CLINTON.	March 28, 1891.
1883.	HOUGHTON, GEORGE WASHINGTON WRIGHT.	April 1, 1891.
1891.	FERRY, JEDEDIAH BALDWIN.	July 28, 1891.
1885	BENJAMIN, FREDERICK A..	Oct. 3, 1891.
1889.	LATHROP, FRANCIS H..	Nov. 15, 1891.
1890.	WOODRUFF, HENRY DWIGHT.	Nov. 29, 1891.

www.ingramcontent.com/pod-product-compliance
Lightning Source LLC
Chambersburg PA
CBHW020509270326
41926CB00008B/802